THE
SACRED
FIRE

THE SACRED FIRE

Christian Marriage Through the Ages

DAVID and VERA MACE

ABINGDON PRESS

NASHVILLE

THE SACRED FIRE

This book is printed on acid-free paper.

Library of Congress Cataloging-in-Publication Data

Mace, David Robert.
    The sacred fire.

    Bibliography: p.
    1. Marriage—Religious aspects—Christianity—History. I. Mace, Vera.
II. Title.
BV835.M224   1986   261.8'3581   86-8051

ISBN 0-687-36712-3 (alk. paper)

MANUFACTURED BY THE PARTHENON PRESS AT
NASHVILLE, TENNESSEE, UNITED STATES OF AMERICA

*We dedicate this book
to each other
in joyous celebration
of our
fifty-three years of marriage*

"The civilization of Christendom—the civilization of which we are the heirs—was founded on Christian marriage. . . . And where the Christian ideal of marriage prevails, the family, strengthened by supernatural sanctions, will hold good through every crisis, and even in the greatest political convulsions provides the principle of eventual recovery."

—Charles H. Joyce
Christian Marriage

CONTENTS

PREFACE

After a busy life together, spent in efforts to improve the quality of marriages, including our own, we have at last been able, in retirement, to fulfill a long-deferred wish and to put this book together.

We should make it clear that we make no claim to be either historians or theologians. We call ourselves behavioral scientists and family specialists. But we are also very much concerned about *Christian* marriage and family life. We take seriously the warning of Emil Brunner, in his book *The Divine Imperative*, that the most serious crisis facing the churches today is the widespread breakdown of marriage and the family.

The insights we have gained by our extensive reading and studies have proved highly rewarding to us. We have learned a great deal, and we have gathered so much material that it has been difficult to decide just what to include in the book and what to leave out. We have simply had to decide in terms of what we personally found most interesting and most helpful.

Our hope is that the book will prove to be a useful addition to the literature about Christian marriage. No other book, to our knowledge, puts the subject in so broad a context. We have tried to include the kind of material that we personally would have been very glad to read when, long years ago, we began to work in this field, and we have tried to conclude with an emphasis on the practical steps we think the churches could take here and now to give to Christian marriage, and to Christian family life, the emphasis they deserve in today's world.

Through the years we have been working on this book, a number of others have been working with us—librarians who directed us to resources; typists who coped cheerfully with several drafts; friends who generously shared their expertise on our subject; editors who took the final steps toward publication; and most of all, friends who demonstrated Christian marriage. You are all a part of the fabric of this book, and we want you to know how deeply we appreciate your help.

DAVID AND VERA MACE

PROLOGUE
The Changing World (and Time Lines)

Our purpose in this book is to look at one of the basic human institutions—marriage—as it was viewed and organized within a particular tradition—the Christian religion and culture. This tradition has now been part of human history for a period approaching two thousand years.

Before we begin our investigation, it may be helpful to gain some perspective. Let us, therefore, see how the Christian era fits into the broader picture of world history and how the two thousand-year period can be divided up into a few significant segments.

At the time when Christianity began, it was not possible to look back very far. The Hebrews could give you a precise date, a fairly recent one, in which the world took shape out of nothingness, responding to God's act of Creation. There are still those who accept this explanation of how it all began.

Our present scientific viewpoint, however, looks back over a vastly greater stretch of time. Even the history of man's immediate ancestors, based on discoveries in Africa and the Middle East, has been progressively pushed back over a few million years, although what information we have is fragmentary. One theory is that early man first lived in trees, but under changing climatic conditions was forced to come down to ground level, stand erect, and become a wandering nomad, picking up morsels of food where he could and using whatever natural shelter was available.

The turning point of human history came, it is affirmed by most archaeologists, about ten thousand years ago, when nomadic man became a farmer, growing crops and keeping domestic animals. From the making of the simplest tools out of flint or wood, he gradually progressed to the building of homes, the use of metals, and living in settled communities. This marked the dawn of what we call civilization.

By the year 3000 B.C., two civilized systems—the Sumerian and the Egyptian—had reached a fairly advanced stage of development. Around the fringes of those developed cultures, wandering tribal groups moved about, picking up a living as they could. Among them, according to tradition, were the Hebrews, and the Bible story of Abraham tells us of his pioneering journey. One estimated date for this is about 1950 B.C., almost exactly the same length of time *before* Christ appeared as our own lifetime is *after* that event!

Over a period about which we have little in the way of historical record, the Hebrews, believing themselves to be a people chosen of God to fulfill a special destiny, founded in time a powerful and prosperous kingdom. Here, recorded history tells the story of the great kings, David and Solomon, about the year 1000 B.C.

From that point the Hebrews experienced changing fortunes as the great empires of the Middle East rose and fell. During this period, the descendants of Abraham held firmly to what they believed to be their divinely appointed destiny, despite such setbacks as a period of exile in Babylon and a split into the two separate kingdoms of Judah and Israel. They were incorporated into one empire after another (Babylonian, Assyrian, Egyptian, Persian, Greek) until they finally came under the rule of the mighty Caesars of Rome. And now the hour of destiny arrived—the date from which our historical events are now reckoned, backward or forward—the year when Jesus was born in Bethlehem. The precise date of that event seems to have been 5 B.C.

The Hebrews had long cherished an expectation that one day their hour of destiny would strike. A heaven-sent messenger, whom they called the Messiah, would appear in their midst, become their champion, and bring in a new world order. But there was no recognizable resemblance between that expected Deliverer and the carpenter's son who played in the village streets of Nazareth. How could they know that the date of his birth would become the dividing line of history—B.C. before, A.D. after?

So he came and went, crucified, some thirty years later, as a common criminal. And then, forty years after that, the day of doom came for the city of Jerusalem; the Hebrew people, now called the Jews, were scattered across the face of the earth, not to be gathered in their homeland again for nearly another two thousand years.

But the boy Jesus had become a man and had delivered the message he had been sent to proclaim. As the years passed, that message was taken by faithful men and women from land to land, all around the Mediterranean

Basin and beyond. The Christian church took shape. Many of the messengers perished in violent persecutions, but as Tertullian predicted, the blood of the martyrs became the seed of the church. In A.D. 313 Constantine, the Roman emperor, was converted, and Christianity became the official religion of the empire. Less than two centuries later, barbarian hordes from the East poured into Europe, and in the year 476 Rome fell.

But the Christian faith lived on. The barbarians who had conquered the Roman legions were won over by the followers of Jesus of Nazareth, and in the years that followed, the nations of Europe, one by one, became Christian, ending with Scandinavia, nearly a thousand years after the Christian era had begun.

So the changing world moved on from the first three centuries of the early church and the closing years of the Roman Empire into the so-called Dark Ages of medieval Europe to the Renaissance, beginning in the fourteenth century, to be followed in the sixteenth century by the Reformation, when European Christendom split in half and Catholics and Protestants went their several ways, barely maintaining mutual tolerance of each other.

With the accelerating increase in scientific knowledge and skill, the Western nations entered the Industrial Revolution, and the wider world was opened up. Meanwhile, a steady stream of missionaries had taken the Christian message to the uttermost ends of the earth—to the mighty continents and the distant islands of the sea.

And so, finally, humanity entered the twentieth century—an era of vast enterprise and brutal wars, of the unveiling of the atom's power and of man's first ventures into outer space. Two thousand years have now passed since the Christian era began, three thousand since King David ruled in Jerusalem, four thousand since Abraham set off to find the Promised Land, five thousand since the ancient kings of Egypt built the pyramids, and ten thousand since primitive man ceased to be a wandering nomad and civilization began. Now we are approaching the end of yet another century and the beginning of another thousand-year era of the ever-changing human world.

During all those vast years of history, multitudes of our fellow-men and women have passed through the human life-span—have been born, have grown up, have lived their lives, and have died.

And the vast majority of them have married. What has this experience, the sharing of life with a partner of the opposite sex, meant to them? Even to begin to tell that story would require many volumes. It never can be, never will be, fully told.

Here, in this book, we shall try to look at just one part of the story—how marriage has been understood, experienced, and organized by the Christian church and by the Hebrew culture out of which it came, as generation after generation of men and women have lived their lives in faith, in hope, and, where possible, in love.

(In order to make the historical record as clear as possible, we have put together a diagram in the form of two "time lines." It covers the two periods, each of two thousand years, before and after the time of Christ. A few significant dates have been included.)

TIME LINES

B.C.   A.D.

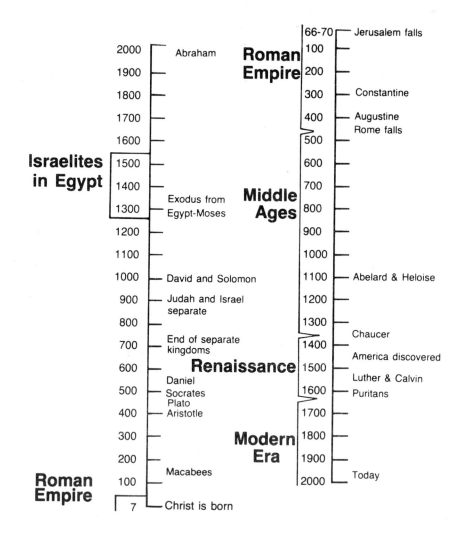

B.C.		A.D.	
		66-70	Jerusalem falls
2000	Abraham	100	**Roman Empire**
1900		200	
1800		300	Constantine
1700		400	Augustine / Rome falls
1600		500	
Israelites in Egypt 1500		600	
1400		700	**Middle Ages**
1300	Exodus from Egypt-Moses	800	
1200		900	
1100		1000	
1000	David and Solomon	1100	Abelard & Heloise
900	Judah and Israel separate	1200	
800		1300	
700	End of separate kingdoms	1400	Chaucer
600	**Renaissance**	1500	America discovered
	Daniel		Luther & Calvin
500	Socrates / Plato	1600	Puritans
400	Aristotle	1700	
300		1800	**Modern Era**
200		1900	
Roman Empire 100	Macabees	2000	Today
7	Christ is born		

PART I

What the Bible Teaches

Chapter 1

MARRIAGE IS GOOD FOR EVERYONE
(The Old Testament)

When Jesus grew up as a boy in the village of Nazareth, he learned from the local rabbi that the Hebrew race into which he had been born had a long history. The Christian era, which dates from his birth, now covers a period of nearly two thousand years. But as far as we can estimate, the first Hebrew settlers, represented by Abraham and his family, had made the journey from Ur of the Chaldees another twenty centuries earlier. So the historical period to which the Jews looked back at the time of Jesus was possibly as long as the entire span of Christian history.

This being so, it would surely be quite unrealistic to begin our investigation of Christian marriage with the New Testament record. Long before a single Christian document had appeared, a whole system of standards, values, laws, and customs had been developed to define what the Jews believed about marriage and family life. This whole social and religious system was known, understood, and simply taken for granted by nearly all the men and women who became the first generation of Christian believers. For them it was not just a social system. They believed that it was a system that represented the revealed will of God.

In this opening chapter, therefore, we must begin our inquiry by looking briefly at what the Old Testament teaches about marriage. And we will hope to demonstrate that it is impossible to understand what we mean by *Christian marriage* unless we first take a look at the foundations upon which it was built. As we shall see later, the new structure the Christian church developed changed the earlier tradition in many ways, and not always for the better. But to understand these later changes, we must begin where Jesus, himself, the founder of Christianity, began. Humanly speaking, he was the child of a Jewish marriage who grew up in a Jewish home.

WHO WERE THE HEBREWS?

A curious ritual in the Old Testament refers to a statement that required a Hebrew farmer, when he brought his first fruits to the priest, to say, "My father was a wandering Aramean" (Deuteronomy 26:5). The Arameans were one of at least four groups of nomadic tribes who came from the East and finally settled in what we now call Asia Minor. According to T. H. Robinson, in *Record and Revelation*, they were "a Semitic migration who, after wandering round the desert edge of the Fertile Crescent, from the far South-East, at last made their home on the borders of Egypt." Earlier, they had come under the influence of the great Babylonian-Assyrian culture that occupied the region of the Tigris and Euphrates rivers where Iraq is today. This was one of the two earliest of all human civilizations (Egypt was the other), dating back to at least thirty-five centuries before Christ. Scholars have traced close connections between the Old Testament laws and the ancient Code of Hammurabi, the Babylonian king who reigned in the eighteenth century B.C., and there are Babylonian equivalents of the Genesis stories of the Garden of Eden and of the Flood.

It is entirely clear, however, that although the Hebrews shared many traditions, customs, and laws with other peoples with whom they came in contact, they had a deep sense of their own uniqueness. They believed in one God, whereas the other tribes around them believed in many. They believed that their God was righteous and that he had called Abraham and his successors into a unique relationship with himself in order that they might fulfill a special purpose. They believed that in the fullness of time he would send his own messenger, the Messiah, to make that purpose clear. In the meantime, they must be faithful to his commands and live at a higher level than their less enlightened neighbors.

According to the Hebrew tradition, it all began with Abraham, Isaac, and Jacob, the first three generations of their common ancestors. This remarkable family developed in time into a nation. They called themselves "the children of Israel." Israel was the special name God gave to Jacob after the mysterious encounter described in Genesis 32:24-32. The word *El* means God; Philo, the Jewish philosopher, has suggested that Jacob's new name could be translated as "He Who Sees God."

The nation that grew out of this very special family has also been called the Hebrews, which means *the people who have crossed over.* Later, they called their God *Yahweh,* and they came at his command to possess the land of Canaan. For a time they had been captive in Egypt, but under their leader Moses, Yahweh led them back to what they called the promised land.

The family became a nation, but the nation continued to be a family. After their deliverance from Egypt, they entered into a covenant with Yahweh, who declared, "If you will indeed obey My voice and keep My covenant, then you shall be My own possession among all peoples, for all the earth is Mine; and you shall be to Me a kingdom of priests and a holy nation." When Moses delivered this message, the people responded "All that the Lord has spoken we will do!" (Exodus 19:5-6, 8 NASB).

It is impossible to understand the Hebrews apart from their strong sense of family unity. Also in *Record and Revelation*, A. Lods, the distinguished Old Testament scholar, expressed it well: "To such an extent did the Semite of historical times regard the patriarchal family as the norm of social organization, that he thought of all mankind under this form. For him, every nation was a family that had increased and multiplied, and traced its descent from a single father, to whom the name of the people whom he was supposed to have begotten was usually ascribed." What this meant to each individual Israelite was well described by another distinguished Old Testament scholar, W. A. L. Elmslie, in the same book: "They felt themselves physically one, for in their way of thought the individual had life solely because there was in him part of the mysterious blood that ran in all their veins. . . . By instinct and reason they knew their sole hope of security and success depended on their complete cohesion."

This remarkable sense of solidarity among all the people was founded on the unity of each individual family. The members of the family lived together in mutual dependence and cooperation. But at the center of every family group, large or small, there was one member whose importance was so great that it could hardly be exaggerated.

That person was the *father*. Always, he occupied the central place. To quote yet another authority, J. T. E. Pederson, "The man forms a complete unity with the whole of his family. . . . Psychic community means, above all, a common will and so a common responsibility. The man is the center of this common will. He does not act for himself alone, but for the whole of his house. Whatever he has done, the house, the family, has likewise done, for together they form an organism so closely knit that no single part thereof can be separated as something independent" *(Israel)*.

The key, therefore, to the Old Testament concept of the nation, of the family, and of marriage is the role of the patriarch, the father. Because this concept of family life has been largely lost in our contemporary communities, we have emphasized it as strongly as possible and quoted distinguished Old Testament scholars to make it very clear.

THE HUSBAND AS FATHER

The Old Testament begins, very properly, with the story of the Creation. A vital part of the story is the appearance of Adam and Eve. They represent the crown of God's handiwork, because, unlike the lower animals, Adam and Eve were made in God's own image. We will admit that all did not go well in the Garden of Eden, but we will defer discussion of the Fall until later. In the meantime, let us focus on the positive side of the story.

The Hebrews were fascinated with the idea of procreation. If we spell the word as *pro*-creation, it can mean the act of creating on behalf of another. God began the creative process and made the first couple. Then he handed over to Adam and Eve the power to make others in their own likeness, which was also in God's likeness. In other words, by coming together sexually, they continued the process of creation.

It is tempting to suggest that this was the reasoning from which the Hebrews developed their very positive view of sex. Of all the powers with which humans were endowed, surely this was the greatest. And since it was achieved through the man's sex organ, surely that must be a very special part of his body. This idea is confirmed by the fact that, in Genesis 24:2, Abraham makes his servant, in the process of taking a solemn oath, place his hand on his master's genitals, or, as one commentator expressed it, "in contact with organs that are the sacred seat of life."

It is significant in this connection that circumcision has always been the rite of initiation that makes the Hebrew male a member of the chosen people. May we not, therefore, suppose that this rite is in fact the santification of the sacred organ with which a man was privileged to continue God's creative work? The cutting away of the foreskin would then fit the pattern of a sacrificial action similar to tithing, in which dedication of the part sanctifies the whole.

We have no final proof of this explanation, but it is in complete accord with the very positive Hebrew attitude toward sex, which stands out in striking contrast to the negative and unworthy attitudes that developed later. Not only did the Hebrew man take pride in his sexual powers, but also he believed that God was actively present when husband and wife had intercourse, opening or closing the womb according to his approval or disapproval of the proceedings and of the participants. There are many references to this in the Old Testament (Genesis 16:2; 29:31; 36:22; Judges 13:3; Ruth 4:13; I Samuel 1:5-6; I Samuel 2:22; and so forth).

Because sex is good and fatherhood is a God-given privilege, all Hebrew men, including priests and prophets, were expected to marry. They generally did so soon after puberty, and got busy at once with the task of begetting sons. A newly married young man could even defer military service for a year in order to get his marriage established and his family started (Deuteronomy 24:5).

The hope of every husband was to beget sons. This was a matter of affirming his identity. In the early Hebrew period, there was no clearly defined doctrine of immortality. The Old Testament tells us that when a man died usually he "slept with his fathers." His ongoing life was assured through his sons, who continued the family name and the family line. "When your days are fulfilled and you lie down with your fathers, I will raise up your offspring after you, who shall come forth from your body, and I will establish his kingdom" (II Samuel 7:12). The worst fate that could befall any man, therefore, was to die without issue, because his name would then be "blotted out" (Psalm 109:13).

So, if a Hebrew husband found himself married to a childless wife, he faced a major crisis. It is important to understand this clearly, because it explains so many things which otherwise don't make sense. The basic Hebrew ideal for marriage was monogamy and life-long devotion. But if no children came, desperate measures might be taken.

Such a measure is represented by the levirate marriage. It does not figure prominently in the Old Testament and was probably an ancient custom in decay. But it fits into what we have been saying about the importance of a man's having sons. Unless it is explained, it may be quite unintelligible to the average Bible reader. If a man dies without sons, the worst has happened. His line is cut off, his name blotted out. Is there *anything* that can be done to redeem this disaster?

Yes, there is a desperate last hope. A brother of his takes the widow into his home and marries her. Of course, he already has a wife of his own, so it becomes a polygamous marriage. But the situation is desperate, and polygamy can be excused in the circumstances.

The former widow now becomes pregnant. A son is born. The son, begotten by a brother of the deceased, is given the name of the dead man and grows up to continue his family line. Because a brother's seed was used, it can be counted as being that of the deceased, because they had the same father.

Fragmentary instances of this practice are found in Genesis 38, where the *levir* ("a husband's brother") tried to cheat the system, with fatal consequences, and in the book of Ruth, where a widow tried to save the name of her dead husband by marriage to Boaz, who was not a brother but a more distant relative of the deceased Elimelech.

Both stories are fragmentary instances of the levirate. But they illustrate the length to which it was possible to go to avoid a man's dying without leaving a son as his heir. We shall understand some of these issues more clearly if we now turn our attention to the wife.

STATUS OF THE HEBREW WIFE

Many people have formed the impression that women in Old Testament times were held in low esteem. There is some truth in this, but it is certainly not at all true of women in their roles as wives and mothers. Never, perhaps, in human history have these particular feminine roles been more highly esteemed.

What we need to understand is the Hebrew view of the reproductive process—a view widely shared among agricultural peoples in the ancient world, and even in more recent times.

Until the invention of the microscope in the seventeenth century, nothing was known of the sperm and the ovum and the way in which their union produces new life. The nature of reproduction could, therefore, only be guessed at, and it was natural that farming people should reason in terms of processes they thought they fully understood. The Hebrews knew well that to grow crops, seeds were sown in the field, and over a period of time they developed and grew into plants.

What was more natural, then, than to suppose that animal and human reproduction followed the same process? So the male ejaculate was called his *seed* (this is the Latin meaning of our word *semen*), and the act of sexual intercourse consists of "sowing" it within the body of the woman, where it is nurtured over time and delivered when it is ready. The woman, therefore, in her reproductive role, played the part of the "field"; in the Hebrew this word was actually used to refer to her reproductive role.

Support for this view comes from archaeologists. They explain that when primitive peoples changed their way of life from hunting to farming, it was probably the women who started the process. From gathering wild crops, they had the idea of increasing the yield by doing their own planting. They used a digging stick to make holes in the ground, dropped in a seed, and then closed the hole. The similarity between the digging stick and the male sex organ is too obvious for even a primitive mind to miss.

All this was logical and apparently obvious. What it clearly implied, however, was that the child was made exclusively out of the substance of the father. The mother, therefore, contributed nothing of her essential self, but merely provided an incubator. True, she gave her blood—it was, of course, observed that she stopped menstruating during pregnancy—but she really did nothing more than the earth did for the nurturing of the seed. This meant, of course, that one woman was as good as another so far as enabling a man's child to be developed was concerned. Any field would do.

The obvious implication of this apparently simple fact was that heredity could only be traced through male descent, and this was what was actually done. A woman played an important, but purely auxiliary, part in the process of continuing the family line. Inevitably, this made her, in the vital business of reckoning succession, quite inferior. This fact must obviously have contributed significantly to her being given an inferior role in other areas.

Consider now what all this meant to the Hebrew wife:

1. *It was vitally important for her to produce children.* If she failed to do so, the major purpose of the marriage was invalidated. In parts of Africa and elsewhere even today, a "barren" wife can be returned to her family, much as one would return a piece of merchandise to the store if it didn't "work" as advertised. This helps to explain Rachel's poignant cry when she failed to become pregnant: "Give me children, or I shall die!" (Genesis 30:1). A childless wife was branded as a total and tragic failure.

2. *Childless, she faced a bleak outlook.* Her husband could, of course, divorce her and marry again. However, this would have been very hard on her in the early Hebrew period, because there was no very secure place for an unmarried woman in a culture in which virtually everyone married. She could make herself useful in her parental home, or live with a married sister and help raise her children. She might even become a prostitute, which was not considered disgraceful (Rahab the harlot made no secret of her profession; yet, she was honored in Israel for her faith in God). Probably, though, whatever alternative she chose, she would eat out her heart in sorrow. Even if her husband kept her as an extra wife, she would feel rejected as the new wife produced the children who had been denied her.

3. *Her husband must find another woman.* He could do so in three possible ways. First, as we have seen, he could divorce her and remarry, hoping for better luck next time. Second, he could take an additional wife and keep the first—the practice of polygamy, though not favored, was acceptable in these special circumstances. Third, he might take a concubine—either a woman captured in war or purchased as a slave—and hope to have children by her. This was what happened in the story of Abraham's childless wife Sarah, who gave her Egyptian maid Hagar to her husband in order to obtain a child. A tense situation followed (Genesis 16).

4. *She might perceive her childlessness as a judgment.* Since the Hebrews believed that God opened and closed wombs, she would inevitably ask herself what she had done to merit the divine disapproval. No doubt, she could think up faults and magnify them to the point of persuading herself that she was worthless, if not actually wicked.

Children, therefore, were greatly to be desired. Had not God himself said, "Be fruitful and multiply" (Genesis 1:22)?

Even if she had a "quiver-full," how did the Hebrew woman stand in her husband's eyes? Was she totally under his control—in fact, one of his possessions? Isn't she listed in the commandments as an item of a man's property, along with his house, his servants, and his domestic animals (Exodus 20:17)? Besides, hadn't he paid a purchase price for her?

To answer these questions, we need to understand the Hebrew marriage system. Scholars have now thoroughly investigated the so-called bride-price (the *mohar*) the husband paid to the father of his future wife. They have defined it as a "compensation gift" for the father's loss of his daughter and for her loss of virginity. It did *not* give the husband possession of the *person* of his wife, but it *did* give him possession of her *sexuality*. In this he had absolute and exclusive rights because, obviously, he must be quite sure that any child she bore was *his* child, and not that of any other man. Otherwise, the family line and name would be falsified; as we have seen, this was the worst affront a man could suffer.

The German scholar Koschaker defined the *mohar* neatly in the phrase *zweckbestimmtes Eigentum*, which means that the wife belonged to her husband *only for the purposes for which marriage exists*; however, as a *person* she did *not* belong to him. So he couldn't justifiably treat her as a chattel. She was, for instance, in quite a different category from the female slave. He had married her neither by capture nor by purchase. If he ill-treated her, she could appeal to her own family, or to the law, for protection. Normally, she had her own tent or living quarters; she could possess her own personal property, such as the gifts received from her family and from her husband on the occasion of her marriage; and she might have her own private maidservant.

Much depended, of course, on how her husband viewed the matter. It is difficult in any culture to protect a wife from abuse if she is married to an unscrupulous man. However, a Hebrew wife and mother married to a good man could enjoy great happiness and could be something of a queen in her home community.

W. A. L. Elmslie sums it up: "It is certain that in Jewish homes women attained an honor and dignity without parallel in antiquity" *(Record and Revelation)*.

STANDARDS OF SEX MORALITY

The Hebrews, we repeat, had a very positive view of sex. All who read the Old Testament must notice at once how openly and naturally the subject is treated. It would be difficult indeed to find any passage that could be regarded as dirty or offensive. In this respect, there is a striking contrast between the Hebrew literature and that of Greece and Rome in the same historical period. Sex is a gift of God to be valued and enjoyed by both men and women. Indeed, it was a husband's duty to see that he met not only the sexual needs of his wife, but also those of a concubine in his home (Exodus 21:10).

However, the Hebrew view set some limitations on sexual freedom. Incest and rape were punishable offenses. And the seed, being sacred, must not be wasted or misplaced. Consequently, there are warnings against such "unnatural" activities as masturbation, homosexuality, and intercourse with animals. These are not based, as is sometimes supposed, on inhibited sexual attitudes, but actually the opposite. Semen is too precious to be wasted on inappropriate objects. In one instance, a husband was reproved by his rabbi for wasting his seed on a barren wife! Also, the Hebrews share with many other cultures a superstitious attitude toward the "uncleanness" of menstruation, so that marital intercourse is forbidden at such times.

When we consider premarital and extramarital sex relations, we encounter a situation that can be quite puzzling, until we examine it in the light of the Hebrew values we have just tried to explain. We refer to the complete double standard that was operative in Hebrew society.

The word *adultery* is often used in the Old Testament. For the Hebrews, however, it had a very different meaning from what it has in our world of today.

Sexually, and subject to the restrictions already mentioned, men were free to do what they liked. A Hebrew man, married or unmarried, could have sexual intercourse with any available woman without censure or penalty. That sounds very permissive. However, the puzzle was to find an available woman! The restrictions on women were almost total. For a married woman, as we have seen, any sexual contact with another man, unless forced, was a grave offense on her part. For an unmarried girl, loss of virginity virtually put her out of the marriage market. Even a concubine or slave would be the property of some other man, and intercourse with her might involve a heavy penalty. The only real possibility, therefore, without committing an offense, was a prostitute.

What this means is that almost every woman in Hebrew society was either under the authority of or the property of some particular man. In her early years, the authority was that of her father, who was responsible for her virginity until he could get her married, usually soon after puberty. A married woman was under her husband's authority. A widow was under the care of her son.

Adultery, therefore, was for the Hebrews a sexual offense in which a man violated, in effect, the property rights of some other man, and the law had to settle it between them. Guilt was attached to the woman only if she had been a willing partner; that was very difficult to prove unless, as in the case of the woman brought to Jesus (John 8:4), she was "caught in the very act."

The penalty for adultery was technically death by stoning, which was a way of saying that the offense had been committed against the whole community; therefore, the execution was carried out by all concerned. In fact, however, there is no record in the Bible of this penalty's ever being carried out.

THE HEBREW WEDDING

As in most early cultures, the Hebrews brought marriage partners together *by arrangement*. This was obviously desirable, since both boys and girls were married at an early age when their capacity for wise choice would be very limited. But that was not the only reason. Marriages were ways of cementing social links between families, so the usual procedure was for the fathers to get together and make the plans, with or without the assistance of the *shadchan*, or marriage broker.

One of the most delightful stories in the Old Testament describes how Abraham sends his most trusted servant to find a wife for Isaac from among his own people. The happy result is that Rebekah turns out to be as pleasing to Isaac, himself, as to his father (Genesis 24). By contrast, Jacob's brother, Esau, takes the matter into his own hands and disrupts the family unity (Genesis 26:25; 27:46). Shechem makes his own choice of Dinah, but has to get his father, Hamor, to arrange the match (Genesis 34:4). This leads to a great deal of trouble, as does Samson's attempt to make his own choice (Judges 14). Joash, being a young king, took *two* wives, but he allowed Jehoiada, the high priest, to select them for him, and all went well (II Chronicles 24:1-3).

In later times, however, romantic attachment became more acceptable. The book of Proverbs speaks of "the way of man with a maid" (30:19 NASB), which could hardly have mattered in the absence of any possibility of courtship. The Old Testament finds space for what are obviously love songs (Psalm 45 and the Song of Solomon).

The first step toward marriage was the betrothal, at which time the *mohar* was paid. This was binding and required that the man must be circumcised—the word for bridegroom, *hathan*, means precisely this. Once these conditions had been met, the wedding, itself, could take place; so a waiting period was usual when, as often happened, the bride was very young.

Although the wedding was a happy and important event, the Old Testament contains no record of either a written contract or a formal ceremony. We may safely assume that a feast and suitable entertainment were part of the celebration, and it seems likely that the bride wore a veil, because Rebekah did so when her future husband appeared (Genesis 24:65); Laban used this device deceitfully to get Jacob married to Leah instead of to Rachel (Genesis 29:23-35).

The two essential features of the Hebrew wedding, however, coincided with the Roman custom. First, the *traditio puellae* (the transfer of the bride from her parental home to the home of her future husband), followed by the *copula carnalis* (the sexual consummation which took place in the bridal chamber). This latter event involved the proving of the bride's virginity, which, as we have seen, is of central importance. In Deuteronomy 22:13:21 this procedure is described—the "tokens of virginity," consisting of a blood-stained garment resulting from the rupture of the hymen, were handed over to the bride's parents and constituted the necessary evidence that the marriage had been duly consummated. We are not told what happened if, as occasionally occurs, the bride had an abnormal hymen that didn't bleed, or the nervous bridegroom suffered from premature ejaculation or impotence!

And so, we hope, they were married and lived happily ever after.

MARRIAGE AS COMPANIONSHIP

C. Ryder Smith, in his book *The Bible Doctrine of Womanhood*, was one of the early writers in this field. He found in Hebrew marriages three goals for the husband and his wife: a source of sexual pleasure, a means of producing children, and mutual companionship. As we have seen, a great deal of emphasis was placed on the first two. But what about the third?

Obviously, in a marriage that was fulfilling in the first two areas, the chances would be high that the third would follow. On the contrary, sexual maladjustment, and even more, childlessness, would make the achievement of close and warm companionship difficult and even unlikely.

Obviously, the temperaments of the two partners, and their facility for effective communication and for being pleasing and supportive to each other, would count for a good deal.

There is evidence, indeed, that truly happy marriages occurred in Hebrew society. The Creation story leaves us with no doubt that one of God's original purposes in creating Eve was because Adam was lonely and unable to find kinship with the lower forms of creation. His immediate response to Eve was, "This at last is bone of my bones and flesh of my flesh" (Genesis 2:23), and we can sense the enthusiasm and excitement in his utterance. Now he had someone to talk with, someone who would understand his thoughts and feelings, his joys and sorrows, his hopes and fears.

True, it is in later biblical literature that we encounter husbands who warmly praise their wives as persons. The book of Proverbs has several: "A good wife is the crown of her husband" (12:4), which we may suppose means that he feels like a king; "He who finds a wife finds a good thing, and obtains favor from the Lord" (18:22), which rashly suggests that *all* wives are good, which is open to doubt; and "House and wealth are inherited from fathers, but a prudent wife is from the Lord" (19:14).

The supreme example, however, is the wife described in Proverbs 31:10-31, who is so full of good works that her husband, in the words of C. Ryder Smith, "appears only as 'trusting in her,' as 'praising her,' as 'sitting complacently in the gate,' proud of being the husband of such a paragon!"

Perhaps the most delightful tribute to marriage is found in the Apocrypha in the book of Ecclesiasticus (26:1-4, 13-18, and 36:21-26). It will be sufficient to quote only the first passage:

> A good wife makes a happy husband;
> she doubles the length of his life.
> A staunch wife is her husband's joy;
> he will live out his days in peace.
> A good wife means a good life;
> she is one of the Lord's gifts to those who fear him.
> Rich or poor, they are light-hearted,
> and always have a smile on their faces. (NEB)

CONCLUSION

It has been possible in this chapter only to select, out of an abundance of material, some of the more important teachings about marriage which the Old Testament contains. Also, limitations of space have made it impracticable to take account of the inevitable changes that have occurred in Hebrew attitudes over the long years covered by the Old Testament literature. Despite these shortcomings, we express the hope that readers of the Bible have obtained a better perspective on what the Old Testament, in its totality, has to say about marriage and a better understanding of the value systems on which that teaching is based. A more comprehensive account is contained in our book *Hebrew Marriage*. With these resources, we believe that later development of the concept of Christian marriage will be much more clearly comprehended.

The Old Testament makes up more than three-quarters of our Christian Bible, and Christianity has its roots in Hebrew religion. To the first generation of Christian believers, what we have discussed in this chapter was an integral part of what they had learned since early childhood, and to them, the message of Jesus represented the fulfillment of all that had gone before.

The sad truth, of course, is that Jesus was rejected by his own people; after the first generation of Christian converts, the new faith moved out beyond the land of Israel to the Gentiles, until it became the official religion of the Roman Empire. Meanwhile, the fall of Jerusalem in A.D. 70 led to the end of the nation of Israel, to be restored only in our own time.

But during those long centuries, the Jews managed to maintain their religion and their social identity, despite much suffering and persecution. Scattered as they were across the world, they held fast to the faith of their fathers. Many reasons can be given for this. The one provided by Moritz Lazarus, who lived from 1824 to 1903, may fittingly conclude this chapter:

> In the days of horror of the late Roman Empire, it was not war alone that destroyed and annihilated all those peoples of which, despite their former world-dominating greatness, nothing remains but their name. It was rather the ensuing demoralization of home life. This is proved—it cannot be repeated too often—by the Jews; for they suffered more severely and more cruelly by wars than any other nation; but among them, the most inmost living germ of morality—strict discipline and family devotion—was at all times preserved. This wonderful and mysterious preservation of the Jewish people is due to the Jewish woman. This is her glory, not alone in the history of her own people, but in the history of the world. *(A Book of Jewish Thoughts)*

Chapter 2

INTERLUDE: THE THREE
CHRISTIANITIES

The Hebrew attitude toward marriage presents to us a
clear, consistent picture. It is also a very positive picture,
in spite of some features to which Christians today would
justifiably take offense (for example, polygamy, giving
men sexual freedom while setting rigid standards for
women, the toleration of prostitution, divorce available
only to the husband, and curious customs, like the
levirate). These can all be explained. The basic conception
is of a very sound, healthy marriage and family system in
sharp contrast to those of neighboring peoples.

This high regard for marriage and family life has
continued in Judaism through the long years of the
Diaspora. Still today, Jews all over the world who practice
their religion attribute a high and honored place to
marriage and family life.

The Christian faith grew out of Judaism; there can be no
question about that. The Old Testament has an honored

place in the Christian Bible. Christianity began among the Jewish people in their native land. Jesus grew up in a Jewish home and in a Jewish community. He accepted the local traditions and customs. He spoke in the synagogues, and his twelve disciples were all of the Jewish faith. His ministry was gladly received by the common people, though not by many of their religious leaders. He, himself, said that he came to fulfill an ancient promise contained in the prophecies of the earlier Jewish tradition.

It might be expected, therefore, that the Christian community, as it came into being, would naturally reaffirm the traditional Hebrew ideals of marriage and family life.

This, however, was not so. As we move across the bridge from Hebrew roots to Christian beginnings, we are in for some surprises.

CONTRASTS BETWEEN THE OLD AND NEW TESTAMENTS

Let us suppose that we have just completed our survey of what the Old Testament says about marriage and family life. We now pick up the New Testament, which we have never seen before, and read it for the first time. As we continue to read, we soon discover that, although we are still in a Jewish setting, the same one in which the Old Testament events had taken place, we are now confronted with some striking differences.

First, we find that the three major figures in the New Testament story—John the Baptist, Jesus, and Paul—are all unmarried men! And we have just learned that according to Jewish custom *all* men were automatically expected to marry, and to do so by the age of twenty! Yet, these three towering figures in the New Testament were men well over twenty, and there is no record of any of them having had, or now having, a wife!

Moreover, as we read on we learn that Jesus, when he began his ministry, chose twelve men to be his disciples. Their task was to proclaim the Christian message across the land; later, some of them became leaders in the church, as its gospel spread to other lands. Yet, the record refers to only one of them—Simon Peter—as having had a wife, and we don't even know her name or anything about her. Anyway, we learn that Jesus had set, as the condition that these twelve men must meet in order to share in his mission, the requirement that they must forsake their homes and families! Later, when Peter says to him, "We have left our homes and followed you." Jesus replies, "Truly, I say to you, there is no man who has left house or wife or brothers or parents or children, for the sake of the kingdom of God, who will not receive manifold more in this time, and in the age to come eternal life" (Luke 18:28-30).

As we consider this astonishing statement—the Founder of Christianity offering rich rewards to those who will walk out on their families—we might wonder if this was an accurate report. But when we check it out, we find that this same passage occurs in all of the first three Gospels—Matthew, Mark, and Luke!

As we then try to investigate this further, we find an account of how, when Jesus was preaching, a message was brought to him that his mother and brothers—his own personal family members—had arrived and wanted to talk with him. But instead of welcoming them, he responded, " 'Who *are* my mother and brothers?' And looking around on those who sat about him, he said, 'Here are my mother and my brothers! Whoever does the will of God is my brother, and sister, and mother' " (Mark 3:33-35). This story also is repeated in the Gospels of Matthew and Luke.

As we try to come to terms with these astonishing statements, we encounter yet another passage in Luke's Gospel Jesus says to a great multitude, "If anyone comes to me and does not hate his own father and mother and wife and children and brothers and sisters . . . he cannot be my disciple" (Luke 14:26).

How can these attitudes, apparently so different from the emphasis in Old Testament times, be explained?

THE COMPLEXITY OF THE GOSPEL MESSAGE

In one sense, the Christian message is very simple. When Jesus says, "Come to me, all who are weary and heavy laden, and I will give you rest" (Matthew 11:28), we need not doubt the genuineness of his offer. To simple souls, bearing burdens beyond endurance, coming to Jesus is in truth a deeply satisfying experience.

For the individual soul in distress, that may be enough. But when we try to view Christianity in the broader perspective as God's answer to the human dilemma, it can become far less simple. One person interprets it in one way, one in another. Probably that is why it is so hard to achieve the *unity* of the church. The message admits of such wide diversity of interpretation that it seems impossible to unite all Christian believers.

This may indeed represent the *richness* of the Christian message, but we had better face the issue of diversity now, before we go any further; it will confront us again and again as we try to define the attitude of the church to the relationships between men and women.

As we confront our task in this book, we find the Christian message taking three alternative forms. It might even be said that we find three Christianities. Let us look separately at each of them.

1. *KINGDOM-BUILDING CHRISTIANITY*

This is the easiest one with which to begin. It is well illustrated in the Hebrew tradition, as we outlined it in the last chapter, and it is summarized in the Lord's Prayer: "Thy kingdom come on earth as it is in heaven."

Kingdom-building Christianity takes the view that God has a purpose for the world he has created. There is a goal toward which we are summoned to strive. It is partly a matter of faith. Abraham, responding to God's call, went out, not knowing whither he went, but trusting that the way would be revealed. He died still trusting, having been obedient, and handed leadership over to his son Isaac, and in turn to Jacob. Generations later, the people found another great leader in Moses and a clearer revelation of God and his purpose. Still, the promise was that the chosen people would, under divine guidance, lead the way to the establishment of God's will in his world. In the fullness of time came Jesus, the promised Messiah, to make the way clearer than it had ever been before. And now, since his life, death, and resurrection, a further two thousand years have passed.

Kingdom-building Christianity represents a continuous, on-going process. Since individual men and women are born, live through the life-span, and die, the goal could be for as many people as possible, in each successive generation, to live according to the teaching of Jesus. What happens beyond this life need not then be a matter of major concern. If we are in God's care, we can trust him for what follows death, whether it be a dazzling prospect of eternal bliss, a period of higher service, or just to rest in peace.

This concept of religion very well represents the early Hebrews. They had not had the full Christian revelation, but that was not their fault. They were not disobedient to the heavenly vision, insofar as it was granted to them. They earnestly strove to act justly, to love mercy, and to walk humbly with their God. For those who were faithful, the life of marriage and the family was rich and satisfying, and they left the world content that their children would remember them with gratitude and continue the family succession into the unknown future.

In our present era, also, this is a widely accepted concept of a Christianity that fully approves of marriage and family life. May sincere Christians seek to serve the present age, to bear witness to the truth as they perceive it, striving in all things to do the will of God and to come to life's end with a sense that they have made their contribution to the building of the kingdom of God on earth. They are somewhat reticent about their expectations of what will happen after death, but they are content if their master can say to them, "Well done, good and faithful servant."

2. *LAST JUDGMENT CHRISTIANITY*

The term used to describe this is *eschatology*. The Greek word *eskatos* means "the end." In the Bible, it refers to the final termination of the present world order. It is as if God has cried "Enough!" and has called for a great judgment in which the wicked will be punished and the righteous justified. The implication seems to be that the sinfulness of man has disturbed the divine plan for so long, and so seriously, that God himself will now take over and establish his kingdom in this world by direct action. It might also mean that the appointed time has elapsed, and that the righteous have now earned their rewards in the new order.

Expectations of a final judgment have been common in religious communities. Something like this is described in the story of the Flood, where the wicked were all drowned, while Noah, under divine guidance, built the ark and preserved the necessary complement of man and beast to start the world all over again when the water subsided.

The Jewish expectation of the Messiah also had an eschatological component. God's anointed messenger, it was believed, would come with power and right the wrongs that had been done against the chosen people. A whole literature describing this kind of event is found in Jewish writings: it is described as *apocalyptic*, which means "unveiling" or "disclosure." Usually, this predicts a future event. The book of Daniel in the Old Testament and the book of the Revelation in the New Testament are well-known illustrations of such writings. Other manuscripts of this kind have been discovered outside the Bible.

What has all this to do with Christian marriage? It is important because it gives us a vital clue to the otherwise puzzling attitude of Jesus (and also of John the Baptist and Paul) to marriage and the family. We can best explain this by referring to what are called the Dead Sea Scrolls.

Most Christians now know of the exciting discovery in 1947 of some documents that proved to have been written at the very beginning of the Christian era, or even just before. A religious community, living on the shore of the Dead Sea, had inscribed the documents on leather, and some on copper, intending them to last a long time. They had then been hidden in a cave, where some Bedouins discovered them in sealed jars. These scrolls were later deciphered by experts, who confirmed their great age with scientific precision.

These records have established beyond doubt that a Jewish religious community existed at the time of Jesus near the northeast shore of the Dead Sea; it now seems likely that John the Baptist, and possibly even Jesus, had been associated with this group, who in turn were linked with a sect called the Essenes—people who lived a life of strict religious discipline, shared all their worldly possessions, and followed in many respects some of the ideals that Jesus both lived and taught.

The Essenes were *ascetics*, which our dictionary defines as "persons who renounce the comforts of society and lead a life of austere self-discipline, especially as an act of religious devotion." We know that John the Baptist fits this description, and the record shows that Jesus also renounced many worldly comforts—spending forty days and nights in the wilderness, wearing simple garments, possessing no worldly wealth, and fasting on occasion.

One of the disciplines practiced by the Essenes was that many of them, in sharp contrast to their Jewish brethren, did not marry. Pliny the Elder, a distinguished Roman scholar who lived at the time, and who visited Palestine, reports of the Essenes: "They live without women, renouncing all sexual love." Actually this was not entirely true, but women were few and very much in the background.

This may well provide us with the clue to the fact that Jesus, while recognizing that marriage was normal and blessed by God, decided that the demands of his special mission would make it undesirable for him personally—particularly since he seemed to expect that his life would end at an early age in a violent and tragic death. By the same token, he may have decided that his specially chosen disciples must also be prepared, for the sake of their great mission, to make the same sacrifice.

However, the matter must be taken a step further. The teaching of Jesus includes some unquestionably apocalyptic passages. He not only claimed to be the promised Messiah, but also from time to time he made predictions about a coming judgment. In one such passage he says:

> And there will be signs in sun and moon and stars, and upon the earth distress of nations in perplexity at the roaring of the sea and the waves, men fainting with fear and with foreboding of what is coming on the world; for the powers of the heavens will be shaken. And then they will see the Son of man coming in a cloud with power and great glory. Now when these things be into take place, look up and raise your heads, because your redemption is drawing near. (Luke 21:25-28)

Other similar passages may be found in Matthew 24 and in John 4:21-26.

In such passages as these, Jesus seems to suggest that he expected some great upheaval to take place, which would fulfill the Messianic expectations of the Jews, and that after his death he would come again in power and glory to usher in the kingdom of heaven. There is, perhaps, no more difficult task for the theologian than to comprehend the Messianic consciousness of Jesus, and we are certainly not qualified to make any such attempt. In recent centuries, at least, interpreters of the Bible have tended to avoid this difficult subject, with the conspicuous exception of Albert Schweitzer in his challenging book *The Quest of the Historical Jesus,* in which he openly confronted the eschatological component in the gospel. However, what is clear is that Jesus left the early Christians convinced that he would soon return in glory. And it is equally clear that this did not occur in their lifetime. But, of course, the impression was left that the end of the world was near; in that setting, such issues as whether or not to marry and have children seemed, as Paul later pointed out, not to matter very much.

Jesus did say quite plainly that marriage was a concern only for this life, because "in the resurrection they neither marry nor are given in marriage, but are like angels in heaven" (Matthew 22:30); so, if the faithful are all soon to be caught up into that higher region, why devote time and attention to defining how Christian couples should behave on earth?

The hope of the Second Coming has never entirely been extinguished, and we still hear from time to time of groups who live in continuing expectation of the great event. However, this form of Christianity is not prominent in our own time; though, as we shall see later, it had a profound effect on attitudes toward marriage in the early church.

3. SOUL-SAVING CHRISTIANITY

This third form of Christianity follows naturally when the hope of divine intervention fades. If heaven is not going to descend to where we are, at least in our lifetime, then we must prepare ourselves to ascend to where it is. Our time here on earth must be used to qualify ourselves for the rewards we shall reap hereafter. Or, to view it from another angle, everlasting hell awaits the wicked, so we must flee from the wrath to come.

Behind this there lies, of course, the concept of a just God. During long stretches of both Jewish and Christian history, life in this world was pretty bleak. People had to work long and hard. In the Roman Empire, a vast system of slavery was in operation, and many early Christians were slaves. The life-span was often very brief, because disease, starvation, and the destruction of war took a heavy toll. For every privileged person there were many for whom life was harsh and bitter. This world was often called a "vale of tears," and the dazzling hope of a heaven hereafter, where full compensation would be paid, was a goal worth striving for. In that heaven, however, as Jesus made clear, marriage would have no place.

For the medieval church, as we shall see later, this kind of Christianity proved to be a very workable proposition. The desire to gain heaven was reinforced by the even greater desire to escape hell; so, longing and fear together produced powerful motivation. As we shall see, in medieval times, this view of Christianity excluded almost every other, and no price was too high to pay for the assurance of salvation. In the end, the profits which the church gained by pushing up the price proved demoralizing and led to the Reformation.

Before that happened, however, the idea of Christian asceticism as the high road to heavenly rewards produced such a negative attitude toward marriage that it was downgraded in the medieval church almost as much as it had been esteemed in the Jewish culture. We must now give some attention to this vital issue.

ASCETICISM AS A CHRISTIAN IDEAL

Before we are ready to examine what the New Testament says about marriage, we need to gain some perspective on the whole question of asceticism and the role it plays in religion.

The Greek word *askeo* has several meanings: to practice, to strive or endeavor, to exercise, to reach out toward a high goal. It is used in the areas of being a good soldier, of prowess in athletics, and in achieving scholarship. In a religious context, it suggests striving for virtue or piety.

The basic idea of Christianity is living a disciplined life, either at the physical or at the spiritual level. This usually means rising above natural inclinations, so as to achieve self-conquest, and shunning every kind of self-indulgence.

Asceticism plays an important role in most of the world's religions, particulary in Hinduism and Buddhism. It was also considered important in some of the Greek philosophical systems—among the Cynics and Stoics, for example. Usually, it was linked with a dualistic frame of reference. The world was seen as an arena where the opposing forces of good and evil were locked in combat for the souls of men, and it required discipline and determination to resist the subtle and beguiling temptations of worldliness.

The tendency was to identify the noble impulses with the soul, and the lower urges with the body and its appetites—food, drink, and sex in particular, but also sleep and the urge to seek physical comforts. Bodily indulgence of all kinds was viewed as demoralizing; the ascetic, therefore, learned to endure hardship and discomfort by frugality and simple living. For the religious ascetic, this meant disciplined periods of prayer, obedience to authority, willingness to be humiliated, and self-denial in every form. In these ways, the powers of evil could be warded off and holiness attained.

Life goals of this kind make little appeal in the Western world of today, except perhaps in the field of athletics and sports. It is, therefore, difficult for people who have lived in our affluent society to comprehend this kind of life-style. But until we do, we simply cannot understand the attitudes of the people who developed the Christian church in the early centuries, and indeed in the Middle Ages and up to the time of the Reformation. To many modern Christians, the value systems that prevailed in that long period of history are almost incomprehensible. Yet, until we grasp this clearly, we cannot begin to understand the attitudes toward marriage that we shall examine later in this book.

In view of all this, it is a striking fact that the Hebrew tradition was so world-affirming and so positive in its attitude toward marriage. This can perhaps be attributed to the central importance, for all Hebrew thought, of the Creation story with which the Bible begins. The essence of Hebrew philosophy was that God is good, that he made the world, that he made man and woman in his own image, and that he enjoined them to marry and to continue his creative work by begetting and rearing children. The Hebrews were not unaware of the darker side of life, because the Creation story includes an account of the Fall, and a tragic murder occurred in the first human family. The wickedness of humankind was further dramatized in the story of Noah and the Flood. However, there are only a very few instances of asceticism in the Old Testament. In the broad picture, nothing could shake the strongly positive faith of the Children of Israel in God's purpose and in the essential goodness of the world over which he reigned.

We may be tempted to wish that this simple faith and trust in the goodness of marriage and family life could have been carried over into the Christian tradition. There is evidence, however, as we have seen, that asceticism already had a foothold in Hebrew society during the period between the Old Testament and the New Testament; such ideas were bound to influence early Christian beginnings. We must, therefore, be prepared to find evidences of this in the New Testament and increasingly in the early church during its first three centuries. After that, the influence of Christian asceticism, chiefly manifested in the celibacy of the clergy, became a dominant force in the shaping of the Christian church for well over a thousand years of its history and did not even end with the Reformation. We shall see all this in greater detail as the story unfolds.

SUMMING UP

This chapter has tried to explain something that we, ourselves, in preparing to write this book, found difficult to understand: Why, after such a high ideal of marriage and family life had been developed in Old Testament times, does the New Testament seem not to follow through and give much attention to the theme of Christian marriage? Actually, what the New Testament teaches about ethical behavior, and about personal relationships, really provides us with all we need to develop a clear picture of how the Christian husband and wife should live together in love and harmony. But the fact must be faced that marriage is not given much prominence in New Testament writing, which is concerned rather with the momentous story of the life of Jesus and the founding of the early church. What happened in those years of crisis had far-reaching implications for world history, but those implications had to be worked out, through much toil and struggle, in the long centuries that followed; some of them are still being sought and found in the very different conditions of our world today. We shall return to this in the later part of the book. But now we must examine the New Testament teaching.

Chapter 3

MARRIAGE IS GOOD: BUT NOT FOR EVERYONE (The New Testament)

What Is the New Testament?

For Christian believers, it is the record of an event of such importance that it eclipses every other event. Into this confused and waiting world came Jesus, the Christ. Human history was thereby changed for all time. Any historian, whatever judgment she or he may personally make about Jesus of Nazareth, must concede that this is true.

We can go to the Old Testament and find in it a well-developed system of marriage, of parenthood, and of family life that has been fashioned by a people dedicated to the service of God. That system has worked well for them, and we can study and learn from it. Like all the rest of their religious beliefs, it has found expression in a massive and complex accumulation of laws and commandments.

The New Testament is quite different. We cannot go to it and find a complete set of rules. It is concerned with a way of living that would, as Christians believe, if put into practice universally, fulfill God's will for the world he made and for the people he placed in it. But it is not a detailed set of rules and regulations to which we can turn for instructions about how to manage a given human situation two thousand years later.

This means that it doesn't give us directions about how to manage our marriages in today's world. What it does is to give us the basic values from which we must work out for ourselves, with the guidance of the eternal Spirit, how to bring any and every aspect of our lives into conformity with the way to which Jesus called us, in his teaching and in his living, to relate to God and to one another. What the New Testament provides is the broad picture—we must work out all the practical details for ourselves.

This attitude toward the Bible is, for us personally, a vital principle. It has been well expressed by Leander E. Keck, Dean of Yale's Divinity School:

> If the specific prohibitions and commands in the Bible were to be enforced, men would stop shaving and women would give up permanents and jewelry (Leviticus 19:27, I Corinthians 11:2-16, I Timothy 2:9); no clothes would contained mixed fibers (Deuteronomy 22:11); no farmer could develop hybrids or cross-breed his stock (Leviticus 19:19); meals would no longer include pork, crabs, lobsters, or rabbits (Leviticus 11); banks could charge interest on loans made only to foreigners (Deuteronomy 23:19f.) and any unpaid loans to fellow citizens would be cancelled every seventh year (Deuteronomy 15:1-3); juvenile delinquents would be executed (Deuteronomy 21:18-22); and illegitimate children would be ostracized (Deuteronomy 23:2). *Taking the Bible Seriously*

Notice that these striking instances come mainly from the Old Testament. But the New Testament also, as Keck goes on to say, has a few similar injunctions that seem to carry the same weight as Old Testament laws. One instance he gives is Paul's command that women remain silent in church (I Corinthians 14:33b-36).

This difference between the Old Testament and the New Testament must, we believe, be clearly understood. It is of special importance when we try to define what Christian marriage should be like. The ways in which New Testament writers instructed early Christian married couples to behave were governed, in part at least, by the social customs of the Eastern Mediterranean two thousand years ago. It would make no sense to try to transfer these values, honored and necessary in the past, to the very different kind of society in which we live today.

Accepting this approach, then, let us see what the New Testament has to say about Christian marriage.

WHAT JESUS TELLS US ABOUT MARRIAGE

Anyone reading the Gospels will soon recognize that Jesus never set out to provide systematic teaching about marriage. All we have are his responses to provocative questions from the Pharisees or Sadducees, or to questions addressed to him by the disciples. In addition, we can ocasionally pick up nuances from his responses to related issues or situations.

Although conclusions gathered from these varied sources cannot be considered to be comprehensive, it seemed to us worthwhile to make this kind of investigation. What we did was to look up all Gospel references to such key words as *marriage, wedding, husband,* and *wife.* All these passages were then examined, and the following statements summarize what they seemed to be telling us about the attitude of Jesus.

1. *Marriage is not desirable for all Christians.* Jesus, himself, as we have seen, chose the single life, and he considered it appropriate for some of his followers to do likewise, in order to concentrate on some special kinds of

ministry and service. This represents a definite departure from the Hebrew tradition.

2. *Those who do marry, however, must take it very seriously.* Responding to the Pharisees in Mark 10:2-12 and Matthew 19:3-9, Jesus takes a firmly negative attitude toward divorce. Those who are truly married (we need to consider what that means) have been joined together by God and may not be put asunder. It is true that in Old Testament times divorce was permitted, but that was only a concession to "hardness of heart." In the new Christian order, no such concessions can be made; although in Matthew's Gospel, one exception *is* given—divorce may be allowed where adultery has occurred. This statement of Jesus has led commentators into endless controversy.

3. *Marriage is for this world only.* Replying to the Sadducees, Jesus says decisively, "In heaven they neither marry nor are given in marriage." In Matthew 24:38 he even seems to suggest that marriage is for worldly-minded people and can become a distraction, turning the attention away from more important issues, as in the time of Noah when the people, heedless of the sinful state of society, went on marrying as if it didn't matter.

4. *Marriage can even be a hindrance to full discipleship.* In the parable of the invitation to the banquet in Luke 14:20, one of the invited guests excuses himself because he has just married and can't spare the time to come. The implication is that those who become true disciples should not be diverted in any way from their calling, and marriage can be such a diversion. This is more strongly expressed in Luke 14:26, where the disciple must be willing to *hate* his wife as a test of his devotion to the gospel. In Luke 20:35 it is recognized that people may marry in this present age, but that those who are "counted worthy" to enter the new age and to share in the Resurrection life neither marry nor are given in marriage

(the double reference presumably covers both men and women). Again, in Matthew 19:12, there is a reference to those "who have made themselves eunuchs for the sake of the kingdom of heaven"—a very decisive way of turning their backs on the possibility of marriage. One tradition suggests that self-castration was actually practiced later by Origen, one of the great scholars of the early church.

5. *Sexual desire must be firmly controlled.* As though emasculation were not really the issue, Jesus makes two references to the control of sinful desire *at its source.* In Matthew 15:18-20 he explains that "what comes out of the mouth proceeds from the heart, and this defiles a man." He then lists the kinds of evil thoughts that originate in the heart—after murder come adultery and fornication. This emphasis is repeated in Matthew 5:28, where Jesus says that "every one who looks at a woman lustfully has already committed adultery with her in his heart."

Although these references are only fragmentary, they seem to communicate that Christians need to think very seriously about marriage, because it could divert them from the straight and narrow path of discipleship. Jesus certainly departs from the traditional Hebrew attitude of advocating and commending the married state, both in his teaching and in his example. Indeed, it must be acknowledged that the position he adopts provides some justification for the ascetic view of sex and marriage which was so widely adopted by church leaders in the later centuries. Perhaps his teaching is summed up in the exchange with his disciples reported in Matthew 19:10-11: "The disciples said to him, 'If such is the case of a man with his wife, it is not expedient to marry.' But he said to them, 'Not all men can receive this saying, but only those to whom it is given.' "

Although the stance Jesus adopted toward the inner circle of his disciples was firm, and even rigid, his attitude toward the common people was warm, charitable, and tolerant. The story of the woman taken in adultery (John 8:3-11) may be of questionable authenticity, but it is a beautiful example of the character of Jesus as it is revealed in other instances of his dealing with people—openly challenging toward false piety and warmly forgiving toward the penitent sinner. Again, in the story of his conversation with the Samaritan woman at the well, he accepts her respectfully without any harsh judgment of her wayward marital record, receiving from her appreciation and regard rather than defensive self-justification. His behavior in both these situations vividly models for us the principle of hating the sin but loving the sinner.

In his relationship with his own family members, Jesus displays the same combination of firmness about his calling, combined with loving care and respect for those closely related to him. The story of his boyhood experience in the Temple concludes with a gentle reminder to his parents that he has other goals to meet beyond his family obligations. He is always ready to enjoy the friendship and hospitality of families and to take time out for children. His first miracle is performed to meet a crisis at a wedding feast. And in his final agony on the cross, he reaches out to make provision for his mother by putting her under the care of his beloved disciple John.

We can sum up the attitude of Jesus by saying that he definitely departed from the Hebrew policy of recommending universal marriage. He did support the married state, while making it clear that some must be ready to reject it for themselves in order to fulfill the duties of discipleship; however, for those who felt called to marry, marriage must be taken seriously, and it could bring happiness and fulfillment. He certainly did not adopt the negative antimarriage attitudes that later developed in the church; yet, there is just enough in the position he adopted to provide some tenuous justification for the extreme ascetic opinions about sex and marriage that became so widely adopted in succeeding centuries.

THE ATTITUDE OF PAUL

There can be no doubt that Paul of Tarsus was a remarkable man—a towering figure who is justly recognized as the greatest of the apostles and, in a sense, the architect who shaped the church, which sought to carry the message of Jesus outward in space and onward in time. Adopting again the policy of portraying a broad picture rather than going into a mass of detail, how can we summarize what he had to say to Christians about marriage?

1. *Like Jesus, he was himself unmarried.* Given his background in the Hebrew community, this was unusual, if not remarkable. We need not accept the rumor that he had once been jilted by the high priest's daughter. But it is noteworthy that he apparently chose the single life, although this may have proved to be providential in the light of his extensive travels and gigantic labors after he became a Christian. The fact remains that, since he was viewed as the natural model for all later apostles, his state of singlehood must surely have given the early church a decided tilt in the direction of clerical celibacy.

2. *He provides some support for ascetic attitudes to sex and marriage in the Christian community.* There is a broad consensus among biblical scholars that Jesus, although he certainly adopted some ascetic practices in the life-style he personally chose, did not encourage the renunciation of marriage for Christians generally. The same can hardly be said for Paul. He took no extremist position, to be sure, and was commendably cautious in some of his statements on the subject. Yet, as Sherwin Bailey has expressed it in *Sexual Relation in Christian*

Thought, "He represents marriage as something of a concession to human frailty—a means whereby those not endowed with the gift of continence can avoid the sin of fornication." We shall see how this was avidly picked up and exaggerated in the later centuries.

3. *Whatever views he held on marriage were profoundly influenced by his conviction that the world was soon coming to an end.* It is not clear by what gradual development of his thought he became entirely convinced of this, nor how far he continued to hold that conviction later. But there seems no doubt that he was fully persuaded of it at the time when, writing to the church at Corinth, he made his most extensive statements about the marriage of Christians. In I Corinthians 7 he uses such terms as "by reason of the present distress" and "the time is shortened"; in the light of these facts, it seems he very definitely expresses a preference for the single state over marriage.

4. *He must have been outraged by the low standards of sexual behavior in the Mediterranean ports where some of the first Christian churches were established and by the morals of the Roman Empire in his time.* Greek culture, as we shall see later, had accepted generally low standards of sex morality and had tolerated prostitution, both male and female. Under Roman influence, claims Bailey, "The baser elements of Greek sexual life . . . produced a parody of the spontaneous naturalism of Hellenic sensuality in the coarse, brutal, and calculated vice for which the imperial city has ever since remained notorious. . . . The cities and ports of the Mediterranean seaboard rivaled or instructed the capital in licentiousness." In several of the New Testament letters, we find urgent warnings to the Christian converts to beware of these enticements to sexual vice. It could, of course, be argued that a good marriage might be the best safeguard (Paul suggests this in

I Corinthians 7:2). However, some Christians tended to feel that strict abstinence from all forms of sexuality was a better solution.

5. *While he clearly accepted Jesus' teaching that a Christian marriage should not end in divorce, he takes a different view of marriage between a Christian and an unbeliever.* In I Corinthians 7:12-15 Paul is careful to say that it is he who speaks, not the Lord; he then goes on to express an opinion that has been called the "Pauline privilege" and has been much debated. What he appears to say is that if the unbelieving partner stays in the marriage, this arrangement must be accepted; however, if the unbeliever breaks the marriage bond and departs, the believing partner is not bound and can presumably remarry.

6. *He took the view that the sexual relationships of married couples were spiritually debilitating.* Paul has been commended for his emphasis on the importance of the husband and wife meeting each other's sexual needs (I Corinthians 7:3). But this injunction is followed up, only two verses later, by the suggestion that if the couple wished to spend time in prayer, normal sex relations should be discontinued during that period. Whatever his intention, this has been interpreted as meaning that the intimate life of the couple is incompatible with their spiritual relationship; a view that was strongly held in medieval times and even by Martin Luther, who said it was impossible to pray upon the marriage bed.

7. *Despite these negative influences, it is to Paul's credit that he made some very positive statements about marriage.* It was the anonymous writer of the epistle to the Hebrews who said, "Let marriage be held in honor among all" (Hebrews 13:4), but Paul, if he wrote the epistle to the Ephesians, is surely saying something very similar (Ephesians 5:21-33). The analogy which likens the

relationship of husband and wife to that of Christ and the church could not have been used if Paul had not held a high spiritual view of marriage, and we can reasonably conclude that he did indeed take this view. Although not directly linked with marriage, mention must also be made of Paul's magnificent tribute to the power of love in I Corinthians 13.

In summing up, however, we must recognize that Paul made enough negative statements about marriage to provide some support to those who came after him to adopt the sadly distorted attitudes that gained favor in the centuries that followed.

OTHER NEW TESTAMENT ATTITUDES

Scattered through the rest of the New Testament are about twenty additional passages which have something to say about marriage. Only a few of them need be mentioned. They raise four further topics—three negative and one positive. Here they are:

1. *Status of the Wife.* Both in the Old Testament and the New Testament, wives have very little status outside the home. We have seen that Paul instructs them to be silent in the church (I Corinthians 14:35). In I Peter 2:7 the wife is described as the "weaker vessel," and therefore to be treated indulgently by the husband, whose greater strength is implied. This is, of course, part of the almost universal idea, in the ancient world, of women as inferior to men. It is significant in this connection that in the New Testament as a whole, a total of one hundred eighty men are identified by name, as compared to only thirty-five women; six of the latter were not *Christian* women! Although there are vague hints about Christian men and their wives working together in the church of New Testament times, only one couple, Aquila and Priscilla,

are clearly identified and named as being engaged in a shared ministry.

2. *Second Marriages.* In I Timothy 3:2 there is a description of the credentials required of a man who aspires to be a church leader. Among the desired qualities listed, it is made clear that he must be "the husband of one wife." There seems no reason to think that a polygamist would even be considered for such an office; so the obvious interpretation is that it was regarded as improper for a Christian widower to remarry. The implication can only be that getting married once is permissible (though we have seen that even this is only reluctantly conceded in some quarters), but for the Christian man to marry a *second* time makes him unfit for responsible service in the church. A similar opinion seems to be adopted about the remarriage of widows. Romans 7:2-3 makes it clear that the law *allows* widows to marry again. But in I Timothy 5:9 it is suggested that a Christian woman who *does* marry a second time has done something discreditable; in the following verses it is hinted that the *young* widow who feels the urge to remarry is yielding to improper, if not actually sinful, impulses.

3. *Fitness for Heaven.* Revelation 19:7 and 21:2 use the analogy of a wedding to describe the coming of the New Jerusalem, which will usher in the final triumph of God's purpose. However, in Revelation 14:1-5 we read about the outstanding Christians—144,000 of them—whose record on earth fits them for the highest honors in heaven. At first it is implied that these paragons of virtue might include both men and women. But in verse 4 it is clearly stated that they have kept themselves pure by not having sexual relations with women. Valiant attempts have been made by scholars to explain away this embarrassing verse. But an honest appraisal would have to assess it as the most anti-marriage statement in the Bible.

4. *False Teachers Will Come.* In I Timothy 4:3, we are very firmly told that the church in the future will be infiltrated by false teachers who are dangerous people and must be identified as such. One way they can be recognized is that they will try to forbid the marriage of Christians. This is an unqualified positive affirmation of marriage for Christians.

SUMMARY OF FINDINGS

We have now looked, albeit briefly, at what the New Testament has to say about marriage. Each passage could be much more intensively analyzed; many could be, have been, and are likely still to be, endlessly debated.

What we want to do here is to try to gain a broad impression, as objectively as possible, of what Christian teaching about marriage really is. If the first Christians broke away somewhat from Hebrew concepts, we need to recognize that this was so, and if possible, we need to know the reasons.

Some of these reasons seem to be fairly clear. By way of summary, here is, though not necessarily complete, a list:

1. Some groups within Judaism, notably the Essenes, had already broken with the traditional view that all men and, if possible, all women should marry.

2. Jesus, although reared within the faith and culture of Judaism, had apparently departed from the rule that all young men should marry. He had presumably done so because he believed that his special mission was incompatible with the duties and responsibilities involved in marrying and establishing a home. Instead, he had adopted celibacy and a simple life-style that bordered on the ascetic.

3. Jesus did not, however, in any way *discourage* marriage, except for those who felt called by God to special service of a nature that would preclude, as it did in his case,

assuming the duties and responsibilities of family life.

4. The first disciples called by Jesus found it necesssary to leave their homes and their marital responsibilities in order to assume their new roles. They became a close-knit group who shared in supporting the ministry of Jesus. Thus the beginning of the Christian community, the twelve first disciples, turned out to be a group of dedicated men withdrawn from life's normal avocations and resembling the later monastic orders.

5. Paul, who became the first of the apostles, was also unmarried and remained so. His extensive travels involved such hardships as imprisonment and eventual martyrdom, which would have been inconsistent with the settled life of a family man.

6. Paul was, in addition, not favorably disposed toward marriage, either for himself or for other Christians. He expected the world to end soon, so marriage was irrelevant. Paul was also inclined to favor asceticism as a sign of spiritual strength and to see celibacy as the best life for most Christians. However, he was careful to recognize, also, that for some Christians marriage was a way of life that could be divinely blessed, and he supported and sought to guide those Christians who had chosen the married state, and specially recommended marriage to the sexually incontinent.

7. Other New Testament writings are either supportive or discouraging of marriage for Christian believers. There is a tendency, however, to repeat some of the less positive opinions we have noted in Paul's writings.

8. Despite its equivocal stand, however, there is very little in the New Testament to support the negative views of marriage that developed later in the Christian community. The New Testament as a whole seems to make marriage entirely optional for Christian believers, while it is discouraged for those called to special ministries.

PROSPECTS FOR CHRISTIAN MARRIAGE

The New Testament writers were naturally not considering how Christian believers should think and believe in other parts of the world two thousand years later. They were recording, under the guidance of God, the essential facts about the life, teaching, and ministry of Jesus, whom they had accepted as the Son of God and the Savior of the world. And they were dealing, in letters to scattered Christian groups in the Eastern Mediterranean, with day-to-day issues and problems for which appropriate action was required. Much of what they wrote, therefore, has little direct application to our world of today. We would be misguided if we tried to copy their behavior in terms of what they wore, how they built their homes, the food they ate, their educational system, their social customs, or even how they conducted their weddings. Clearly there are aspects of married life that are equally irrelevant to us today.

Our proper use of the New Testament, therefore, is to get behind these circumstantial and situational facts to the basic beliefs and principles that motivated them, then to apply these to our behavior as Christians in the very different environment in which we live today.

The best way to do this is to listen attentively to the message of Jesus, just as the people who heard him did, and to watch how he lived, just as they did. We have no more than a fraction of the information we would like, of course. But most of the people who decided to follow Jesus had far from complete information and plenty of unanswered questions. Even Paul, for example, never met Jesus in the flesh. Neither they nor we will ever have all the answers. That doesn't really matter, because it was promised by Jesus himself that "when the Spirit of truth comes, he will lead you into all the truth" (John 16:13 TEV). All Christian men and women through the ages made their decision to be Christians only on the basis of what they learned from the New Testament and through the witness of others who had learned before them from the same source.

There are, of course, distinctive characteristics that make a Christian marriage what it is, and we shall try to identify them in due course. But knowing what these are will not take us much nearer to *experiencing* a Christian marriage, simply because it *is* a matter of experiencing. Knowledge is a necessary and good beginning, but until knowledge has been translated into experience, through *acting on the knowledge,* we are still far from our goal.

Christianity is a way of life, which means a way of *behaving.* A Christian married couple are no different from any other married couple, except that they are living the Christian life and applying its principles, day by day, to their relationship with each other and in their united relationship to the people around them.

Suppose for a moment that Jesus *had* married. We may be sure that it would have been a good relationship, simply because in the marriage Jesus would have lived by the same principles of behavior as he did when unmarried. He would have been loving, honest, caring, considerate, and forgiving just because these are the ethical standards by which he lived and by which he called on all his followers to live.

What this means is, as we said earlier in this chapter, that we go to the New Testament not to find rules and regulations that applied in Palestine two thousand years ago, but to find principles for behavior that we can build into the marriage system of our own time. The New Testament won't tell us how to allocate roles between the modern husband and wife, how to budget our money, or how to manage our time. What it will tell us is how to express love, how to be sensitive to the needs of another, how to be open and honest, how to act considerately and unselfishly, how to deal with anger and conflict, how to forgive and be reconciled after an experience of alienation, and above all else, how to reflect the love of God for us both in our love for each other. It is these vital principles put into practice that make a marriage truly Christian, just as it is these same vital principles which alone can make any other human institution truly Christian, and could ultimately make the life of the whole world truly Christian.

What the New Testament makes possible for a man, a woman, or a married couple is an *encounter* with Jesus of Nazareth. When the Christian church started, it was no more and no less than a company of people, single and married, who had experienced such an encounter and had decided as a result to change their way of living. Wherever the Christian message has reached people, this has been true. When the church has been a vital institution, it has been because its members were seriously living the Christian life. When the church has failed, it has been because its members were *not* living the Christian life. The same has been true of marriages.

Albert Schweitzer closed his great book *The Quest of the Historical Jesus* with an account of what it means to encounter Jesus of Nazareth. His words provide a fitting conclusion to this chapter:

> He comes to us as One unknown, without a name, as of old, by the lake side, He came to those men who knew Him not. He speaks to us the same word: "Follow thou me!" and sets us to the tasks which He has to fulfil for our time. He commands. And to those who obey Him, whether they be wise or simple, He will reveal Himself in the toils, the conflicts, the sufferings which they shall pass through in His fellowship, and, as an ineffable mystery, they shall learn in their own experience Who He is.

It is, therefore, those, and only those, who have encountered the ever-living Christ and have surrendered their lives to him who will surely know how to make their marriages truly Christian.

PART II

The Early and Medieval Church

Chapter 4

INTERLUDE: THE ENCIRCLING GLOOM (The Pagan World)

In or near A.D. 30, Jesus of Nazareth was sentenced to death by Pontius Pilate, who officially represented the Roman emperor ruling over Palestine at that time. The accusation against Jesus was that he had claimed to be king of the Jews, which represented a challenge to the power of Rome. He was nailed to a cross—crucifixion was at that time the official way to execute criminals.

Less than three hundred years later, in the year A.D. 313, Roman Emperor Constantine accepted the Christian faith, and Christianity became the official religion of the empire. Constantine explained his action by saying that at a critical point in his life, he had seen a cross silhouetted against the sunlit sky. The "pale Galilean," to use Swinburne's phrase, had finally conquered.

The victory had not been easily won. It had taken the dedicated efforts of a host of apostles and martyrs, who had proclaimed the gospel and offered up their lives in a sustained witness to the new faith.

The young churches, therefore, had to develop in a pagan atmosphere that was not at all helpful to the Christian message. In all the territories surrounding the Mediterranean, the standards of marriage and family life were desperately low. Unless we clearly realize this fact, we shall not be able to understand some of the attitudes about sex and marriage that developed in the early church. So, in this chapter, we must make a brief survey of the moral standards that existed in the Greco-Roman world at the time Christianity began.

MARRIAGE AMONG THE GREEKS

The stories of early Greece told by Homer could stretch as far back as 1200 B.C., but these are mainly myths and legends. The period best known to us is the so-called "Golden Age," from about 600 to 300 B.C., in which the famous philosophers, writers, and artists flourished. The contributions made to later thought by these great men—Socrates, Plato, Aristotle, and the rest—are so outstanding that it is rather disconcerting to discover that "the glory that was Greece," to use Poe's words, was often far from glorious at the domestic levels.

The picture we present here is mainly that of Lucius F. Cervantes and Carle C. Zimmerman, co-authors of *Marriage and the Family.* Both men were distinguished scholars at Harvard University. Cervantes brings to our attention several aspects of Greek life that were not conducive to high marital standards:

1. GREEK RELIGION

We are probably all familiar with some of the gods and goddesses, ruled over by Zeus, who were believed to inhabit Mount Olympus, which for the Greeks was the equivalent of heaven. According to Homer, Zeus set a deplorable standard of family life. The stories about him record that he killed his father, devoured his first wife, Metis, married his sister, Hera, had sexual intercourse with his other sister, Demeter, and had a child by his daughter, Persephone. He had various children by other goddesses, too, and from time to time he descended to the earth to have sexual relations with especially attractive women.

In fact, Cervantes asserts that "the marital manners of the Greek deities were undignified, coarse, and even brutal. . . . In general, gods and goddesses carouse, fornicate, lie, intrigue, fight like the worst of ordinary humans." Their relationships were both heterosexual and homosexual. (Several of the early Greek statues were of homosexual gods.)

2. SEXUAL BEHAVIOR

If the gods you worshiped behaved like that, what inducement would there be for you to accept higher standards of behavior than they did? It is hardly surprising that one shrine, dedicated to the goddess Aphrodite, was served by a thousand temple prostitutes, whose task it was to be available to male worshipers. In Old Testament times, several of the neighboring tribal groups also provided religious prostitutes as symbols of fertility, and a special Hebrew word *(kedeshah)* was used to distinguish them from ordinary harlots. Similarly, sexual orgies were an accepted part of the worship of the Greek gods and goddesses.

The goddess Aphrodite was the model for all sacred prostitutes, and the famous temple at Delphi, dedicated to Apollo, had a gold-covered statue of her, carved by the great sculptor Praxiteles. Two other statues by Praxiteles represent a smiling prostitute beside a weeping wife, dramatizing the way in which women were viewed in Greek society.

A special kind of prostitute, the *hetaera*, was a cultivated and highly intelligent woman who became the companion of married men, sharing their intellectual and social lives. The wives of these same men were generally ignorant girls who had been deprived of any chance of education, and who were confined to their homes and served no other purposes than to bear and raise children for their husbands.

3. PEDERASTY

The word, *pederasty*, from the Greek word *pais*, which means a child, describes a special feature of Greek sexual relations—the use of young boys as sex objects. In the Golden Age of Greek culture, the use of boys as prostitutes, or as special companions, became widely accepted, and this practice came to be called "the Greek vice." The boys were usually slaves and could be purchased by patrician families as bed companions for their teenaged sons. Edward Westermarck, who investigated this system, reports in *The Making of Man* that "the attachment was not only regarded as permissible, but was praised as the highest and purest form of love."

Given these publicly accepted standards of behavior, what then happened to marriage? Inevitably, it was not held in high esteem. Moreover, it was a rite highly restricted. V. F. Calverton, in his book *Sex in Civilization*, estimates that in Athens in 300 B.C., with a total population of 515,000, only nine thousand of these were legally entitled to marry. The reason—most of the people (one estimate is between three and twelve for each household in Athens) were slaves with no legal rights. Even legal wives, however, were strictly confined to the women's quarters of the house. The wife took care of her daughters and of her sons, but only until the latter reached the age of seven. A statement attributed to Demosthenes puts it like this: "Mistresses we keep for pleasure, concubines for daily attendance upon our person, wives to bear us legitimate children and to be our faithful housekeepers."

It might almost seem that among Greek women, the lot of the prostitute was better than that of the wife. While she was still young and attractive, this may well have been true. But once the prostitute had passed her prime, she was no longer needed or wanted by anyone.

For those of us who greatly admire the Golden Age of ancient Greece, and all the high standards of culture and art for which it stands, it seems difficult to believe that in such a culture women should often have received such miserable treatment and that esteem for marriage should have been so low. Yet, careful investigators are unanimous in the judgment at which they have arrived. Here are three of them:

V. F. Calverton writes: "In . . . a civilization that has become renowned for its intellectual genius and progressive tendency, the position of woman was a tragic spectacle. . . . She was regarded as a form of property with rights no more exalted than that of a slave. Hipponax declared that 'a woman gives two days of happiness to a man: her bridal day and her burial.' Women were treated with open contempt in the works of Plato, Pindar, Lucian, Thucydides, Antiphanes, Menander, Isomachus, and Aristophanes" *(Sex in Civilization)*.

Carle C. Zimmerman writes: "Even after making all possible allowances, we cannot excuse the men of Pericles' time for the selfishness, lack of appreciation, and—from our point of view—downright cruelty, which too often characterized their attitude to the other sex. Her sad and isolated life, during the brilliant period of Athens' political and intellectual supremacy, constitutes one of the most astonishing phenomena in the history of the Greek states" *(Family and Civilization)*.

Finally, Robert Briffault sums it up: "Greek woman was the most degraded and abject to be found in any civilized country of the Western world" *(The Mothers)*.

And now we turn to Imperial Rome.

MARRIAGE AMONG THE ROMANS

Founded in 753 B.C., Rome finally fell to the barbarian hordes in A.D. 476. In that long period of more than twelve hundred years, there were many changes.

The family system in the early centuries was characterized by the *patria potestas*, which might be translated as "the all-powerful father." This was literally and legally true. The male head of the family had the power of life and death over his children; also, through the *law of manus*, the man had control over his wife and all other legitimate members of the family group.

This is, however, a somewhat dramatic way of putting it. We are not to assume that this power was often used. In the Old Testament, Abraham assumed that, at God's command, he had the right to sacrifice his son Isaac, but he didn't actually do so. The point is that the Roman family *began* by being fully patriarchal—the authority of the father was supreme. This was based on religious belief, just as it was among the Hebrews. And, like the ancient Hebrews, the ancient Romans counted the worship of God to be focused on honoring the ancestors and continuing the family line. Similarly, too, the Roman wife and mother didn't count as an ancestor, since she had only been the bearer of the children. In life and in death, she was counted simply as a part of her husband.

In *The Ancient City*, Zimmerman and Cervantes quote De Coulanges' neat summary of the rites of the early Roman father as the religious head of the family. He is empowered:

1. To accept or reject a child at birth. There was a widespread custom in the ancient world that allowed unwanted children to be "exposed"—that is, left alone to die.

2. To repudiate the wife, either in case of her childlessness or of her adultery.

3. To give his son or daughter in marriage.

4. To adopt a stranger into the household.

5. To name, at his death, a guardian for his wife and children.

Marriage in the early days was very stable. Romans boasted that for over five hundred years they had not had a single divorce. But as the empire grew in power and influence, great changes occurred. The early laws were modified over time, and in the last years of the empire, as we shall see, the whole system collapsed.

A major cause of these changes was the fact that the number of slaves greatly increased until they became, as they had done in Athens, the majority class, and marriage was not legally permitted to slaves. A time came, too, when the religious basis of marriage was weakened; Roman women, like those in Greece, could register as prostitutes and become concubines in upper-class families.

These changes began as early as the Punic Wars in the third century B.C., and continued through the time of Christ to the final fall of the empire. "By the end of the second century B.C., marriage was no longer considered a social and religious obligation; the insolent air of luxury and world conquest began to clog the moral atmosphere; slaves and other forms of property poured into the public coffers . . . the middle class disappeared; the birth rate dropped . . . the process of social disintegration was in full sweep" (*Marriage and the Family*).

To understand this situation, we need to focus on the expanding number of slaves. In A.D. 50, as the first apostles were taking the gospel message out into the empire, there were twenty-one million slaves in Italy and only seven million freemen—a ratio of three to one. When Paul was in Rome, the average upper-class family had fifteen slaves. At that very time the prefect of Rome was murdered by a slave who resented his treatment of a slave girl. The punishment was that all the slaves in the entire household—four hundred of them—were put to death.

Imagine what this meant to the life of the city. Slaves couldn't marry, but many of them came from communities where every kind of sexual excess was commonplace. Corruption inevitably spread throughout the empire.

At the time of the Julian legislation of 18 B.C. to A.D. 14, a second type of marriage was introduced. It was called the *concubatus*, and it lasted for five centuries. It was legally a marriage, but one that was easily terminated. The idea was to recognize the sexual freedom that was now an accepted state of affairs, but to build in some controls. However, this seems to have done very little to check the widespread breakdown of standards. In the later years of the empire, there was hardly a woman in Rome who had not been divorced at least once. There is one case on record in which the woman was married to her twenty-third husband, while she was his twenty-first wife.

It was obviously impossible to protect human values in marriage while moral principles were being violated on every hand. An anonymous oracle at that time sounded an ominous warning: "Woe to you, Rome: punishment will overtake you, because you have yearned for poisons, practiced adultery, and nefarious intercourse with young boys. Oh city, a cesspool of vices, iniquitous, evil. Woe to you, impure city of the Latin land." The warning was not heeded. The empire, rotten to the core, collapsed.

CONCLUSION

This chapter has not been a pleasant one to write, and we have kept it as short as possible. It will not be pleasant to read either. However, unless the widespread decay of morals in the early centuries of the Christian era is clearly understood, it is difficult to credit the negative attitudes about sex that developed as the church tried to establish itself in the Roman Empire. We shall address that issue in the next chapter.

Chapter 5

MARRIAGE IS ACCEPTABLE: BUT SEX CAN MAKE IT SINFUL
(The Early Church)

We now turn from the New Testament to follow the development of the early church. This period of Christian history covers about five hundred years, until the final fall of Rome in A.D. 476. During this time we shall be confronted by the emergence of some negative ideas about marriage that are not at first easy to understand. When we ask how they arose, we find that they focus on one major issue which has caused confusion throughout most of the history of the church—the Christian interpretation of human sexuality. Before we confront this, however, let us see how the church developed during those early centuries.

After the death of Jesus, some waited eagerly for his triumphal return in power. But gradually it became clear that the urgent task was now to get the message out to others. Beginning in the Jewish communities, the first apostles won converts in ever-widening circles, and the Christian community grew and spread until the church extended to the outer limits of the then-civilized world. It is a magnificent and triumphant story which vindicated the authenticity and the power of the Christian message beyond further dispute.

How were those early Christian communities organized? The question is well answered in William Stewart McBirnie's very informative book *The Search for the Early Church.* He tells us how the first apostles founded local congregations, ministered to their converts, and helped them to grow in grace.

Jesus had left no clear directions for the organization of the churches. The only one he can be said to have founded is the one in Jerusalem, and in A.D. 70, when that city was virtually destroyed by the Romans, the Christian community fled and scattered. Paul had founded a chain of churches across Asia Minor, reaching even to Rome; some of his letters, included in the New Testament, give us valuable information about them. The chief activities of the churches were witnessing, praying, evangelizing, baptizing converts, teaching, and ministering to the needy—the kinds of programs in which dynamic Christian churches, wherever in the world they have been established, have been involved ever since.

Often, a beginning church would meet in the home of a Christian family, as happened in Jerusalem at the home of the mother of John Mark. So, Christian married couples were involved together in a kind of informal ministry; although, following the traditional Jewish pattern, the wife usually played a subsidiary role and stayed well in the background. There seems every reason to believe, however, that convert couples established beginning churches in Christian households, and that this was accepted as a normal and natural arrangement. With apostles, of course, the situation was different. It was not practicable to take a wife with you on rough and extended missionary travels, and to add a brood of children would have been virtually impossible. So the apostles, like their predecessors, the first disciples, had to sacrifice the normal fulfillments of marriage and family life for the propagation of the gospel.

THE DEVELOPMENT OF THE MINISTRY

In the New Testament, we find many references to the people who became leaders in the churches. Various terms were used; the words *deacon* and *minister* both mean "servant," so these men didn't assume authoritative roles. Some women also served as deaconesses. The word *elder* obviously means a senior person, one who has gathered enough experience to provide leadership. The chairman of the elders in these early churches began to be called the *bishop*, from a Greek word meaning "overseer." The word *pastor* clearly denotes a shepherd of the flock. At a later time, the word *priest* began to be used, and the comprehensive word *clergy* included all ranks.

At first these Christian ministers maintained themselves—Paul as a tent-maker—and gave their services without recompense. But inevitably, as churchs became bigger and longer established, the need arose for full-time service, and the congregation had to maintain its pastor. Then, all churches in a geographical area linked up with one another, and bishops were appointed to supervise them and coordinate their activities.

What has all this to do with Christian marriage? A great deal, because these leaders modeled the accepted life-styles for settled Christian families. At first the ministers were mainly married men, with wives and families, and this was accepted without question.

However, over time the pattern began to change. The many influences we have already considered—the fact that Jesus and Paul were unmarried, the greater freedom of singles to travel and to cope with crisis situations, the increasing influence of asceticism as a way of demonstrating zeal for the gospel, negative attitudes about human sexuality—these and other influences clearly began to shift the preferred pattern for a minister, and his chances of being successful in his task, toward an emphasis on celibacy.

In those days, also, the heroes tended to be the extremists. The religious climate, strongly influenced by Neo-Platonism from Greece and extreme ascetic cults from the Orient, in reacting negatively to the low standards of sexual morality in the empire, strongly favored those whose renunciation of worldliness went to the greatest lengths. The desert hermits of North Africa, abandoning all worldly comforts and devoting their lives to prayer and fasting, seemed to model true dedication to spiritual ideals. Then, when persecution fell upon the churches, it was those who had given up all earthly ties and set their hopes only in heaven who suffered torture with resignation and went to their deaths with matchless courage. It is easy to see how, in this atmosphere, truly dedicated men and women would aim at totally renouncing all worldly pursuits and pleasures and how their example would motivate others to follow in their footsteps.

Elaine Pagels, in her book *The Gnostic Gospels*, argues that the early church at first accepted not only the right of ministers to be married, but also the right of women Christians to share with men in positions of leadership in the church.

> In its earliest years the Christian movement showed a remarkable openness toward women. Jesus himself violated Jewish convention by talking openly with women, and he included them among his companions. . . . In earlier times men and women sat together for

worship. However, in the middle of the second century . . . orthodox communities began to adopt the synagogue custom, segregating women from men. By the end of the second century, women's participation in worship was explicitly condemned; groups in which women continued on to leadership were branded as heretical. . . . The orthodox community came to accept the domination of men over women as the divinely ordained order, not only for social and family life, but also for the Christian churches.

Tertullian, who lived from about A.D. 160 to 230, was particularly vehement on this issue. He described as a "viper" a woman teacher who led a Christian congregation in North Africa, and he violently attacked the heretic Marcion for appointing women as priests.

Obviously it was a simple, logical step from declaring that women were unfit to perform spiritual functions to adopting the attitude that men set aside exclusively to perform spiritual functions should not share an intimate life with a woman by being married to one.

As the centuries passed, more and more of the clergy voluntarily chose celibacy as the right way of life for them. By the beginning of the third century, the movement for the celibacy of the clergy was becoming organized, and attempts were made to persuade married bishops, presbyters, and deacons to abstain from sexual intercourse with their wives. A century later, synods passed resolutions requiring this of all clergy, and a number of the married ones had now been persuaded to cease living with their wives altogether.

It should be noted in passing that celibacy applied only to the *Western* church. In the Greek Orthodox tradition, only bishops have been required to be celibate. And even in the West, the rule was not successfully and universally applied until the sixteenth century.

The attempt to *enforce* the celibacy of the clergy met with varying success. For a time it would seem to be widely accepted, then it would break down. Often it was honored more in the breach than in the observance. There were periods, and geographical regions, in which large numbers of priests, though not married, lived openly with women. Over the centuries, many priests, including a number of popes, fathered children and lived grossly immoral lives. The whole story has been vividly recorded by Henry C. Lea in a volume of over six hundred pages, *History of Sacerdotal Celibacy in the Christian Church*, first published in 1867. It certainly represents a massive study of the subject, but some critics feel that it is somewhat biased against the Catholic church, and for that reason does not always present a really fair picture.

It is not easy to see this issue with a full and clear perspective. Certainly, the cause of Christian marriage suffered a cruel setback for well over a thousand years. Yet, when we view the hardships suffered by the Christian cause, first by persecution in the Roman Empire, then by the fall of Rome and the ravaging of Europe by the barbarians, then the Dark Ages when human values seemed to stagnate in a climate of ignorance and indifference—in such conditions, it was again and again the dedication of celibate priests, monks, and missionaries that brought the world back to sanity.

IMPACT ON THE LAITY

Meanwhile, relegated to the background, there were the lay members of the churches, the ordinary Christian believers who married and raised children. What eventually happened was that the Christian community was divided up into three fairly separate groups: first, the parish clergy, who served the churches at the pastoral level—bishops, priests, and deacons; second, the monks (and some nuns), who were dedicated to the monastic life and had withdrawn from the world into religious communities; and third, the lay members of the churches. The first two groups wielded almost all the power and made most of the important decisions. And, since all of them were ultimately vowed to celibacy, they naturally viewed their parishioners as being spiritually inferior. Through the confessional, the priests were able to keep in close touch with the personal lives of Christian married couples, and what they learned helped them to formulate the code of canon law—a complex legal system of rules and regulations administered by the church. So, what the Roman Catholic church developed was *a means of controlling the lives of married couples by a set of standards put together by men who had never themselves been married and who regarded married life as an inferior level of Christian living.*

Naturally enough, such a system was mainly concerned with the requirements for entry into marriage, the nature of the contract between the parties, the church's jurisdiction over matrimonial causes, the consummation of marriage, the prohibited degrees of kindred and affinity, the indissolubility of the relationship, and similar issues. Little or no attention was given to *the quality of the relationship.* For example, in the monumental six hundred forty page *Christian Marriage: An Historical and Doctrinal Study* by George Hayward Joyce, first published in England in 1933, the index contains no reference whatsoever to words like *love, affection, companionship, communication, conflict, forgiveness, reconciliation, growth, relationships, mutuality,* and the like. The approach is purely legal, and intentionally so, because the way two married persons interact and feel about each other is outside its terms of reference.

It must be added, however, that Catholics today are re-examining their traditional policies and have made significant contributions to married couples by developing such a movement as the Marriage Encounter. But during the long centuries when the church had firm control over the marriages of its members, scant attention was given to relational issues, except in terms of their conformity to the rules. There is a tragic touch of cynicism in the famous saying of Jerome: "I praise marriage, because it brings me virgins." It might have been more honest to substitute the word *tolerate* for praise.

We shall have more to say about this question later. The point we wish to make now is that as long as marriage was viewed as a spiritually inferior form of Christian living—which has been true for most of the history of the church—there has been litle serious attempt to help husbands and wives to develop their relational potential in terms of Christian love. Apart from the Puritans, it has been only in the modern era that this important question has, to our knowledge, been given any serious attention.

This brief summary of what actually *happened* to Christian marriage in the early church during the nearly five hundred years to the fall of Rome must, of course, be supplemented by an account of the development of theoretical and theological ideas on the part of the church's leaders. We must now look at this very important part of the picture.

CHRISTIAN TEACHING ON SEX AND MARRIAGE

In its early centuries, the Christian church produced not only a multitude of dedicated witnesses and apostles who spread the message throughout the Roman Empire, but also a succession of brilliant scholars who set about the task of formulating the intellectual concepts that became Christian doctrine. No religious system in world history has been so well served by dedicated thinkers—the early church Fathers, or patristic writers, as they are called. If we can confine ourselves to a round dozen who were much involved in hammering out the church's teaching about marriage, we might list Ambrose, Augustine, Basil, Clement of Alexandria, Cyprian, Gregory of Nyssa, Ignatius, Jerome, John Chrysostom, Justin, Origen, and Tertullian—and that would be omitting many who also deserve recognition. They wrote mostly in Latin; a few wrote in Greek. A good many of their extensive writings have now been translated into English.

Sherwin Bailey, who studied this material closely, offers this judgment:

> The interest of the Early Church in sexual and matrimonial questions was generally occasional, limited, and practical. . . . It is particularly significant that no dispute arose of such magnitude as to demand a thorough and systematic treatment of the theological principles governing marriage and sexual relationship. Reaction against the prevailing ascetical mood of the time provoked a few light skirmishes; but a short treatise or two usually sufficed to refute, silence, and disgrace any who had the temerity to challenge current assumptions or prejudices. Apart from such brief contentions, however, and an unflagging zeal in exalting and commending the virgin state, the patristic concern with sexual matters was relatively slight and narrow. (*Sexual Relation in Christian Thought*)

As Bailey indicates, the focus of these exchanges was invariably the question of sex and sin. The aim of every true Christian, he adds, was "to attain perfection through renunciation of the world and subjugation of the body. To this end, every means was employed—fasting, solitude, prayer, mortification; but always the decisive test, the critical discipline, was that of sexual continence."

SEX AND SIN

The focus of much of the discussion of the sinful nature of sex is the story of Adam and Eve in the Garden of Eden.

So, let us go back to that old story and consider how it was treated, first by the Hebrews and then by some of the leaders of the early church.

The Bible begins with two accounts of how God created the world. It then moves on to describe how mankind came into the picture, together with the animals and birds.

The man Adam was made, as the Bible teaches, in God's image—a partaker of the divine nature. God is, of course, considered as masculine, and Adam, his first created human being, was likewise masculine.

The next stage was for God to provide Adam with a partner. The main reason stated is that it was not good for Adam to be alone; he needed a companion.

Adam's companion, Eve, was female, which meant that the possibility existed that they could, through sexual intercourse, produce children as the animals did, in order to be fruitful and multiply. But at first, apparently, this was not intended, and they seemed not to have been aware of the possibilities of their sexual differences.

The assumption is that Adam and Eve were at first intended to enjoy an endless state of bliss in the Garden of Eden, where all their needs would be fully provided. But a warning was sounded. There was a particular tree in the garden, the fruit of which they must not eat, or dire consequences would follow.

We all know what happened next. At least, we *think* we know. Tempted by the serpent—which presumably had a wicked streak in its disposition—Eve plucked the forbidden fruit and shared it with Adam. The result was that they lost their innocence and became aware of the possibility of good and evil. This made them afraid and guilty, and they tried to hide from God's presence. But of course God knew what had happened, and they were punished by being banished from Eden. Not only so, but they were now subject to the need to toil for food to sustain life, to suffer pain, and to endure a life cycle ending in death. Since death would come, however, they must now use their sexual powers, and by so doing, produce children to succeed them. Thus the continuing chain of human parenthood began.

Whether we regard this story as literal fact or view it as a symbolic explanation, it serves very well to explain the present condition of human life in this world and provides an appropriate opening for the Hebrew scriptures. It explains many aspects of the human condition—marriage, sex, parenthood, pain, work, sorrow, sin, and death. What we need to explore, however, is an issue which had a profound influence on the Christian teaching about marriage: the relationship between sex and sin.

The Hebrews were, of course, well aware of the fact of sin, and of how it could incur the disapproval, and even the wrath, of God. At the same time, as we have seen, they had a very positive attitude toward sex, seeing it as the means by which the married couple could continue God's work of creation to perpetuate the divine image from one generation to another. To them, sex was sinful and disapproved of by God *only when it was misused* by the man's wasting of his precious seed or violating the sexual rights of another man. There is no evidence that sexual intercourse in a legal marriage was viewed as in any way undesirable, let alone sinful. As E. C. Messenger expressed it, "No passage in the Old Testament implies in reality that the sexual act is in itself impure or sinful" *(The Mystery of Sex and Marriage in Catholic Theology)*.

NEGATIVE ATTITUDES ABOUT MARITAL SEX

However, in the early church, and even in the later Hebrew culture and to a small extent in the New

Testament, this positive attitude toward sex in marriage began to be questioned. We have seen that a number of factors supported a change of attitude—the development of asceticism, specially among the Essenes; the deplorably low standards of sexual behavior in the Greco-Roman world; dualistic attitudes in Greek philosophy and Oriental religion, which viewed the body and physical life as inherently opposed to the well-being of the soul. In New Testament times, these ideas had done no more than to introduce an ambivalent attitude toward marriage; it was essentially good, but it could also be a hindrance to those who sought the full cultivation of the spiritual life.

As time passed, however, and the early church began to formulate Christian doctrine and to organize the life of the Christian community, a marked increase took place in negative attitudes about marital sex. A few examples follow, all taken from chapter 4 of *The Theology of Marriage,* by Joseph E. Kerns, a Jesuit scholar.

> Justin the Martyr, born in Palestine only some seventy years after the death of Jesus, compared the pagan attitudes about sex to the Christian ideal and suggested that Christian couples should use sex only with the specific intention of having children. Athenagoras, a Christian apologist, echoed the same sentiment a generation later, and early in the third century Clement, the Bishop of Alexandria, said that a Christian husband should "practice continence, not even seeking pleasure from his own wife, whom he ought to love, but with honorable and moderate desire having but one intention, children."
>
> In the third century, Origen, one of the greatest scholars of the early church in Africa, urged married couples to stop having sexual relations once the wife had conceived. Jerome, who in A.D. 390 began to

translate the Bible into Latin, said that defective children—lame or blind—could be the result of neglecting this warning. He further declared that marital sexual relations which are not undertaken with the express intention of producing children are no more than "filth and lust."

The great Augustine (A.D. 354 to 430), Bishop of Hippo in North Africa, expressed a similar opinion. Speaking of the holy men and women of the Old Testament, he says that they "were inflamed, not with the desire of intercourse but with a faithful desire to have children. Indeed, they would not have sought intercourse if they could have had children in some other way."

Ambrose, the distinguished Bishop of Milan in the fourth century, said to his people, "Although marriage is good, it includes something that makes even married people blush at themselves."

As a result of this frequently repeated attitude, "the stain of carnal pleasure," as Cyril of Alexandria (A.D. 375 to 444) called it, led some priests to require married couples to stay away from church for several days and not to approach the altar after they had had sexual intercourse. Much later, in the sixteenth century, a Spanish priest at the Council of Trent spoke of "the inborn embarrassment" of a husband after having sex with his wife, and said that "a man who does not feel this is lower than every beast."

THE FALL AND ORIGINAL SIN

These derogatory attitudes were closely linked to theories about the sin of Adam and Eve. So, let us look again at what happened in the Garden of Eden.

Some early writers have hinted that the Fall story could be given a strongly sexual interpretation. The suggestion is that what Adam and Eve did was not to eat an apple, but to have sexual intercourse. Let us try to reconstruct the story along these lines:

We may suppose that God's original purpose was to make Adam and Eve immortal. But to earn this right, they had to be tested; so, they were told that there was one thing they must not do. Suppose that thing was to have sexual intercourse. How does this fit by analogy the drama that is described?

The serpent was frequently, in the ancient world, used as a sexual symbol. Its shape and the appearance of sliding toward Eve could easily be suggestive of the male sex organ. The tree is described in terms of "knowledge." When Adam and Eve came together sexually outside Eden, the term for what they did is that he *knew* her.

The forbidden act is related not to the tree as such, but to its *fruit*. Sex, in human terms, symbolizes fruitfulness. If trees in Eden bore fruit, the sexual principle was already established in the vegetable world as in the animal world. And there were animals in Eden to be observed.

Could Eve, therefore, encouraged by the serpent, have entertained the idea of sexual intercourse and made the suggestion to Adam? In the story, she was the one chiefly blamed for the offense.

After the event, they knew that they had yielded to temptation and disobeyed God. Their reaction was to try to hide the fact. How did they do so? By covering up their sex organs, hoping that God wouldn't notice. Why did they do this, unless their guilt was associated with sex?

The threat of God had been that their disobedience would lead to death. Why? Obviously, continued reproduction would mean more and more human beings, and in time the original ones would have to make room for the newcomers. So the capacity for reproduction implied vulnerability to death. As Milton expressed it in *Paradise Lost*, the "disobedience" of Adam and Eve "brought death into the world, and all our woes."

So, if sexual intercourse was first a sinful act of disobedience toward God and initiated the cycle of death and new life, obviously the sex act carried with it a renewal of the life process through birth, growth, aging, and death. So the "original" sin was repeated in every act of sexual intercourse, renewing the cycle. Human beings are sinful; therefore, they are doomed to die, but reproduction continues the line.

However, Milton's theme was not only "Paradise Lost," but also "Paradise Regained." The possibility existed that, after all, fallen man could be redeemed and could get to heaven in the end through salvation by the mediation of Christ.

But clearly the chances of gaining heaven would be enhanced for those who could resist the original temptation to which Adam and Eve succumbed— namely, the sexual urge. Therefore, there was an obvious spiritual advantage in practicing continence.

THE VIEWS OF AUGUSTINE

It should be made clear that interpreting the sin of Adam and Eve as sexual intercouse has never been the official teaching of the church. According to Augustine and Aquinas, the most highly respected authorities, the sin committed in the Garden of Eden was spiritual pride. Man wanted to put himself above God. "Pride," said Augustine, "is the beginning of all sin."

However, Clement of Alexandria, who has already been quoted, gave the Fall a definitely sexual significance. He saw Adam and Eve as acting like children. They were not yet ready for sex, but yielded to its impulse. He supports this view by pointing out that "the serpent writhing on his stomach figuratively symbolizes pleasure."

Earlier Jewish writers had suggested the same idea. The *Book of Jubilees* (3:26-27, 31) implies that having sexual relations caused the expulsion of Adam and Eve from the Garden of Eden. Philo, a Jewish philosopher who lived during the time of Christ, wrote "Love came to Adam and Eve, and gave to both of them the desire to unite themselves to each other. This desire engendered the fleshly pleasure which is the source of all wickedness" *(De Opificio Mundi).*

E. C. Messenger, in volume two of his book *The Mystery of Sex and Marriage*, quotes a Professor Coppens of Louvain as suggesting that "the sacred author modified the story in such a way as to put the sexual motif in the background, so that the sexual character of the sin is now no more than hinted at."

Augustine (A.D. 354–430) taught that "concupiscence"—sexual desire—is the means by which original sin is *transmitted* from parent to child. A later view, slightly modified, is that what concupiscence transmits is human nature in its fallen state.

Since Augustine was one of the greatest figures in Christian history—both scholar and saint—we may pursue this theme a little further. In his *Confessions* (toward the end of the tenth book) he gives an account of the death of his beloved mother, Monica. He feels acute grief, but cannot allow himself to cry or otherwise reveal his feelings because, as a Christian, he shouldn't feel sadness at his mother's going to heaven. He and the others around him restrained themselves from grieving.

But he is really under great stress, and cannot find relief. He tries a hot bath, but that doesn't work. Finally, he allows himself *just one hour* privately and completely alone to pour out his grief. After this cathartic experience, he feels better and needs no further mourning.

This feeling about grief is very revealing. Clearly, for Augustine life must be purely rational, expressive only of what is *believed* and never of what is *felt*. This principle sheds much light on the ascetic attitude toward sex. The early church fathers often attacked concupiscence *because it produces a flood of feeling that overwhelms rational control*.

This leads to a further reflection. The Christian ascetic is focusing attention on the spiritual world, seeking to live, here and now, the life of heaven. What separates the ascetic from that life is only the body which the soul now occupies. Therefore the demands of bodily existence must be firmly reduced to a minimum. Obviously, one must breathe, eat, and sleep—though eating and sleeping can be kept to a minimum. However, one bodily function that can be *completely* suspended is sex. It represents a pleasurable experience that strengthens the tie to this world. Therefore, its renunciation represents a critical test for the Christian, a way of demonstrating convincingly that one chooses the life of the spirit rather than the life of the body.

It is easy to see how, by this kind of reasoning, sexual suppression could become the acid test of Christian dedication. And once that position has been adopted, all sources of sexual stimulation come to be seen as temptation to sin. This could, and did, lead to the renunciation of marriage and to the avoidance of women, especially attractive women, by holy men.

This basic argument can be supported by others. Marriage introduces new obligations and commitments to wife, to children, and to home. Such mundane concerns are distractions in a double sense. They demand time and attention that could otherwise be spent in prayer and devotion; this would be very frustrating for a monk or a nun. Also, the claims of marriage focus attention on home and family obligations, so that the freedom to devote oneself to ministry to the needy is hampered, and of course this could hinder the work of a priest.

Obviously, these concerns give strong support to the idea that chastity, virginity, and celibacy represent high spiritual ideals. This had a special appeal to the early church at a time when rejection, harassment, and persecution were often suffered by new converts. All these manifestations of dedicated self-denial represented taking up the cross for the sake of the gospel, and they were seen as manifestations of virtue that increased the likelihood of inheriting eternal life hereafter.

Yet the Hebrew tradition, out of which the Christian faith has come, emphasized marriage as a gift of God and as a means of blessing. The church could hardly reject this traditional teaching, because the New Testament had not rejected it. Christians could not be asked to give up something good provided by God, as an evidence of religious devotion. So the church found a solution by suggesting that *marriage* was essentially something good, but that *sex* was something evil—even an instrument of the devil—and the vehicle through which original sin is transmitted from generation to generation.

This unfortunate stratagem, of course, landed the church in a quandary. In order to frighten the faithful away from sex, it was necessary, also, to degrade marriage, women, and parenthood, which in the end led to a complete reversal of the standards of the early Hebrews.

Faced with this dilemma, the church tried at a later time to balance its teaching by making marriage a sacrament.

But against the negative views of sex, this never carried much conviction; Christian writers had to get tied into knots, such as the attempt to teach the laity that sex in marriage was acceptable *only when it was not enjoyed,* and that the minds of the couple should be focused exclusively on the concept of having a child. This, of course, led later to the strong condemnation of contraception, because it enabled couples to separate the enjoyment of sex from the duty of parenthood.

To begin to deal with all the implications of what the patristic fathers said about sex and marriage would require another book on that subject alone. This is a confusing and disturbing aspect of Christian history, and most church members know very little about it and prefer to leave it alone. But it is impossible to ignore it in making any attempt to write a book about Christian marriage in a changing world. We need to remember that the early church fathers were doing their best to formulate Christian teaching on all aspects of human life, and they had to do so in a world that had no developed knowledge of human biology or psychology such as we have today. Moreover, all their thinking was affected by the dualism that permeated the Roman world.

Augustine was a man of towering intellect, but he had to use the materials that were available to him. He was also a man of saintly character, ready to open up his inner life as he strove valiantly to become a better Christian. In his earlier years, sex had been his major obstacle, as he describes vividly in his *Confessions;* the complete victory he gained over it was for him the keystone of his conversion. It was, therefore, natural that he should support the view already adopted by the early church, that the hallmark of a true Christian was the renunciation of sex and marriage, and that those who would not or could not do this, though acceptable to God, must be thought of as belonging spiritually to a lower order.

Another point must be repeated. In the early centuries of its existence, when the church was suffering rejection, hostility, and sometimes brutal persecution, the survival of the Christian faith had to depend upon men and women whose dedication made them ready for any sacrifice. The lives of those early Christians leave us in no doubt about their being ready to meet this test. Many of the early church fathers ended their lives as martyrs for the faith they proclaimed. Who are we, living in more comfortable circumstances, to say that their willingness to forego the fulfillment and comforts of Christian family life may not have been necessary, in their time, to enable them to meet the final test of their faith?

In our world of today, however, much has changed. The church has had to adapt to those changes. Concepts of sex and marriage have had to be modified as Christian leaders struggled to interpret the meaning of the gospel for the lives of those who sought to witness to their faith in an ever-changing world.

William Graham Cole sums up the patristic teaching on sex in marriage, as Augustine tried to interpret it: "Augustine regarded all sex except that required for reproduction as venially sinful. . . . It would be unfair to lay the sole responsibility for this on Augustine. He simply accepted the tradition as it was passed on to him from earlier hands, but he did systematize and solidify it, making it definitive for the medieval Church" *(Sex in Christianity and Psychoanalysis)*.

Our next task will be to see how the medieval church dealt with the beliefs and attitudes to sex and marriage which were passed on to it. The collapse of the Roman Empire was to lead to many changes.

Chapter 6

INTERLUDE: LIFE IN
THE MIDDLE AGES

We now enter a stretch of a thousand years during which millions of Christian men and women were born, lived, and died. In order to understand what life was like for them, we must first look at some of the historical facts.

When the western Roman Empire finally collapsed in the fifth century A.D., Europe was thrown into confusion. Barbarian peoples who had been kept under control by the powerful Roman armies now went on the rampage, fighting one another and ravaging the land.

This marked the end of what has been called Antiquity—the classical Greco-Roman civilization—and the beginning of what we call the Middle Ages. We usually date this period roughly from the fall of Rome in A.D. 476 to the discovery of America—the "New World"—in 1492. These dates are shown on the time line at the beginning of this book.

The medieval era was, therefore, a long stretch of history. It covered what Edward Gibbon, the English historian who wrote *The Decline and Fall of the Roman Empire*, described as the "Dark Ages." It was finally followed by what is called the Renaissance, a French word meaning "rebirth," which ushered in the Protestant Reformation and the revival of learning in the Western world.

It is clearly impossible for us to devote time and space to the *political* developments that occurred during this period—the Frankish kings preceding Charlemagne, the establishment of the Holy Roman Empire, the popes and their policies and intrigues. However, we cannot understand the developments in the field of marriage and of the relationships between the sexes without some knowledge of the *social* conditions in which people lived during those years. That will be our task in this chapter.

MEDIEVAL EUROPE TAKES SHAPE

The fall of Rome was followed by a period of confusion. With the empire shattered, there was no legal system to see that justice was done, and land could be grabbed by force. With no central authority to supervise and support them, groups of families had to join forces to protect themselves. So, over time, the feudal system developed. A powerful leader would occupy, or build, a castle or other stronghold and divide up his land among tenants. If the tenants were attacked, they all withdrew to the central stronghold for mutual defense, though sometimes they were besieged and starved out.

The mighty Roman army was no more; so the nobles, as they came to be called, had to train their own fighting forces. This led to the system of knighthood, which we shall discuss later.

While the feudal system was taking shape, the church was active. Dedicated monks went out as missionaries, and gradually the barbarians became Christians. Parish churches were built. Often land passed into the hands of the religious orders, and monasteries were established to administer estates, maintaining themselves by the labor of the monks and of peasants who settled under their protection.

From the ninth to the fifteenth centuries, therefore, the feudal system was in operation in most of Europe. The Latin word *feudum* means an estate. As we have seen, the roots of the system had developed in the late Roman Empire, when central control was breaking down, and during the ensuing period of the Germanic invasions. But under Charles Martel and the Frankish kings who followed him, it now became the dominant political system. The idea was to put the church lands under the control of vassals, who in return would organize military services to protect them. With the decline in royal power, this arrangement spread widely over much of Europe and continued until the twelfth century. After that, feudalism began to decline and the Roman system of sovereign kingdoms, taking responsibility for maintaining public order, was revived. Europe now saw the development of towns, each with its own militia, and by the thirteenth century, the feudal system was definitely in decline. However, the concept of landed noble families, subservient to the king, has continued in some European countries until the present time. (According to Marxist doctrine, feudalism laid the foundations of the capitalist system, which was then challenged by the workers in the name of socialism.)

One factor in the decline is that well qualified artisans were no longer willing to donate their labor to nobles or to monasteries. Towns developed in which the craftsmen formed themselves into independent guilds and organized their own militia.

Meanwhile, two important changes occurred. When heavily armed knights fought on horseback, they were able to finally defeat the Viking invaders from the North, who had hitherto caused such havoc by their harassing raids on peaceful European communities. At the same time, improved methods of agriculture and the development of trade brought prosperity and a steady increase in population. Now the land began to be divided up into a number of sovereign and independent kingdoms, destroying the hope of a secular empire, but still under the religious authority of the pope. Finally, the Reformation challenged the papal system and produced a division of religious authority. Likewise, the Renaissance led to a flowering of art, literature, and scientific inquiry which ended a long period of cultural stagnation.

This very brief account is no more than a summary of a thousand years. We must now fill in the outline with a little more detail.

SECULAR AND RELIGIOUS SOCIAL SYSTEMS

In all human societies, people tend to be divided into different classes. The following rough diagram will identify how this happened in the medieval world. A clear distinction is made between those who were allowed, and those who were not allowed, to marry:

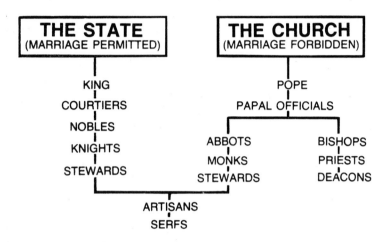

DIAGRAM OF MEDIEVAL SOCIAL SYSTEMS

In the left-hand column, we have the lay members of the community; these, of course, made up the great majority of the population. They included both men and women, and all of them were free to marry. The kings invariably married because they needed to have sons to succeed them. The same was generally true of courtiers and nobles. In fact, as we shall see, the main purpose of marriage of upper class persons in those days was to assure legal succession to title and property.

We shall postpone discussion of knights, although we have already referred to their function as warriors. They had attendants who were called squires; often these were young men who would themselves later become knights.

A steward, or major, was put in charge of an estate and was responsible for all the organization—supervising the work, collecting taxes, making payments. It was a heavy task. Sometimes instead of appointing stewards, a large estate was divided up so that portions of it were taken over by supervisors, who functioned as landholders in return for meeting agreed obligations.

Under the stewards were two classes of workers: those who were skilled, the artisans (like carpenters, blacksmiths, and stonemasons), and the serfs, who plowed the land, gathered the crops, and looked after the animals. Wives of the serfs were responsible for cooking, washing, and cleaning.

The special name for all low-grade workers was *villeins*, a word originally meaning farm worker, that has come down to us today in the pejorative form of *villains*. They were to some extent the property of the nobles, and often were treated very badly.

Now turn to the right-hand column—the clergy. Although they were far fewer in number than the laity, the difference was nothing like as great as it is today. Sherwin Bailey reports in *Sexual Relation in Christian Thought* that in the thirteenth century one in twelve of all adult males was a cleric, compared with about one in five hundred today for England, and about one in four hundred for the United States.

The pope had supreme power, but unlike the king, he was *elected* to office by the cardinals. There were some great popes, and some very bad ones. Under the pope were many officials. Together, they were called the Curia, and they managed the business of the church. A pope might be as powerful, and as wealthy, as a king.

At the next point, the right-hand column divides. On one side, we have the parish or "secular" clergy, beginning with the bishops. As we have seen, they were the overseers of groups of churches, supervising the parish priests in each diocese, and often attached to a cathedral. At a lower level were the deacons, or inferior clergy. The task of all of them was to minister to the laity, which included everyone from the king to the serfs.

The other section of the clergy, in the left-hand column, included those who were involved in the monasteries. The abbot or abbess was in charge; women, as nuns, were included here, though not in the parish clergy. Monks and nuns took the threefold vow of poverty, chastity, and obedience, following a probationary period or novitiate. A few of the men's religious orders (Franciscans, for example) allowed their monks to travel freely; these itinerant monks were called friars. Some of them served as missionaries.

The monasteries usually owned land, and this was managed in very much the same way as the estates of the nobles—with stewards, and employing artisans and serfs who could, of course, marry. However, the monks themselves supplied a good part of the labor.

As already indicated, all branches of the clergy, with a few exceptions in the very lowest orders, were required to renounce marriage, which was permitted only to the laity. This distinction inevitably added to the low spiritual esteem in which the marriage relationship was held on account of the negative attitudes which had already developed in the early church.

THE ORDER OF KNIGHTHOOD

We have seen how, when the western Roman Empire broke up in the fifth century, law and order could no longer be enforced. So, for protection, many people had no option but to surrender their land and liberty to some powerful overlord and to become dependent upon him.

Each of these lords maintained a small army to protect his territory, and those dependent on him, from marauders. The Lord lived in a castle or other stronghold, to which his vassals and their families could withdraw if necessary. In order to have sufficient military strength to protect themselves, the men of the community were trained in the use of arms. They were led in battle by their overlords, who were well equipped with weapons and trained for combat. This naturally led to the system of knighthood.

As Henry Osborn Taylor expresses it in *The Mediaeval Mind*, a "warrior class" emerged, whose "ideals accorded with the feudal situation and tended to express themselves in chivalry." The knights and their ladies developed high ideals of behavior which were very different from the low standards of cruelty, greed, and lust which had been all too common. Feudalism, according to Taylor, "presents everywhere a state of contrast between its principles of mutual fidelity and protection, and its actuality of oppression, revolt, and private war."

The church soon became involved in this system in two ways. First, some landowners chose to turn over their property to a local monastery. Marauding bands hesitated to attack church property. Also, monks were ready to work the land, and there were spiritual benefits to be reaped by putting your family under the care of a religious institution.

The second way in which the church became involved was that the ideals of knighthood took on a distinctly religious flavor. When a young man of noble birth approached manhood, becoming a knight was a very attractive goal. He would be recognized as a warrior, would learn skills that promised exciting adventures, and would achieve high social status. The entry into this illustrious brotherhood was by way of a ceremony of investiture that was replete with religious meaning and symbolism—a night-long vigil of prayer and a pledge to fulfill the knightly code of honor in striving for the protection of all who were abused or exploited.

In this way, the idealism of young men from the best families was ingeniously integrated with the religious ideals of the church. And when, in the late eleventh century, the crusades became a prominent feature of Christian policy, the thirst for adventure and conquest, and religious zeal, were conveniently combined.

When he was ready for combat, the knight was formidably equipped. Here is how Barbara Tuchman describes him in *A Distant Mirror:* "To fight on horseback or foot wearing 55 pounds of plate armor, to crash in collision with an opponent at full gallop while holding horizontal an eighteen-foot lance half the length of an average telephone pole, to give and receive blows with sword or battle-ax that could cleave a skull or slice off a limb at a stroke, to spend half of life in the saddle through all weathers and for days at a time." And when not in combat, the knight traveling alone must eat whatever he could find, sleep in the open with his armor on, and be ready to defend himself at any time.

Bands of knights, of course, would be better provided for when at war. They were then, to all intents and purposes, soldiers who were part of an army.

All the knights serving one lord were bound together by an oath of loyalty, and must be ready to risk their lives in order to support or rescue one another. For many in the wealthy classes, fighting was considered a manly way of spending time, like hunting and hawking. When there was no other chance to fight, tournaments were organized. We shall have more to say about these later, because they were closely associated with the cult of courtly love.

Roles of the Knight

The system of knighthood, which ushered in the "age of chivalry," reached its height in Europe in the twelfth and thirteenth centuries. Beginning in France and Spain, it spread rapidly, representing a fusion of Christian and military idealism. It initiated, in the upper levels of society, the standards of gentlemanly conduct that have persisted until our own time. The main virtues marking the true knight are piety, bravery, loyalty, and honor.

The idea was that people who wield power should not be ruthless oppressors, but considerate and helpful toward those of lower social standing. Since most of the nobles became knights, this proved to be a welcome corrective to their previously imperious behavior.

The church viewed the priest and the knight as cooperating to maintain social order. The knight served as policeman and soldier combined. He was often a landlord, a noble, a courtier—the succession reached all the way up to king or emperor. With him, the priest had a cooperative role to play. The priest could read. He could keep records. He was in regular and close contact with the common people. And he knew, through the confessional, what was going on behind the scenes and beneath the surface. As Crane Brinton expressed it in *Anatomy of a Revolution,* "The Middle Ages regarded both the knight and the saint as complementary facets of a single ideal, the Christian; both were needed servants of God and of His order on earth."

So far as marriage was concerned, most of the knights had wives. Only two orders—the Templars and the Hospitallers—took vows of celibacy. For the others, the concept of "gentlemanly" behavior had some influence on their wives also, encouraging them to adopt "ladylike" behavior and status. However, marriage played no part in the system that earned the name of courtly love, which we will consider in the next chapter.

The Crusades

No account of knighthood can omit reference to the crusades—those enthusiastic campaigns, often poorly planned and brutally executed, directed against the infidels, who were viewed as the deadly enemies of the Christian faith.

One of the marks of virtue in a medieval Christian was to go on pilgrimage to some holy place. To do so was an act symbolizing respect for the place and its associations. In addition, making the trip was counted penance, and was, therefore, a virtuous act. Chaucer's famous collection of stories, *The Canterbury Tales*, for example, is about a group of pilgrims visiting the shrine of St. Thomas à Becket in Canterbury, England. Naturally, the most important of all pilgrimages was to Jerusalem, to the Holy Sepulchre, and many Christians counted this pilgrimage as the supreme event of a lifetime.

In the eleventh century, bands of Turkish nomads began to harass the Christian pilgrims, and this stirred among Christian leaders a wish to free the Holy Land, and particularly Jerusalem, from the hands of the Muslims. What more appealing adventure could be offered to zealous Christian knights?

So, a rather motley army of Crusaders (soldiers of the Cross) began to assemble in Constantinople late in the year 1096, and during the next three years various battles were fought with the Saracens, who were Muslims. The Crusade reached its climax in 1099 when, after stubborn resistance, the city of Jerusalem fell to the Christian invaders. A victory of this kind, despite the carnage, brought together the love of fighting and the desire to serve God. As the Crusaders continued, this fighting came to be the supreme fulfillment of Christian knighthood. To die on a crusade almost guaranteed a direct entry into heaven, and the Christian knight who returned was covered with glory. At least, that was so at the beginning. But as the Crusades continued for another century and a half, and then trailed off, enthusiasm finally dimmed. The view of most historians is that more harm than good was done to the Christian cause. The chief benefit of the Crusades was to stimulate East-West trade.

DAILY LIFE IN MEDIEVAL TIMES

We now need to take a look at the lives of ordinary people, as they went about their business from day to day.

Wherever you were placed on the medieval social ladder, most of the comforts and conveniences we take for granted would have been denied you. Most of them could not even have been imagined as possible.

You would start your day with morning light and end it when the sun went down. In a castle or palace, you might occasionally sit up late by the light of a flaming torch, or in a poorer home, with a flickering candle. Nearly all the work you had to do, however, would depend on daylight.

You would wash yourself under primitive conditions, unless you lived in a town that had public baths. People rarely bathed because water was thought to carry disease. Your home might have formidable stone walls, as in a castle; but more likely it would be a rude structure of wood and plaster, with few windows and a thatched roof. The earthen floor would have a layer of rushes, only occasionally renewed, often filthy and swarming with vermin. Winter heating would be provided by an open wood fire, and the smoke would sometimes choke you. Food would be eaten from a plain wooden table, and you would sit on a hard wooden bench. Sofas and padded chairs would be rare luxuries.

Rarely would you experience privacy. All members of the household—guests and even servants—might sleep in the same room, often two or more to a bed, if there were, indeed, beds! A comfortable mattress would be a luxury. There would be no effective way of dealing with pests. Fleas and lice would be everywhere, and rats and mice your constant companions. The Black Death, the terrible plague that decimated Europe in the fourteenth century, spread only because the necessary conditions—plenty of rats and fleas—were everywhere to be found.

There would be no sanitation system except open sewers running along the narrow streets, causing a constant stench and ending in piles of rotting garbage. Personal habits often matched the environment—wiping of the nose on the tablecloth, spitting on the floor, wiping hands on the backs of dogs instead of napkins, wearing sweaty garments for days on end. Pets were common, but they were little cared for—dogs, cats, monkeys, and hawks.

Travel, compared to modern standards, was a nightmare. Roads were rough and uneven; yet they thronged with beggars, messengers, peddlers, merchants, wandering minstrels, friars. Most people had to walk. The more fortunate traveled on horseback. Comfortable carriages were only for great ladies and were poorly sprung. Wagons and carts were used for local transportation, and there were few bridges. Often tolls had to be paid. For a major journey, a mule train was best. Night stops were at inns, monasteries, or castles, with few creature comforts. Food was unappetizing and not always fresh. Drinks were beer, ale, cider, and spiced wine—tea and coffee were unknown.

Little was known about disease. Hygiene was not understood. Mental illness was viewed as devil-possession. Physicians were ignorant and greatly feared for their drastic remedies, which were seldom effective. Sickness and death were never far away. Many mothers died in childbirth. Nearly half of all babies died in their first year. People didn't live long. Half of the total population was under twenty-one, in spite of the high death rates for children. Because life was short, childhood was over at age seven. Then boys and girls became apprentices or servants, often leaving home to do so.

Education was only for the privileged. Books were rare and had to be copied by hand until the printing press was invented in the fifteenth century. Information was received by word of mouth, usually from sermons, poems, and legends. There was almost no scientific knowledge as we understand it today. Superstition was rife, and most people believed in magic, sorcery, and witchcraft. There was no evenhanded system of justice as we know it today. If innocence and guilt couldn't be decided on the basis of evidence, torture might be used as a means of getting a confession.

Attitudes about money were different from ours. The church condemned usury—lending money at interest—as a sin. Jews were invariably the money-lenders and had little or no competition. So the Jewish people grew rich, but they were considered unholy and were segregated. The concept of a Christian businessman hardly existed, because making a profit was considered reprehensible. But giving money to the church was applauded and giving alms to the poor earned you spiritual credit. The church, itself, made money in a big way by granting special favors or by authorizing remission of sins, *pardons*, in return for payment. The system of *indulgences*, sold to the relatives of the departed to shorten their stay in purgatory, so enraged Luther in the sixteenth century that it precipitated the Reformation.

LIVING THE CHRISTIAN LIFE

If you lived in a medieval community, you didn't have to decide about being a Christian. That had been settled for you soon after birth, when you were baptized. You might later decide after all *not* to be a Christian, but then you would soon be in very serious trouble.

The church controlled almost every event in your life. After baptism, you were confirmed. When you reached the age of seven, you began confessing your sins to the priest, who would prescribe an appropriate penance and grant absolution. On Sunday, everyone in the parish was expected to go to mass, which was read in Latin. If you didn't show up, you paid a fine. And only essential work was done on Sunday.

If you defied the system, you would first be warned. Then, if you continued not to fulfill the prescribed duties, you could be excommunicated. In that event, you would find yourself shunned by all your neighbors. If you still persisted in your defiance, you could be branded as a heretic and brought to trial. The penalty could be death—often by burning.

In order to get the picture clear, let us suppose you were a young man or woman from a pagan background, and you had indicated a serious desire to become a Christian. After some instruction, you had been baptized. You then asked the priest to explain clearly to you what living the Christian life would mean. What options did you have?

His reply, translated into modern terminology, would probably have been something like this:

"You must understand that in this world you are on probation. Human life is a time of trial and of testing. You have a body, and you have a soul. The most important task in life is to save your soul.

"The duration of your human life is brief. It will soon be over. How you spend it will decide how you will spend eternity. You have three options—heaven, hell, and purgatory.

"Heaven offers everlasting bliss. You will be where God is completely in control, with Christ, the saints, the angels, and all who have been faithful in their lives in this world. There will be no sin or sorrow there.

"Hell is a place of punishment and torture, where the devil is in control, served by his attendant demons. Once there, you can never escape. You will pay a very bitter price for your sins, and you will go on paying it forever.

"Purgatory is also a place of suffering, but you may still have a chance to make good and finally get to heaven. You will need to do penance there, or continue penance begun on earth. Help is available from the Virgin Mary and the saints—not directly from Christ, because he will be the final Judge.

"Human life is brief, and it would be wise for you to use your time on earth to make sure you are going to heaven after this life. The best way is to forsake the world *now* by joining a religious order and spending your life in a monastery. This would mean giving up all worldly ambitions and taking the threefold vow of poverty, chastity, and obedience. Your time would be devoted to prayer, meditation, and appointed work of some kind, ranging from manual labor to study. You might later, if a man, became a missionary.

"You would have to give up all worldly comforts by fasting, cutting back on sleep, and avoiding all forms of pleasure. You would have no personal possessions. In particular, no kind of sexual experience would be tolerated. You would have to go regularly to confession and do penance for any sinful behavior.

"A second possibility, if you are a man, is to become a priest. You would then serve in a parish and supervise the lives of the laity. You would be forbidden to marry, and would be under the orders of your ecclesiastical superiors. As a woman, you couldn't enter the priesthood, but as a nun there might be some special services open to you.

"If you are not prepared in either of these ways to devote yourself to a religious life, you can still be a Christian, though at a distinctly inferior level. Of course, you will have to attend church, go regularly to confession, and submit to whatever disciplines your priest requires.

"As an ordinary Christian believer, you may marry, although spiritually that is an inferior status. If you do marry, it must be a commitment for life. There is no possibility of divorce. And sexual intercourse is acceptable only when you and your partner come together with the specific desire to have children—sex that is *enjoyed* is concupiscence, and that is sinful. Once your children are born, to be on the safe side, it is best to give up sex altogether.

"These are your options—now you must choose."

THE CHURCH'S LOST OPPORTUNITY

It seems ironic that at a time when the church had more influence and worldly power than at any other period in history, it should have interpreted the Christian message not in terms of kingdom-building, but almost exclusively as a soul-saving process. According to Barbara Tuchman, "for nearly a thousand years [the church] had been the central institution that gave meaning and purpose to life in a capricious world. It affirmed that man's life on earth was but a passage in exile on the way to God and to the New Jerusalem."

What the medieval church offered was not a gospel that could make this world a good place to live in—a kingdom where the Lord's prayer would be fulfilled and God's will would be done on earth as it is in heaven. What it offered was, in Barbara Tuchman's terms, "salvation, which could be reached only through the rituals of the established Church and by the permission and aid of its ordained priests."

Certainly, the hope of heaven must have meant a great deal to people living in the wretched conditions that were the lot of the poor and the sick. There were plenty of these people, and the church certainly did its best to relieve their misery in this world. But, surely, with almost unlimited power to influence human events, much more might have been done to create a community where people lived together in continuing love and peace.

As a matter of fact, the hope of heaven did not prove, by itself, to be an adequate dynamic to induce most church members to toe the line. Again and again, the church had to rely, as the motivation for righteous living, on a more powerful dynamic—the fear of hell.

Even Geoffrey Chaucer, who lived in the fourteenth century and is acknowledged as the father of English literature, concludes his *Canterbury Tales* with what was called a *retraction*—a confession of sin for writing and publishing the book. As he grew older, the fear of eternal punishment began to prey on his mind. So he concludes:

> I beseech you humbly, for God's mercy, to pray for me so that Christ will have mercy on me and excuse my sins, particularly any translations and compositions dealing with worldly vanities, all of which I revoke." [I ask for] the grace to bewail my sins and to study for the salvation of my soul . . . so that I may be one of those who shall be saved at the day of judgment.

115

All who have seen medieval portrayals of the Day of Judgment know how dramatically and vividly this awesome process was portrayed. To quote Barbara Tuchman again,

> In Hell the damned hung by their tongues from trees of fire, the impenitent burned in furnaces, unbelievers smothered in foul-smelling smoke. The wicked fell into the black waters of an abyss and sank to a depth proportionate to their sins. . . . Some were swallowed by monstrous fish, some gnawed by demons, tormented by serpents, by fire or ice or fruits hanging forever out of reach of the starving. In Hell men were naked, nameless, and forgotten.

This was not a dreadful fate reserved for only a few abandoned sinners. The teaching of the church was that this was the destination of the great majority. "Few saved, many damned" was the judgment of such esteemed theologians as Augustine and Aquinas. Indeed, a parallel was drawn with Noah's family, who survived the flood, and such estimates as one saved to a thousand damned were offered to terrified believers. All the way up from the parish priest and the official "pardoner" to the sumptuous palaces of the popes, the church collected contributions and fees for its offers to lighten the load of accountability for the awful sum of human sin.

NO MARRIAGE FOR THE CLERGY

The burden laid by the church on tortured souls was demonstrated also by the enforced celibacy of the clergy. The massive investigation of Henry C. Lea makes it all too clear that during much of the medieval era the denial of the right to marry was a burden too heavy to be borne, and the parish priests, who had not all wanted to be priests, were unable to resist the temptation to live with concubines.

After all, if one in twelve of all adult males was ordained in the thirteenth century, then something like the same proportion of women would have been deprived of wifehood and motherhood, which were the only respectable occupations open to them, apart from becoming nuns.

To quote Barbara Tuchman yet again:

> In all popular literature of the time, clerical celibacy is a joke. Priests lived with mistresses or else went in hunt of them. "A priest lay with a lady who was wed to a knight," begins one tale matter-of-factly. In another, "the priest and his lady went off to bed." In the nunnery where Piers Plowman served as cook, Sister Pernell was "a priest's wench" who "bore a child in cherry time." Boccaccio's rascally friars were invariably caught in embarrassing situations as victims of their own lechery. In real life their sinfulness was not funny but threatening, for when a friar failed so far in holiness how could he save souls?

Of course, all this is only one side of the picture. The medieval church also produced a host of devout Christians and a significant quota of saints. It was Saint Francis of Assisi—whose life, according to Henry Osborn Taylor, was a poem—who set the pattern for friars, living in total poverty and simplicity and doing good wherever he went. And there were plenty of parish priests who were tireless in ministering to the sick and needy—one of them appears in Chaucer's *Canterbury Tales*.

But the tragedy of the medieval church remains. It lies in the fact that in those thousand years of unparalleled opportunity, the meaning of the Christian life was so weighted on the side of soul-saving and hell-avoiding that a great opportunity was lost to encourage and help ordinary Christian believers to practice the Christian virtues as these had been so clearly taught and demonstrated by Jesus of Nazareth, and to develop, on the foundations of loving Christian families, something like a working model of the kingdom of heaven.

The judgment of history was vindicated when, at the end of the long centuries of the Middle Ages, the power of the church finally waned, and there was ushered in a flowering of the human arts and graces which has been called the Renaissance.

What the world needed then, and still needs today, is a Christian renaissance—the flowering in human nature, in human relationships, and in human society, of the gospel of love, peace, and joy.

Chapter 7

LOVE IS ROMANTIC:
BUT NOT IN MARRIAGE
(The Middle Ages)

As we have seen, love between man and woman came under a heavy shadow during the early centuries of Christian history. The deplorably low standard of sexual behavior in the Greco-Roman world, the close association between sex and sin in theological thinking, and the low view of marriage which resulted, provided little opportunity for any idealization of human love. As has happened at other times, any romantic feelings that young people might have experienced were either immediately dissipated in crude types of sexual encounter or were sublimated into esthetic or religious idealism.

Behind the scenes, of course, tender and affectionate exchanges must often have occurred between youthful lovers, and even between apparently staid married couples. It was simply that the cultural climate had made no provision for such sentiments to be acknowledged or recognized.

Henry Osborn Taylor, with his usual perceptive insight, saw clearly what was happening beneath the surface in medieval culture: "Unquestionably in the monk's eyes passionate love between the sexes was mainly lust. Within the bonds of marriage it was not mortal sin; but the virgin state was the best. . . . Monasticism did not stop the human race, or keep men from loving women. Such love would assert itself; and ardent natures who felt its power were to find in themselves a love and passion somewhat novel, somewhat raised, somewhat enlarged. In the end the love between man and woman drew new inspiration and energy from the enhancement of all the rest of love, which came with Christianity" *(The Mediaeval Mind)*.

In the end. Yes, but that end didn't come to be recognized in *marriage,* not in the medieval era, not entirely even after the Reformation. Recognition was to come much later. Its full coming, in fact, was not to be until our own time.

What *did* come in the Middle Ages was an idealized projection of this intense emotion *outside* marriage in the form of romantic chivalry. It was closely associated with the ideals of knighthood, but it spread more widely than that. It found expression in poetry, in music, in legend, in drama, and in art. It saw Christian experience humanized and emotionalized, in contrast to the patristic era when the emphasis was rigidly confined to rational thought and dogma. "The Fathers of the Latin Church from Tertullian to Gregory the Great," continues Taylor, "had been occupied with doctrine and ecclesiastical organiza- tion . . . the constructive mind of the Latin West . . . stood forth mainly as the creation of those human faculties which are grouped under the name of intellect. Patristic Latin Christianity hardly presents itself as the product of the whole man. Its principles were not as yet fully humanized, made matter of the heart, and imbued with love and fear and pity."

CHIVALRY AND COURTLY LOVE

What has all this to do with marriage? The long absences from home that were part of knighthood brought little satisfaction to the wives of knights, who had to cope as best they could, and they knew well that at any time they might find themselves widowed. However, the components that were built into the concept of knighthood—the sense of dedication, the thrill of adventure, the desire to prove worthy, the acceptance of frustration and hardship—produced a result that might have been hard to predict, yet is not difficult to explain.

It seemed that, as Christians developed greater freedom to express emotionally their religious feelings of love, they came to realize that despite all the negative teachings of the church about sexual desire, there could be an idealized form of love between man and woman that might have spiritual significance.

So, in association with knighthood, an interesting and important development occurred. It was part of a new willingness to recognize, in the attraction of men and women to each other, something more than crude sexual desire. It was this romantic idealism to which Freud once referred when he said that "love is aim-inhibited sex." It meant being attracted by sexual desire to a person of the opposite sex, recognizing the attraction, but not acting on it directly. The result is not frustration, but a sublimated and exalted state of ecstasy that is sometimes called "romantic love." The sexual energy is then translated into the desire to be worthy of the lover and to honor and please her by acts of devotion and sacrifice. This, of course, is closely related to the courtship process.

For the knight, this meant choosing an attractive lady in whose service he could do mighty deeds, win trophies and lay them at her feet, and thus earn her approval. Ideally, it would be a great lady of striking beauty and noble character. It would seldom, if ever, be the knight's own wife, because love and marriage were not often associated in medieval society.

So, the knight chose his lady. But how was he to show his devotion by mighty deeds? Going off on a crusade meant a very lengthy absence, and in those days communication over great distances was almost impossible. He might get involved in a minor war nearer home, or by chance find some wrong to right in the local community. But these were not adequate. Something better must be found.

The something better was the *tournament*. This was an organized event at which knights came together and fought one another according to prescribed rules. Of course, such events were viewed as popular entertainment. They normally lasted a week and were the great sporting events of the time, corresponding to the football matches of today. However, in those days the combats were perilous. The knights really fought one another with deadly weapons, and were often seriously wounded or even killed. The tournaments were justified as ways of training soldiers, but in fact the conditions were very different from those of the battlefield. The church disapproved of tournaments, but they went on just the same. Crowds attended them, and of course, the fights—sometimes single combat, at other times opposing teams—were very exciting to watch.

It was here that romantic love was prominently acted out. According to the picture often portrayed, the ladies would be watching, and the knights would be wearing some token of the favor of their chosen ones. It would be a colorful scene—brilliant decorations, banners, trumpets, parades of the combatants, glittering armor. The ladies would throw scarves to their admirers as tokens of their devotion. This was the supreme moment of courtly love for the knight. Openly, in public, he was to prove his devotion to the lady of his choice by a display of military prowess. Here is how Barbara Tuchman describes it:

> Courtly love was considered to ennoble a man, to improve him in every way. It would make him concerned to show an example of goodness, to do his utmost to preserve honor, never letting dishonor touch him or the lady he loved. . . . He would be inspired to greater prowess, would win more victories in tournaments, rise above himself in courage and daring. . . . Guided by this theory, woman's status improved, less for her own sake than as the inspirer of male glory, a higher function than being merely a sexual object, a breeder of children, or a conveyer of property.

That, at any rate, was the idea! But we repeat, it had nothing to do with marriage. As long as marriage was kept on an idealized level, it could be tolerated. But all too often, it toppled from such noble heights.

What happened, in fact, was that the awakening of romantic love developed in opposite directions. Let us see how this took place.

MAN-WOMAN LOVE AS SPIRITUAL IMAGERY

May I find your breasts like clusters of grapes on the vine,
  The scent of your breath like apricots,
And your whispers like spiced wine
  flowing smoothly to welcome my caresses.
                                    (Song of Songs 7:8-9 NEB)

The inclusion of this ancient love song in the Scriptures provided all the sanction that was needed to justify the allegorical use of marital love as a symbol of the soul's communion with God. And in the records of monastic life in the Middle Ages, the use of this kind of symbolism is found from time to time. Two illustrations will suffice.

First, the great Saint Bernard of Clairvaux, who lived in the twelfth century. Here are some excerpts from one of his sermons:

> [Conversion] marries the soul to the Word, whom it is like by nature . . . loving as it is loved. If it loves perfectly it weds. What more delightful than this love, through which thou, O . . . soul, cleavest to the Word. . . . Spiritual is the contracting of these holy nuptials, wherein always to will the same makes one spirit out of two. . . . Love aboundeth in itself. . . . Wherefore she who loves, loves, and knows nothing else. . . . The Bridegroom is not only loving, but very love.
>
> This love is the Bride's, because she is what she is by love. Love is the Bride's sole hope and interest. In it the Bride abounds and the Bridegroom is content. He seeks nothing else, nor has she ought beside . . . the Bridegroom's love—for He is love—asks only love's return and faith.
>
> Rightly renouncing all other affections, the Bride reposes on love alone, and returns a love reciprocal. And when she has poured her whole self out in love, what is that compared with the perennial flood of that fountain? Not equals in abundance are this loving one and Love, the soul and the Word, the Bride and the Bridegroom. . . . What then? shall she therefore despair, and the vow of the would-be Bride be rendered empty? . . . No. For although the creature loves less, because she is less, yet if she loves with her whole self, nothing lacks where there is all. Wherefore, as I have said, so to love is to have wedded; for no one can so love and yet be loved but little, and in mutual consent stands the entire and perfect marriage. *(The Mediaeval Mind)*

Second, a passage from *The Flowing Light of God* by Sister Mechthild, a nun who lived in Germany early in the thirteenth century. In the following passage, the Soul speaks to her guardians, the senses.

. . . Lady, would you with love cool yourself, approach the Child in the Virgin's lap?

That is a childish love, to quiet children with. I am a full-grown bride and will have my Bridegroom.

Lady, there we should be smitten blind. The Godhead is so fiery hot. Heaven's glow and all the holy lights flow from His divine breath and human mouth by the counsel of the Holy Spirit.

. . . God has granted to all creatures to follow their natures; how can I withstand mine? To God will I go, who is my Father by nature, my Brother through His humility, my Bridegroom through love, and I am His forever. . . . I would glady die of love, might that be my lot; for Him whom I love I have seen with my bright eyes standing in my soul.

These were both devout Christians, utterly dedicated to the celibate life. But their use of such language breaks through the negative rejection of marital love and uses it by analogy to express the noblest spiritual longings.

While a few monks and nuns were using the language of romantic love to express their religious experiences, that same language was increasingly becoming part of the language of chivalry. It all started through the romances.

THE CULT OF COURTLY LOVE

The French term *chanson de geste* means a "song of great deeds." Beginning toward the end of the eleventh century, a whole series of historical tales, beginning with the *Chanson de Roland* in praise of Charlemagne and his knights, began to be put together in rhyming couplets. They describe the adventures of brave knights, their courage and devotion, and above all, their chivalry in performing noble deeds. The songs were composed or sung by wandering minstrels, and by the twelfth century, these songs had become immensely popular because they reflected the courage and valor of the knights as they righted wrongs and performed prodigious feats.

Soon, however, we encounter the theme of courtly love. The ladies were high-born, sometimes queens. They were adored and worshiped from afar. Of all the legends that were put together, the best known were those about the court of the fictitious King Arthur and his knights of the round table. There were also French associations with Eleanor of Aquitaine, who presided over court readings of love poems, and romantic legends like that of Tristan and Iseult, later enshrined in Wagner's opera.

Of all the heroes of knightly virtue, Lancelot is one of the best known. He performed many feats in honor of Queen Guinevere, the wife of King Arthur, who finally accepted his love.

However, these idealized romances of song and story had very little connection with marriage, because the marriages of those days, as we have seen, had little or no association with love. They were merely arrangements of convenience to establish political or social links between families, or, more often, to acquire property. But during the twelfth and thirteenth centuries, the great awakening of the sentiment of romantic love resulted in poems, songs, and legends, on an increasing scale, in which the love-sick knight finally won the lady on whom he had set his heart.

At this point, the story often ended with a tragic death. To end with a marriage, as it was conceived in those days, would have been an anti-climax. In a few instances, the adventure *did* end in marriage, but if so, that was decisively the end of the story. As in the tales that were read to us as children, "they lived happily ever after" was the *end*—no more questions entertained! A typical example is the conclusion of the Knight's Tale in *The Canterbury Tales* of the fourteenth century English poet Geoffrey Chaucer:

> At once the bond of matrimony was made between them by the assembled council and barons, and Palamon married

Emily in all happiness and harmony. God, who wrought this wide world, sent love to the man who had so dearly paid for it, for Palamon was in all ways content, living in happiness, in wealth, and in health. Emily loved him so dearly, and he served her so courteously, that there was never any word of jealousy or any other difficulty between them.

THE ROMAN DE LA ROSE

One of the well-known medieval romances is the *Roman de la Rose*, a long poem that was popular in medieval Europe over a period of at least two centuries. The first four thousand lines were written in about A.D. 1240 by an author about whom nothing is known except his name. It is a simple story, in the form of an allegory, about the wooing of a maiden. The maiden is represented as a rosebud, protected by prickly thorns in an enclosed garden that represents the aristocratic society of the Middle Ages. The characters represent the emotions that play their parts in the lover's quest and the desired lady's responses—Friendship, Pleasure, Shame, Modesty, Envy, and others. The lover, admitted into the garden, is guided and instructed in the correct courtly behavior he needs to adopt in order to win the response he eagerly seeks.

About forty years after the original writing, the poem was greatly extended by another writer, Jean de Meun, and in its final form it contains over twenty-six thousand lines. The second writer saw the allegory as an excellent way of airing his views on many subjects. His attitude toward love is erotic and cynical. The lover eventually achieves his goal, but it becomes little more than a sexual conquest—the rose turns out to represent the female genital area.

Why was this allegory so popular? The reasons are complex, but let us try to identify them.

First, in all civilized human societies there is a tendency to develop idealized concepts about the man-woman relationship. It has been said that "all the world loves a lover." Love poetry, songs, and legends appear in most developed cultures. They focus on the first awakening of love in youth, when boy and girl are attracted to each other, but are too shy and uncertain to proceed straight to physical sex as animals do. There are built-in restraints in every culture to control the process of procreation, and to see that the right couples get together in the right circumstances. That is what our marriage laws and customs are all about.

In our modern culture, romantic love is understood and accepted in the form of courtship, and marriage, which normally follows, is respected and honored. It is, therefore, very difficult for us to comprehend the conditions that existed in the Middle Ages. Consider them for a moment.

Love and marriage were simply not associated. The main purpose of marriage was to produce children, and we have seen that in the upper levels of society it was a means of forming alliances to transfer property, or to gain social status or prestige. The young people concerned were moved, like pieces on a chessboard, into positions that were considered to be advantageous. This was usually done when they were mere children, before they could have made any responsible choices for themselves. Even if they did have personal preferences, these were unlikely to be considered.

Among the lower classes, there might have been more opportunity for choice based on love. But at that level, crude sexuality was the dominant theme. The people had no education as we understand it. They picked up their knowledge of sex early from domestic animals and from what could easily be observed among their elders in a setting where privacy simply did not exist. You have only to read Chaucer's *Canterbury Tales* to understand how easily and naturally sex was talked about—even by a group of people of both sexes, going together on a religious pilgrimage in the fourteenth century. There seemed to be nothing improper about a man's telling a woman that he would like to have sex with her—even if the man were a priest or the woman were already married to someone else. It was even considered a great joke for another man to conspire with a wife to make a "cuckold" of her husband. Married women were producing children most of the time, anyway. These children were not very welcome, and nearly half of them died in infancy or early childhood, so what did it really matter who fathered them?

Add to all this the fact that the church made it clear that marriage was an unspiritual condition, forbidden to the clergy and to the really virtuous women—the virgins— who became nuns. Even if people *were* properly married, sex for any other purpose than to beget a child was sinful. However, sexual sins were so common that they weren't taken very seriously. Confess them to the priest, and for a few routine prayers and a small cash contribution, he could erase them from your spiritual record.

What seems tragic is that all this interest in love and romance had little or no association with marriage, because medieval society, under the firm domination of the church, had seldom associated love and marriage with each other. How different it might all have been had the church promoted married life as a spiritually sanctified form of Christian love!

This is dramatized in an interesting book written at the time courtly love was in vogue. A French nobleman, de la Tour Landry, decided "to teach my daughters the fashionable convention in love matters." He makes it clear that marriage has little to do with love. On this subject, he reports a conversation he had with his own wife, the mother of the girls. He had ventured the opinion that a girl might, in special circumstances, be justified in falling in love with the man she was going to marry. His wife strongly disagreed on religious grounds. She said, "I have heard many women say, who were in love in their youth, that when they were in church, their thoughts and fancies made them dwell more on the delights of their love affairs than on the service of God, and the art of love is of such a nature that just at the holiest moments of the service . . . these little thoughts would come to them" (see Johan Huizinga, *The Waning of the Middle Ages*).

In other words, happy thoughts of married love and the worship of God are totally incompatible!

REALITIES OF MEDIEVAL MARRIAGE

In spite of all the romantic songs and poems, therefore, marriage in the medieval world was, by contrast, a very prosaic matter.

> Feudal life in the earlier mediaeval centuries did not foster tender sentiments between betrothed or wedded couples. The chief object of every landholder was by force or policy to secure his own safety and increase his retainers and possessions. A ready means was for him to marry lands and serfs in the robust person of the daughter, or widow, of some other baron. The marriage was prefaced by scant courtship; and little love was likely to ensue between the rough-handed husband and high-tempered wife. *(The Mediaeval Mind)*

It must be remembered, too, that marriage, at least in the noble families, was usually contracted early in life. As we have seen, people didn't, in those days, enjoy the life-span we can count on in our time. Death came often, and early, in many forms. So daughters, at last, and often sons also, were married off without delay.

The Christian church had accepted without question the Roman rules about age at marriage. The onset of puberty was the signal that a boy or girl was now marriageable. In terms of age, this was assumed to be twelve for the girl and fourteen for the boy. But since it was customary for marriages to be arranged between families, with the wishes of the young people seldom consulted, the wedding was usually preceded by betrothal, which involved a very serious commitment. Young people could be betrothed at any time after the age of seven, but in some instances, it happened when they were babies and even before birth. To prevent abuse, the church insisted that young people, when they reached the legal ages for marriage, should be free to repudiate the betrothal contract. But obviously a girl of twelve, accustomed to obeying her parents, could be in a very difficult situation if she questioned the choice they had made for her.

Some extreme cases are on record in which the general rules were ignored. Eileen Powers, in *Medieval People,* tells of Grace de Saleby, inheritor of extensive lands, who was married to a nobleman at the age of four. When he died two years later, she was remarried to a second husband who took over the property, and to a third when she was eleven. John Rigmarden, at the age of three, was tutored by the priest to repeat the marriage vows in church, and then released to go and play. James Ballard, who was ten at the time, was bribed by the gift of two apples by a "bigge damsell" to go with her to be married. A somewhat older couple, John Bridge and Elizabeth Ramsbotham, were married when he was eleven and she thirteen. After the wedding, they went together to the home of the bride's brother, but when evening came, John would eat no supper and cried to be taken home by his father.

These were not typical cases, but they actually happened. Obviously, the marriages didn't represent the wishes of the children concerned, who were simply pawns in games involving family property or prestige. By contrast, among the lower classes, the marriages of young people, far from being premature, were sometimes delayed until the two were in their thirties, for the very good reason that the husband, living in poverty, was unable to provide his intended wife, and expected future children, with a home until he had saved the necessary money.

It was not just the husband, however, who had to have money in order to marry. In families with any social status, a daughter had to have a dowry. Madame Eglantyne, the prioress in Chaucer's *Canterbury Tales*, had become a nun, not because of any sense of spiritual vocation, but simply because her father didn't want to go to the trouble or expense of finding her a husband, and there was no other career possible for a high-born lady. In fact, it was also usual to give a daughter a dowry when she became a nun, but probably a smaller amount would suffice for this than for a marriage.

One of the treasures of medieval literature is the book which the Ménagier (Householder) of Paris wrote for his young wife in 1392–94. It attempts to summarize her wifely duties. He is reputed to have been over sixty, and she only fifteen, when they married. This could have been a miserable experience for her, and that was true for many other girls, because older widowers often married teenaged wives. But the Ménagier was an unusual man, and all went well.

The Prologue to this unusual book is often quoted:

> You, being of the age of fifteen years and in the week that you and I were wed, did pray me . . . in our bed as I remember, that for the love of God I would not correct you harshly before strangers nor before our own folk, but that I would correct you each night or from day to day in our chamber and show you the unseemly or foolish things done in the day or days past, and chastise you, if it pleased me, and then you would not fail to amend yourself according to my teaching and correction, and would do all in your power according to my will, as you said.

The book is in three sections—first, religious and moral duties, second, household management, and third, games and amusements, indoor and outdoor. Altogether it provides a fascinating picture of day-to-day life in the world in which the couple lived.

The duties a wife owes to her husband, according to the Ménagier, are summed up in three words: submission, obedience, and constant attention. He illustrates this with an analogy that would hardly be thought flattering by a modern wife, however devoted:

> A little dog, whether on the road, or at table, or in bed, always keeps near to the person from whom he takes his food, and leaves and is shy and fierce with all others; and if the dog is afar off, he always has his heart and his eye upon his master; even if his master whip him and throw stones at him, the dog follows, wagging his tail and lying down before his master, seeks to mollify him. . . . Wherefore for a better and stronger reason women, to whom God has given natural sense and who are reasonable, ought to have a perfect and solemn love for their husbands.

And now it is time to turn from the marital experiences of the common people of the medieval world to the authorities who made the rules.

WHAT WERE THE THEOLOGIANS SAYING?

We have seen how the views of the patristic writers had a profound effect on the teaching and practice of the early church concerning marriage. What new positions were adopted by the scholars of the medieval period? Did they make any changes in the official attitudes of the church during this further period of a thousand years?

Now that universities were being established, the theologians came to be called the "schoolmen." Many of them were able thinkers, and they included the great Thomas Aquinas. Perhaps the greatest scholar in all Christian history, he was respectfully given the title of the "Angelic Doctor."

Sherwin Bailey, in his excellent book *Sexual Relation in Christian Thought,* has again brought together for us the scholarly opinions about marriage that were registered during this period, with all the appropriate references. Here is a brief summary of his findings:

1. *Legal Control of Marriage.* Under the Christian Roman Emperors, jurisdiction over marriage remained with the state. But when the empire was dissolved, the church took over and continued to deal with all aspects of Christian marriage through the Canon Law. That arrangement has continued until the present time, when judgments are made for Catholics by the marriage tribunals, regardless of the attitude of the state.

2. *The Nature of Marriage.* Two issues were involved here. What constitutes a valid Christian marriage? And under what conditions, if any, can it be terminated? The answer to the first question is that the Roman requirement—that the free consent of the parties is basic—was accepted. There were some who also felt that the marriage must in addition be sexually consummated, while others, following Augustine, thought otherwise. A strong point in the argument was that if sexual consummation was essential, this would imply that Joseph and Mary were not legally married, because the church had been committed since the fifth century to the concept of Mary's perpetual virginity. After centuries of debate, the decision was that *consensus per verba de praesenti* (consent in words applicable to the immediate situation) would be the sole requirement. This was a judgment very helpful to the ecclesiastical courts, because consent before witnesses is beyond dispute, whereas certain proof of sexual consumma-

tion is difficult to secure. Bailey also adds that "It is evident that they found the sexual act a source of theological embarrassment."

3. *Sex and Sin.* This issue was again frequently debated. Some schoolmen wanted to take a strict view, insisting that Christian married couples should be free to have sexual intercourse only on two days a week, Tuesday and Wednesday, because all the other days were holy days. Peter Lombard (1100–1160), however repudiated the views of Augustine and Gregory about the sex act being sinful, but conceded that it always includes "an element of evil." According to Aquinas, the element of evil is that the sex act disturbs the exercise of the rational faculty. Bailey sums up this discussion by saying that the conclusion reached was "a great advance upon that of the early Fathers in its realism and comparative motivation, but . . . we still perceive something of the old emotional antipathy."

4. *Marriage as a Sacrament.* Augustine had defined marriage as a sacrament chiefly because Paul had seen it as a symbol of the union between Christ and the church. In the twelfth century, the number of sacraments recognized by the church was fixed as seven, of which matrimony was one. However, there was difficulty in accepting the fact that a sacrament could encourage acts that could easily be sinful. In the end, it was agreed that the sacramental moment, when grace was bestowed, was when the bride and bridegroom, as baptized Christians, exchanged the vows. In this way, the possibility of bestowing grace later, when the marriage was consummated, was avoided.

5. *Impediments to Marriage.* A list was drawn up of the conditions that made marriage invalid. It

included defective consent (based on fear, violence, or fraud), error concerning the identity or condition of either party, an existing union, sexual incapacity (inability to generate offspring), and inadequate age. Others were listed, including being in holy orders and the complicated issue of the forbidden degrees of relationship, based on either consanguity (ties of blood) or affinity (kinship based on marriage).

6. *Second Marriages.* Although remarriage after the death of a spouse had been discouraged as early as New Testament times, and positively thundered against by Tertullian, by the Middle Ages this no longer seems to have been an issue of any importance. It is true that one eleventh century writer considered a second marriage to be adultery, and another called a third marriage "superfluous"; however, most writers, including Aquinas, recognized second, third, and even fourth unions as acceptable. (We may note that Chaucer's "Wife of Bath," who had made an exceptional number of religious pilgrimages, spoke quite openly of having had five husbands!) When the death of a spouse came so often, remarriage was apparently an acceptable sequel.

7. *Divorce and Remarriage.* Insisting that the marriage union was indissoluble had proved very difficult in Roman times, and also among the newly-converted barbarians. It took several centuries to bring this situation under control. Not until the twelfth century were all the issues settled by Gratian's formulation of canon law, which, according to Bailey, "states with final authority the settled and unconditional adherence of the Western Church to the principle that lawful and consummated Christian marriage is absolutely indissoluble." The

one issue that remained unsettled was the so-called *Pauline privilege,* allowing a Christian believer, whose unbelieving partner departed, to remarry. Aquinas took the view that the bond established by a mixed marriage lacked the strength of a full Christian union, and that the stronger bond automatically cancelled the weaker. However, this issue was not finally settled during the medieval period.

8. *Clerical Celibacy.* The continually recurring issue of the clergy who married or lived with concubines came up in a decisive manner in the twelfth century. Up to then, every effort to enforce clerical celibacy had met with failure. At the first and second Lateran Councils (A.D. 1123 and 1139), a new step was taken by declaring that a marriage contracted by a monk or a priest was declared to be no marriage at all. This had no immediate significant effect, but it was firmly followed up at the fourth Lateran Council in 1213, and "thenceforth little is heard of clerical marriage, except in the remoter and more barbarous parts of Europe."

This does not mean, of course, that the clergy gave up living with women; it means only that they could not live with them in the state of matrimony. It produced the curious situation that a priest who, in modern terminology was "living in sin," would be less seriously judged than if he married the woman and lived with her as his legal wife!

Bailey makes an important point in this connection. In medieval society, any man who wished to attend a university or pursue a professional career would be in a much better position to do so if he were ordained. Therefore, many of the so-called priests who kept concubines had in fact no vocation to the ministry and were living under normal conditions with women who were their wives in all but name.

A striking illustration of this situation follows in the story with which we conclude this chapter.

ABELARD AND HELOISE: A LOVE STORY

No account of relationships between man and woman in the medieval church could justly omit the tragic story of Abelard and Heloise. It is a moving account of human love—thwarted, shamed, and finally redeemed. It dramatizes, as nothing else could, the complications resulting from the degradation of marriage which was the inevitable consequence of compulsory clerical celibacy.

Peter Abelard was a brilliant scholar, popular and celebrated, who in the early twelfth century became a teacher of theology and logic at Notre Dame of Paris. Following the custom of the time, he was a cleric, but not a priest. At the time when the story begins, he was thirty-six years of age.

Let him continue in his own words:

"There was in Paris a young girl named Heloise, the niece of a canon, Fulbert. It was his affectionate wish that she should have the best education in letters that could be procured. Her face was not unfair, and her knowledge was unequalled. This attainment, so rare in women, had given her great reputation.

"I had hitherto lived continently, but now was casting my eyes about, and I saw that she possessed every attraction that lovers seek; nor did I regard my success as doubtful, when I considered my fame and my goodly person, and also her love of letters. Inflamed with love, I thought how I could best become intimate with her. It occurred to me to obtain lodgings with her uncle, on the plea that household cares distracted me from study. Friends quickly brought this about, the old man being miserly and yet desirous of instruction for his niece. He eagerly entrusted her to my tutorship, and begged me to give her all the time I could take from my lectures, authorizing me to see her at any hour of the day or night. . . . I marvelled with what simplicity he confided a tender lamb to a hungry wolf. . . . Doubtless he was misled by love of his niece and my own good reputation. Well, what need to say more: we were united first by the one roof above us, and then by our hearts. Our hours of study were given to love. The books lay open, but our words were of love rather than philosophy, there were more kisses than aphorisms; and love was oftener reflected in our eyes than the lettered page. . . . The more I was taken up with this pleasure, the less time I gave to philosophy and the schools—how tiresome had all that become! . . . A passion so plain was not to be concealed; every one knew of it except Fulbert. A man is often the last to know of his own shame. Yet what everybody knows cannot be hid forever, and so after some months he learned all. Oh how bitter was that uncle's grief! and what was the grief of the separated lovers!"

In due course, Heloise disclosed to Abelard that she was pregnant. He arranged to spirit her away to his family home in Brittany, where a son was born.

Fulbert, the uncle, was furious. Finally, Abelard went to him and humbly offered to do anything to make amends. The best plan seemed to be that the couple should marry—on condition that the marriage should be kept secret. Since Abelard was not a priest, this was possible, though in view of the low esteem in which marriage was held, it would be very damaging to his reputation.

Heloise realized this, and opposed the idea of marriage. Abelard continues his story:

> "She strongly disapproved, and urged two reasons against the marriage, to wit, the danger and disgrace in which it would involve me. She swore—and so it proved—that no satisfaction would ever appease her uncle . . . what curses, what damage to the Church, what lamentations of philosophers, would follow on this marriage. . . . She expatiated on the disgrace and inconvenience of matrimony for me and quoted the apostle Paul exhorting men to shun it. . . . Finally she said that it would be dangerous for me to take her back to Paris; it was more becoming to me, and sweeter to her, to be called my mistress, so that affection alone might keep me hers and not the binding power of any matrimonial chain."

Heloise knew well the attitude of the church at that time. Although marriage was sanctioned, it was regarded as a low and worldly estate not fitting for men and women who were dedicated to purity and holiness. For a celebrated religious leader to have an extra-marital affair on the side, and to beget children, was not a very serious matter—even some of the popes did just that. But for such a man to *marry* placed him in a sinful state and meant that his career was irrevocably ruined.

Abelard, however, felt he must keep his promise, and the marriage took place. The hope was, of course, that it could be kept a secret. But Heloise proved right. Her uncle broke his promise and made it widely known. He went further, and in his rage began to treat his niece so badly that, for her protection, Abelard took her away to a convent and had her admitted.

This action brought on the final outrage. The uncle hired assassins, not to kill Abelard, but to wreak on him "by night, while I was sleeping, a vengance as cruel and irretrievable as it was vile and shameful"—the forcible removal of his sex organs.

"I was afflicted," he wrote, "with more shame than I suffered physical pain. I thought of my ruined hopes and glory, and then saw that by God's just judgment I was punished where I had most sinned. . . . But what a figure I should cut in public! how the world would point its finger at me!"

For both, there was only one remaining action to take. Abelard became a monk at the Abbey of St. Denis, and Heloise took the veil and became a nun.

But even as a monk, Abelard's troubles were not over. He was viciously criticized for his teachings, and his first theological book was publicly burned. Although he was recognized as a philosopher, he made many enemies.

His many writings include a partial autobiography, *Historia Calamitatum: A Story of Adversity.* His recorded statements here are drawn from that source.

Heloise, for her part, was greatly loved by the nuns among whom she now lived, and she became their abbess. Abelard ceased to visit her after a time; his appearances only revived scandalous gossip. After she read his autobiography, however, she wrote him a letter that has been preserved. Here are some extracts:

"Your letter, beloved, written to comfort a friend, chanced recently to reach me. Seeing by its first lines from whom it was, I burned to read it for the love I bear the writer, hoping also from its words to recreate an image of him whose life I have ruined. . . . you showed the treachery and persecutions which had followed you . . . the vile acts of those worthless monks whom you call your sons. No one could read it with dry eyes."

(Later, she changes to the intimate form of address.)

"Dearest, thou knowest—who knows not?—how much I lost in thee, and that an infamous act of treachery robbed me of thee and of myself at once. The greater my grief, the greater need of consolation, not from another but from thee. . . . It is thou alone that canst sadden me or gladden me or comfort me. . . . God knows, I have ever sought in thee only thyself, desiring simply thee and not what was thine. . . . I have brought thee evil, thou knowest how innocently. Not the result of the act but the disposition of the doer makes the crime. . . . My intent towards thee thou only hast proved and alone canst judge. I commit everything to thy weighing and submit to thy decree."

This surely is one of the world's great love letters. The correspondence continued. Abelard's responses were not so warm, his language not so intimate. He saw their relationship as lovers as something now in the past. In one letter he says:

"We are one in Christ, as through marriage we were one flesh. Whatever is thine is not alien to me. Christ is thine, because thou art His spouse. And now thou hast me for a servant, who formerly was thy master—a servant united to thee by spiritual love."

After his stormier early days, Abelard found a refuge in the famous monastery of Cluny. In the year 1142, at the age of sixty-three, he died, and the Abbot of Cluny sent a letter to Heloise, of which this is a part:

"God's providence . . . granted us to enjoy the presence of him—who was yours—Master Peter Abaelard, a man always to be spoken of with honour as a true servant of Christ and a philosopher. . . . No brief writing could do justice to his holy, humble, and devoted life among us. . . . When he came to pay humanity's last debt, his illness was brief. . . . The brothers who were with him can testify how devoutly he received the viaticum of that last journey, and with what fervent faith he commended his body and soul to his Redeemer."

His body was taken to the Paraclete, where Heloise was abbess. Later, she asked the abbot to give into her keeping the declaration of Abelard's absolution, so that it might be placed in his tomb. Here it is:

"I, Peter, Abbot of Cluny, who received Peter Abaelard to be a monk in Cluny, and granted his body, secretly transported, to the Abbess Heloïse and the nuns of the Paraclete, absolve him, in the performance of my office, *(pro officio)* by the authority of the omnipotent God and all the saints, from all his sins."

Twenty years later, also at the age of sixty-three, Heloise died. She was buried in the same tomb with Abelard. So they were together at last.

We are indebted for much of the information in this account to Chapter XXVI of Henry Osborn Taylor's *The Mediaeval Mind,* and to Helen Waddell's novel *Peter Abelard.*

PART III

The Reformation and After

Chapter 8

AFTER ALL, MARRIAGE IS GOOD:
EVEN FOR THE CLERGY
(The Reformation)

Something had to happen!

The tragedy of Abelard and Heloise dramatizes the confusion that had developed about Christian marriage. Here were two people—a man and a woman. Both were scholars with exceptional ability. Both were Christians, ready to devote their lives to serving the church. They loved each other deeply.

Today, the course to take would be obvious. The two would marry with the blessing of the church and the goodwill of all their friends. They would become involved in Christian service together, combining their great gifts in a fulfilling team ministry and enjoying the blessings of a truly happy Christian marriage.

But they had the misfortune to have lived in the Middle Ages, when the teaching of the Christian church about sex and marriage was a tangled mass of contradictions. If they had put out of their minds any thought of sex, love, and marriage, all would have been well. But because they allowed themselves to be sexual beings and to let love draw them together into intimacy, they were doomed. And when, because love and sex had become vital components of their relationship, they then took the fatal step of marrying each other, disaster followed. All that the church could offer them was to separate their lives and to spend the rest of their days trying to atone for their misdeeds.

It seems to us almost impossible to realize that this was the Christian church in action. But the story of Abelard and Heloise only dramatizes what was going on all the time.

Heloise had tried to express it in one of her letters to Abelard after they were separated. Here are her words:

> "Love turned to madness and cut itself off from hope of that which alone it sought, when I obediently changed my garb and my heart too in order that I might prove thee sole owner of my body as well as of my spirit. God knows, I have ever sought in thee only thyself, desiring simply thee and not what was thine. I asked no matrimonial contract, I looked for no dowry; not my pleasure, not my will, but thine have I striven to fulfill. And if the name of wife seemed holier or more potent, the word mistress was always sweeter to me, or even—be not angry!—concubine or harlot."

Heloise is, of course, speaking out of her personal anguish. What she is challenging is the so-called Christian teaching that is ready to at least tolerate a situation in which a Christian clergyman has a love relationship, sexually expressed, with a woman to whom he has made no commitments. But if he *marries* that same woman, he is in disgrace, and if he and his legal wife seek to express their love sexually, apart from the deliberate intention of procreation, they may be judged as living in sin.

Yet that was where the Christian church had been for well over a thousand years. There was, perhaps, some justification for taking an extreme position as a protest against the gross immorality of the Greco-Roman world in its years of degeneration; we must pay all tribute to the dedicated Christians who accepted the celibate life as the price they believed had to be paid for divine approval. But such distorted views of human sexuality and love simply do not represent the teaching of the Bible as a whole. So, something had to happen.

Hensley Henson, in his book *Christian Marriage,* reminds us that "the student of Christian history must be prepared for grave disappointment when he turns from glowing eulogies of Christianity to seek their justifications in fact. It is only by very slow degrees, and with long intervals of desolating error, that the Christian Church arrived at such a theory and practice with respect to marriage." And W. E. H. Lecky, the distinguished historian, in his *History of European Morals,* does not mince his words. Speaking of the writings of the early church fathers he says:

> It would be difficult to conceive anything more coarse or more repulsive than the manner in which they regarded marriage. The sex relation was invariably treated as a consequence of the fall of Adam, and marriage was regarded almost exclusively in its lowest aspect. The tender love which it elicits, the holy and domestic qualities that follow in its train, were almost absolutely omitted from consideration. . . . Marriage was regarded as being necessary, indeed, and therefore justifiable, for the propaga-

tion of the species, and to free men from greater evils; but still as a condition of degradation from which all who aspired to real sanctity should fly. . . . Even when the bond had been formed, the ascetic passion retained its sting. . . . Whenever any strong religious fervor fell upon a husband or a wife, its first effect was to make a happy union impossible. The more religious partner immediately desired to live a life of solitary asceticism, or at least, if no ostensible separation took place, an unnatural life of separation in marriage. The immense place this order of ideas occupies in the hortatory writings of the Fathers, and in the legends of the saints, must be familiar to all who have any knowledge of this department of literature.

Early in the present century, the Anglican Bishop of Salisbury, quoted by Henson in the same book, summed it up: "That one great branch of the Church should have so ordered the domestic life of the clergy for a thousand years that a priest should be in virtue of his office a suspected person and his house a suspected house, about which nearly every Church assembly that meets must pass a warning canon, is a standing blot upon Christianity which concerns us all."

So, something had to happen! And it did. We call it the Reformation. It forms the major bridge leading from the end of the Middle Ages to the Renaissance and the opening of the modern era of European history.

WINDS OF CHANGE

When we say that something had to happen, we mean simply that change was inevitable. Much of the medieval period was a long era of stagnation; part of it has been described as the Dark Ages.

Barbara Tuchman, in her book *A Distant Mirror*, describes the fourteenth century as an era of almost unparalleled futility and tragedy in human history. Yet, during those dismal years, a few dedicated people lived nobly and creatively, but failed to secure the recognition they deserved. The factors contributing to spectacular progress in any period of history are complex and largely beyond individual, or even corporate, control. We are well aware that we live in a changing world, but the forces that bring about change are generally too vast and mysterious even to be recognized. Major wars, for example, are often triggered by incidents that may not at the time seem momentous. It is much easier to be accurate when looking backward than when looking forward.

However, as the thousand medieval years drew to a close, winds of change were blowing that can easily be recognized in retrospect. The term *renaissance,* or rebirth, is applied to a period spanning the latter part of the fourteenth century to the early years of the seventeenth. Significant events usually listed are voyages of discovery (including the discovery of America in 1492); the scientific revolution heralded by Copernicus (1473 to 1543), Galileo (1564 to 1642), Newton (1642 to 1727), and a host of others; imperialistic expansion in Africa and Asia; the French Revolution (1789); the explosive development of the arts and the rediscovery of classical literature; and last, but not least, the Protestant Reformation and the Catholic Counter-Reformation which followed.

The really dramatic event concerning us here is the action of Martin Luther and the other reformers in ending clerical celibacy; so, this is the obvious point on which to focus our attention.

THE FIRST PROTESTANTS

Looking back today, we tend to think of the Reformation as a logical transition from a united, but corrupt, religious system to a division of Christianity into two parallel, but deeply different and mutually hostile, organizations. That may be how it eventually turned out, but at the same time, it was a confused and chaotic series of events, often only remotely connected with each other, activated by people with very different expectations, who often were surprised and bewildered by what they seemed to have started.

It is no part of our purpose in this book to try to piece these chaotic events together, but only to focus on what happened to Christian marriage. We will, therefore, direct our attention to three men who played leading roles in the rebellion against the Roman Catholic system, and we will examine their attitudes toward the marriage relationship. The three are Martin Luther, Huldreich Zwingli, and John Calvin—one German, one Swiss, and one French.

Luther was an Augustinian monk who was a professor in a minor German university, but it would be no exaggeration to say that he started a fire that engulfed Europe for about a century. When he began it all in the year 1517 by nailing his ninety-five theses to the church door in the castle of Wittenberg, he had no idea of the tremendous events that would follow.

It began with what were called *indulgences*. We have seen how important it was for medieval Christians to build up merit so as to be sure of a place in heaven, and to avoid a stay in purgatory to expiate an overload of sins. The parish priest, as part of his service to believers, heard their confessions of sins committed and prescribed necessary acts of penance to set their records straight. But in addition, a kind of points system could be used to even up what looked like a heavy debit balance. For an appropriate payment, surplus merits accumulated by the saints, and made available to the church, could be transferred to the sinner's record—whether he was already in purgatory or likely to proceed there. This system, superintended by the pope, proved to be a very lucrative source of income for the church.

It happened that in Germany, in Luther's time, a promotional drive was being conducted for the sale of indulgences. Johann Tetzel, a Dominican friar who was a persuasive preacher, was conducting this drive in the area where Luther lived. Realizing that naïve people were being ruthlessly exploited, Luther was incensed and protested. Beginning with this simple step, he soon became the leader of a campaign against a whole series of abuses the pope seemed to tolerate, and before long the weight of ecclesiastical authority began to descend upon his head. A less courageous man might have pulled back and abandoned the unequal struggle. But Luther was no coward, and he fought back. The result was that some lined up on his side, while others opposed him—and the battle was joined.

Luther had an inquiring mind, and he soon began to find other abuses in the papal system. His published works are not always coherent, and he often shifted his ground, but in essence what he said was that the Christian believer is justified not by his works, but by his faith in Christ; that the complex system of the medieval church had denied the believer direct access to God; and that the authority for Christian truth is not the pope and his minions, but the Bible. On these convictions, Luther took a determined stand and refused to budge an inch.

LUTHER MARRIES A NUN

As he examined the ecclesiastical system for further abuses, the rule of enforced clerical celibacy soon emerged. He denounced this as having no basis in the Bible and encouraged monks and priests to defy the rule, which many of them were very willing to do. It was not, at first, his intention to marry, himself—he was now entering his fortieth year, and he expected to be martyred. The fact that he *did* marry in the end was due to an incident that is both charming and amusing.

151

A group of nuns asked Luther how they might escape from the convent where they lived, and he agreed to help them. Leonard Kopp was a sixty-year-old merchant who from time to time delivered barrels of herrings to the convent. He agreed, after delivering a load, to bundle some nuns into his covered wagon and bring them out. There were twelve of them. Three went back to their homes, but the rest were willing candidates for marriage.

Luther assumed responsibility for placing these nuns, and in the following two years all were settled but one. Katherine von Bora was to marry a young man, but the man's parents firmly refused. Another candidate was found, but Katherine, now twenty-six, was not willing this time. Through an intermediary, she indicated that she would prefer to marry Luther, himself. He treated this as a joke at first, but on a visit to his parents, he found them very much in favor of his continuing the family line.

So, in the end he capitulated. He said plainly that he was not in love, but that he was taking this action for three reasons—to please his father, to spite the pope and the devil, and as a witness that he now believed in clerical marriage.

On June 27, 1525, at ten o'clock in the morning, with all the bells in Wittenberg ringing, Luther and Katherine walked together to the parish church and were joined in holy matrimony. That evening, a banquet and a dance in the town hall followed. So, the leader of the Reformation, as an act of Christian witness, defied the church's doctrine of clerical celibacy. In the years that followed, Martin and Kate enjoyed together a very happy Christian marriage. It was a fruitful union, too. They had six children—three boys and three girls.

Erasmus, the distinguished Dutch theologian, tried to make a joke out of all this. The Reformation, he said, had at first seemed a tragedy, but it turned out to be a comedy by ending in a wedding.

OTHER REFORMERS

In Switzerland, the leader of the Reformation was Huldreich Zwingli, who belonged to a good family. He came under the influence of the humanist movement, which rejected superstitious practices and went back to the early sources of Christian belief. He became a priest and gained an increasingly wide reputation as a scholar and preacher. He nearly died of the plague, but recovered. Coming under the influence of Luther, he spoke out for the marriage of priests, and himself took a wife. He had, in fact, lived with her (Anna Reinhard, a widow) for some two years, and had had a child by her, before the formal wedding. So, it was in his personal interest to support the opposition to clerical celibacy.

Zwingli soon became the recognized leader of the Protestant movement in his own country. With the support of the civil authorities, Catholic practices were given up. Priests and nuns were allowed to marry, and monasteries were converted into schools. Zwingli and Luther disagreed, however, on their interpretations of the Lord's Supper, and this led to an unfortunate breach in the Protestant front.

The Reformation movement in Switzerland became overconfident. The city of Zurich tried aggressively to suppress medieval practices. This was resisted, and civil war followed. In a battle in 1531, Zwingli's followers were defeated and he, himself, was killed.

At the western end of Switzerland lies the city of Geneva. French-speaking and Catholic, it became the scene of violent conflicts. At first, the city authorities resisted the Protestant movement, but finally, in 1536, the monks and nuns were banished. This opened up the way for William Farel, a fiery preacher who had led the cause of reform, to reorganize the life of the city. It happened that a young Frenchman, a friend of his, was passing through at the time. Farel invited him to stay and help with the task of reorganization. The Frenchman agreed to do so. His name was John Calvin, and his age was twenty-seven at the time. Two years before, he had experienced a sudden conversion to the Protestant faith and had followed this up by writing an eloquent and scholarly defense of his new faith, the *Institutes of the Christian Religion.*

Beginning in a quiet way, Calvin developed the idea of making Geneva a model Christian city. With tireless zeal, he worked on at this task, which proved painful and arduous. By 1555, however, he and his followers had won undisputed leadership of the city, and he founded the Geneva Academy, which later became the University of Geneva, and the center for training leaders of the Reform movement.

Before he settled in Geneva, Calvin was persuaded to marry, and his friends offered to find him a wife. Their first choice was a lady of noble birth, but she spoke no French, and Calvin felt she would not be acceptable. They then found another candidate, and the wedding date was arranged. But something went wrong, and it also was cancelled. Finally, Calvin took the matter into his own hands, and married Idelette de Bure, widow of a Frenchman who had been converted to the Reformed faith. She had two children from her previous marriage, and in due course they all moved into a modest home in Geneva. This was in August, 1540, when Calvin was thirty-one. Later, they had a son, but he was prematurely born and, unfortunately, died. Calvin, reporting this to a friend, wrote: "The Lord has certainly inflicted a severe and bitter wound in the death of our baby son. But He is Himself a father and knows best what is good for His children." They had no more children, and Idelette died in the spring of 1549.

Calvin shared his sorrow with a friend. "You know," he wrote, "how tender my mind is. Had not a powerful self-control been given to me, I could not have borne up so long. And truly, mine is no common source of grief. I have been bereaved of the best companion of my life, of one who, had it been so ordained, would have willingly shared not only my poverty but even my death. During my life she was the faithful helper of my ministry. From her I never experienced the slightest hindrance. She was never troublesome to me throughout the whole course of her illness, but was more anxious about her children than about herself."

Calvin was a modest, self-effacing man. He lived frugally, often eating only one meal a day. But he was a brilliant thinker, a gifted writer, and a tireless worker. Some consider him the greatest theologian since Aquinas. In his last illness, he continued to dictate until eight hours before his death, when his voice failed. That was in 1564, and by that time he had won international recognition as one of the most distinguished leaders of the Reformation.

KING HENRY AND HIS SIX WIVES

In any chapter dealing with the Reformation and its impact on marriage, it would be an unpardonable omission not to include some reference to a major event involving the opposite process—the impact of marriage on the Reformation. Apart from the bizarre behavior of King Henry VIII of England, it is an open question as to whether England would have ended up Catholic or Protestant.

Henry's marital adventures have made him a notorious figure and often have obscured the fact that he was a scholar, a gifted organizer, and a vigorous opponent of the

Reformation, to whom Pope Leo X gave the title "Defender of the Faith."

His ventures in the field of marriage, however, were complicated in the extreme. He began by marrying Catherine of Aragon, daughter of the King and Queen of Spain. She bore him six children, but only one of them, Mary, survived. This meant that there was no male heir to the throne, and that might be a serious matter—a woman, up to that time, had never ruled England. In order to have a male heir, it seemed he must get another wife. Of course, he had mistresses, but their offspring wouldn't count.

Anne Boleyn was a lady in the royal court. Henry urged Cardinal Wolsey, his trusted friend, to find a way to annul his existing marriage, but Wolsey died without succeeding in this.

The King now pushed through legal arrangements which gave him wide power over the church. He also appointed his friend Thomas Cranmer as Archbishop of Canterbury. He then secretly married Anne Boleyn and persuaded Cranmer to declare his former marriage annulled. In due course, a daughter—the future Queen Elizabeth I—was born to his new wife.

The pope, responding to Henry's high-handed action, threatened to excommunicate him. The King's response was to break off all connections with Rome and to have himself declared "the only supreme head on earth of the Church in England." Some Carthusian monks who refused to accept the King's new power were executed. So were two distinguished spiritual leaders—Bishop John Fisher and Sir Thomas More.

These actions were followed in 1536 by the closing down of all the monasteries, which brought in needed income to the state, and in that same year Catherine of Aragon, Henry's first wife, died. Soon afterward, Henry accused Anne Boleyn of adultery and had her beheaded.

Eleven days later, he married Jane Seymour, and at last he had a son and heir, but Jane died within days of her son's birth. This was in 1537.

Henry now married Anne of Cleves, his fourth wife, at the advice and support of Thomas Cromwell. The marriage was never consummated, and in 1540 he divorced her and had Cromwell beheaded. He next married Catherine Howard, his fifth wife, but by 1542 she followed Anne Boleyn to the executioner on the grounds that she had had sexual relatons with other men both before and after her marriage to the King. Finally, Henry married Catherine Parr, a scholarly woman who had had two previous husbands. Married to the King in 1543, she survived him when he died in 1547, then remarried and died in childbirth in 1548.

Although Henry's original loyalty to Rome had been strained to the breaking point by his flagrant marital and political intrigues, he was still opposed to the idea of the clergy's being allowed to marry. His son Edward VI, a sickly youth of nine years old, succeeded him and reigned for only six years, but during his reign the ban on clerical marriage was removed, and many ministers eagerly seized the opportunity to take wives. Then, when Edward was succeeded in 1553 by his rabidly Catholic step-sister "Bloody Mary," the ban was reimposed, and large numbers of married clergy had to lose their status or give up their wives. A few, who held firmly to their Protestant faith, were martyred.

One particularly moving story is told in *Foxe's Book of Martyrs*. Rowland Taylor, a clergyman who was married and had nine children, refused to give up his faith and was sentenced to death as a heretic. Early one morning, he was taken from prison to be burned to death in the presence of his former congregation. Outside the prison gates, his wife and children were waiting. He embraced them, and then all knelt down together in the street and repeated the Lord's Prayer, after which, with calmness and courage, he was led away to die.

Mary's turbulent reign lasted only five years, then Queen Elizabeth I ascended the throne. England at last became firmly Protestant, and clergy were again free to marry. Never again was this right denied them.

PROTESTANT TEACHING ABOUT MARRIAGE

From the writings of the reformers, we can gather the main teachings about marriage, and this provides the foundation for what later became Protestant doctrine. We shall try at this point to make a rough outline of this material, extracting it again from Sherwin Bailey's *Sexual Relation in Christian Thought*, where the documentary references are given in full.

1. *Clerical Celibacy.* The major issue related to Christian marriage confronted by the Reformation was the traditional Catholic insistence on clerical celibacy, and we have seen how that was firmly reversed, on the ground that it had no Scriptural authority to support it. Luther strongly insisted that the "gift of continence" is not awarded to most men, and that compulsory vows of celibacy imposed as a condition for exercising Christian ministry represent a cruel injustice. Zwingli said that since God had ordained marriage, it must be lawful for all Christians, including the clergy. Luther also pointed out that vows of chastity carried the implication that salvation depends on works, rather than on faith, and that this is contrary to the teaching of the Bible. Calvin, while holding the same general view, suggested that there *are* life situations in which chastity must be observed, and that with God's help all things are possible. However, he added that an outward appearance of abstinence might only cover up an inward

lack of purity, so that celibacy did not of itself constitute a virtue.

2. *Marriage as Divinely Ordained.* Luther asserted that marriage is God's gift to mankind, authorized in his Word, that human nature is equipped for it, that it was initiated in paradise, that it is confirmed by the fifth commandment and safeguarded by the seventh, and that it is a school of faith and love in which men and women learn and grow. Therefore, it is in marriage, and not in celibacy, that we are best prepared for life everlasting.

3. *Marriage as a Sacrament.* Calvin and Luther both, while accepting the sanctity of marriage, saw no grounds for treating it as a sacrament. This had no scriptural warrant, said Luther. And Calvin wondered how the Roman Catholic Church could call marriage a sacrament, when distinguished patristic writers had vilified it as unclean, polluted, and carnally defiling.

4. *Husband-Wife Roles.* Calvin, although recognizing that marriage is primarily the means for propagation of the species, added that its chief purpose is social rather than generative. Woman is not simply man's bedmate, but his life companion. Luther was more inclined to see the wife as bearer of children, as providing a sexual outlet for her husband, and as occupying a subordinate position in marriage. While both Calvin and Luther stressed the wife's subject status as divinely ordained, they saw no reason why this should exclude her from ministry in the church. However, they pointed out that the Scripture forbids her from preaching or exercising spiritual leadership. Calvin saw her true ministry as that of motherhood.

5. *Monogamy and Polygamy.* For Calvin, anything but monogamy was clearly contrary to God's purpose for marriage, and he went so far as to say that, in this respect, the behavior of the Old Testament patriarchs went "beyond the liberty which is conditioned by love." But he

agreed that in very special circumstances God might approve of suspending the general rules. Luther had landed in a whole heap of trouble by allowing the bigamy of Philip of Hesse, so he presumably agreed with Calvin.

6. *Marital Sexuality.* Luther's opinion of this subject is not entirely clear. He appears to accept the earlier teaching of Augustine and others that sexual desire is a result of the Fall and associated with original sin—marriage is a regrettable necessity. His statement that it is impossible to pray upon the marriage bed reveals his discomfort. On the other hand, he recognizes that most men are unable to suppress their sexual drive, and that taking a wife provides the best remedy for the Christian. Calvin is more positive and views sexual intercourse in marriage as provided by God for good purposes; therefore, it is clean and good in itself. However, he goes on to say that while the Christian husband and wife may enjoy the experience, they should do so not intemperately, but with modesty and propriety.

7. *Marriage and Law.* Following the fall of Rome, and until the Reformation, all legal questions related to marriage had been dealt with by the ecclesiastical courts and had been based on canon law. Both Calvin and Luther favored handing over legal responsibility for marriage to the state. However, it was Calvin's view that the secular court in Geneva should base all its judgments on biblical principles. Luther counted on close cooperation between church and state in dealing with matrimonial issues—a high expectation that was not to be realized.

8. *Unfitness for Legal Marriage.* Both Calvin and Luther accepted the prohibited degrees of relationship found in the book of Leviticus as being based on the natural law, with Calvin advocating some minor adjustments. Luther added three others—impotence, a vow of continence taken before marriage, and an existing marriage—as legal barriers.

9. *Grounds for Divorce.* Luther took as his base the judgment of Jesus in Matthew's Gospel that there could be no "putting away" except for adultery and that even then the innocent party might not remarry. However, this seemed to conflict with Paul's judgment that it was "better to marry than to burn." So, in some cases remarriage seemed to be justified. Both Calvin and Luther also recognized the Pauline privilege that applied to a Christian married to an unbeliever, but they differed in their detailed interpretations of this. Both vigorously denounced the complexities of canon law in deciding individual cases, particularly the dispensations that could be bought by the wealthy, but were denied to the poor.

10. *Responsibility for Parenthood.* The reformers attached great importance to parenthood as one of the supreme blessings of marriage. Luther saw parenthood as the chief end of marriage and viewed parents as being called to serve as "apostle, bishop, and priest" of their sons and daughters.

THE CATHOLIC RESPONSE

The Reformation was a challenge to the Catholic Church, from within its own ranks, to mend its ways. At first, there had been no intention on the part of the reformers to establish a competing organization, and it was unfortunate that this happened. The situation is well summarized by T. H. L. Parker in his *Portrait of Calvin:*

> For a hundred years or more the magnificent structure of Church and common life that the Middle Ages had painfully built out of the ruins of the old Roman Empire had shown signs of wear. And, as will happen when buildings are not well looked after, time only accelerated the decay. In theology, the universal breadth of the thoughts of St. Thomas Aquinas had given place to the 'mummified philosophy' of the 15th century. The odor of

decaying sanctity hung about the cloisters of old monastic orders. . . . Yet the cause for reform met with little response from the Roman court. Here and there a little was put right, and here and there a little was made worse. A few bones were thrown to the dogs to stop their barking. But the radical reform of the Church was not attempted. We may well doubt whether the Roman Church could have been reformed from within at this time. Certainly, she reformed herself in the Counter-Reformation of the 16th century, but not before she had been shocked into action by the wide-spread Protestant revolt.

The "action," unfortunately, did not come until 1546, the year Luther died. Nearly thirty years earlier, when he had nailed his challenge on the church door, he had simply been regarded as an obscure monk making a nuisance of himself. No one at that time would have dreamed that the consequences of his action would split Christendom down the middle for the next four centuries.

Many attempts had been made to call together a council of responsible Catholic leaders, but there were regrettable delays and postponements. When at last the first meeting was convened in Trento in northern Italy, there were only three papal delegates and thirty-one others present. At the twenty-fifth final session just eighteen years later, the total number had risen to two hundred thirteen.

In *The History of Sacerdotal Celibacy in the Christian Church*, Henry C. Lea reports that the issue of marriage of the priesthood was raised in an early session, when a Bavarian delegate estimated that out of one hundred priests, there were only three or four who were not either married or living with concubines. Attempts were made to deal with this regrettable state of affairs. This is illustrated by the action taken in 1548 by the Archbishop of Trèves. He issued an order to all the clergy in his diocese: "All of you, of what grade soever, shall dismiss your concubines within nine days, removing them beyond the bounds of your parishes, and be no longer seen to associate with loose and wanton women. Those who neglect this order shall be suspended from office and benefice, their concubines shall be excommunicated, and they themselves be brought before our synod."

Three weeks later at the synod, it appears that there had been little response, and the archbishop changed his approach from threatening to pleading. A year later, he called another synod in which he renewed his appeals, which apparently had not had the desired effect.

It was not until the twenty-fourth session of the Council of Trent, in 1564, that general issues concerning marriage were settled. These included dogmatic pronouncements that the state of celibacy is spiritually superior to the state of marriage, that a valid Christian marriage is a true sacrament, that marriage cannot be ended by divorce, although it is possible for the couple to separate never to remarry, and that all legal decisions about Christian marriage are made by the church and not by the state. Other decisions concerned what makes a Christian marriage valid and new rules to avoid possible abuses. Last, but not least, it was firmly declared that the clergy are pledged to a life of celibacy, and that this must henceforth be strictly enforced.

So, the lines that separate Catholics and Protestants were firmly drawn. The Catholic Counter-Reformation followed the Protestant breakaway. The two separate branches of the church still had much in common, but in their views of Christian marriage there were significant differences, most of which have continued to the present day.

CONCLUSION

In closing this chapter, we need to remember that the era of the Reformation followed closely the historical period known as the Renaissance. The power of Christianity to shape the destiny of Europe had been impressive, indeed. But power can be repressive, too, and in the medieval period we can sense a pervasive staleness that was very different from the dynamic, liberating energy of the early church. The Reformation brought division, and that was grievous. Yet, dedicated Christian men and women were its leaders, and their motivation had been to bring about renewal from within. Perhaps what they did was to create in Christendom the restless dynamic that characterizes the two party system in politics—an openness to new ideas and new ways of achieving goals.

The situation has been brilliantly expressed by W. H. McNeill in his widely applauded book *The Rise of the West.* We cannot do better than to close this chapter with his words:

> The thundering voices of the Reformation and Counter Reformation contrast sharply with the slender siren song of the Renaissance. Yet the siren song was piercing, too. Even in the midst of the volcanic passions and violent upheavals provoked by religious strife, it could still be heard, tantalizing many of those whom it could not win over. Beauty created by human imagination and skill for its own sake, and truth pursued by an unfettered human reason independent of all external authority, had a seductive charm even for men striving desperately after religious and moral certainty.
>
> The magnitude of European cultural achievements in the sixteenth–seventeenth centuries, together with the violence and scale of the religious, political, economic, and social changes of the age, arouses a sense of wonder and amazement. Old human relations, old habits of thought, and old patterns of sensibility and piety lost their normal rigidity, and individual genius correspondingly enlarged its scope as seldom before in civilized history.

Chapter 9

CHRISTIAN MARRIAGE AS A SPIRITUAL COMPANIONSHIP
(The Contribution of the Puritans)

The struggle that ended in the division of Christendom into Catholics and Protestants began in continental Europe, involving mainly Germany, Switzerland, and, of course, Italy. Later, however, the scene shifted to England. There, the issue of the nature and interpretation of the Christian message led to a fierce battle between the Anglican state church, on the one hand, and the Puritan reformers on the other. The Puritans lost the battle in England, but some of them later, after a sojourn in Holland, took ship across the Atlantic Ocean to the North American continent, and there helped to create a new democracy which later became the United States of America.

As a side issue in this process of revolutionary change, a new and profoundly different interpretation of the meaning of Christian marriage emerged. In this chapter, we shall follow this important development in some detail.

In the last chapter, we described the tumultuous reign of Henry VIII of England, whose actions in marrying six wives resulted in breaking the links between England and the Roman Catholic Church. When Henry died in 1547, his son Edward VI, a sickly youth, succeeded him, but did nothing to end the state of alienation from Rome. Six years later, however, when Edward died, his half-sister Mary, who later earned the nickname "Bloody Mary," came to the throne. The daughter of Henry VIII by his first wife, Mary was a fanatical Catholic. She resumed the broken relationship with the pope and reversed most of the changes that had been made in the Anglican church. Only five years later, her reign, in turn, came to an end, and she was succeeded by her half-sister Elizabeth, who became one of the greatest of all English monarchs.

During those turbulent times, state and church policies led to a bewildering succession of changes, and even reversals, of opinion among leaders in both church and state. Among those who wanted radical alterations in church policy, one group emerged to whom we must now give close attention.

In 1559, when Queen Elizabeth I was firmly established on the throne, this group of dissenters launched a campaign for drastic revision of the policy of the state church. Their first leader was Thomas Cartwright, the Lady Margaret Professor of Divinity at Cambridge University. He was supported by a number of clergy including some who, during Mary's harsh reign, had been forced to leave their parishes and had fled to Geneva, where they had become convinced advocates of the Calvinist philosophy of how to run church and state.

This dissenting group earned the title of "Puritans." According to Thomas Fuller, *puritan* was viewed from the beginning as an odious term, and is still considered derogatory. However, our own investigation has convinced us that whatever else the Puritans did or did not do, they laid new foundations for Protestant thinking about the nature of Christian marriage.

In general, Puritans wanted to replace the formal prayer book services of the Anglican Church with a Bible-based preaching ministry. They stood for an ordered life and strict moral discipline, self-control with no excess or waste, and the responsible use of time and money. They took the view that the church must not become a tool of the state—a goal they failed to achieve in England, but were later able to achieve in the new democratic system they helped to establish in North America.

What concerns us here is that one of their primary aims was to strengthen family life by the application of basic Christian principles to daily activities in the homes of believers. This led them to develop concepts of Christian marriage that were radically different from those widely accepted in the past.

PURITAN VIEWS OF MARRIAGE

The recognition of the Puritan contribution to the formulation of the Protestant view of marriage is in itself a curious story.

In 1929, a book entitled *The Puritan Family* was published in Germany by Levin L. Schücking, a gifted German scholar who made an intensive study of the subject. Fourteen years later, in 1943 during World War II, the type for a revised English translation of the book was all ready to print when it was totally destroyed in an Allied air raid on Leipzig. Following this delay, it was not until 1968, nearly forty years after the book was first written and after the author's death, that a German copy was obtained. This was translated into English by H. J. Hentschel and was published in 1970. It is a scholarly work, ably translated and based on a detailed knowledge of the facts and a clear perception of the issues.

In the preface of his book, Schücking explains that the book "has nothing to do with dogma or ecclesiastical politics, and is only concerned with that which lay nearest to the heart of the members of this movement, namely with the practical conduct of the pious man's life." He describes his task as "an examination of the characteristic mechanics of that family theocracy which constituted the very heart of the religious life and which has by no means received the attention which it deserves."

We need to stress the fact that the attitudes developed by the Puritans represent a striking departure from the traditional view of marriage. This view, in England, was simply that of medieval Catholic Europe.

Let us illustrate some of those earlier English views. According to one writer, marriage was considered to be a "necessary evil." Anyone who has read Chaucer's *Canterbury Tales* will understand what this means. Further evidence is found in William Langland's fourteenth century *Vision of Piers Plowman* in the words: "Those who surrender their wills and lead a chaste life of meditation are more according to the heart of the Lord than those who live according to nature's commands, and following what the flesh desires bring forth fruit." In that same century, Dan Michel's *Remorse of Conscience* (1340) uses the New Testament parable of the sower to construct a scale on which virginity counts as 100, widowhood 60, and marriage only 30.

Later, however, the English attitude toward marriage was somewhat modified by the addition of the companionship concept. William Tyndale, in *The Obedience of a Christian Marriage* (1528), defined marriage as "ordained for a remedy and to increase the world." This is the traditional Catholic view. However, he added the words "and for the man to help the woman and the woman the man, with all love and kindness."

Later still, Archbishop Cranmer, in revising the marriage service in the Church of England Prayer Book in 1549, added to the two traditional Catholic reasons for marriage—children and sex—a third: "the mutual society, help and comfort that the one ought to have of the other, both in prosperity and adversity." These three reasons have been listed ever since in the marriage rituals of most Protestant churches.

It was the Puritans, however, who undertook the major task of developing a new Christian concept of marriage. Schücking, the German scholar, gives a remarkably clear and detailed account of this process. But, as we have seen, as a result of many complications, his book did not appear in English until the year 1970.

In that same year, 1970, an American scholar, quite independently, went over the same ground. Apparently quite unaware of Schücking's work, he also published his findings. James Turner Johnson's book is entitled *A Society Ordained by God*, and his research was carried out at Princeton University. His book is carefully documented, but there is no evidence that he had ever heard of Schücking.

It would be a fascinating task to make a detailed comparison of the findings of these two quite independent studies, but it would take up more space than we can spare in our very broad survey. The main difference between them is that Johnson's approach is mainly theological, while that of Schücking is more general. We shall have to be content to draw a few major conclusions from both sources.

The Puritans, as we have already explained, were dissenters and revolutionaries. They wanted changes in church policy—away from the politics of power, focused instead on the life of the individual Christian believer, which would follow in a disciplined manner the teaching of the Bible. They saw the family as a small community, almost a minor church, where the basic Christian teaching could be lived out and demonstrated. The local church could then be a community of Christian families, inspiring and encouraging one another.

Until the Reformation, the Catholic Church had taken over the control of the lives of individual Christians, and there had been little emphasis on family religion as such. The priest had acted as "father" to all family members, and the worship of God had focused almost exclusively on the sanctuary. The Puritans wanted to change this by shifting the focus to the Christian home, making the church a family of families and the pastor essentially a preacher and interpreter of the meaning of Christian living. Although they failed in their immediate purpose in the Church of England, it could be said that the Puritans played an important part in opening the way for the development of the free and independent Protestant churches of today— mainly Presbyterians, Congregationalists, Baptists, and Quakers.

Given their emphasis on family life, it was inevitable that the Puritans, and those they influenced, should develop a doctrine of the Christian family and of Christian marriage. This they certainly did in an impressive series of publications. All we can offer here is a representative list, with authors and dates of the publications in question. We have chosen to preserve some titles in their original spelling and to list the authors in alphabetical order:

Baxter, Richard. *Christian Directory*, 1673.
Becon, Thomas. *The Golde Boke of Christen Matrimonye*, 1542.

Bullinger, Heinrich. *The Christen State of Matrimonye.* Translated from the German by Miles Coverdale, 1541.

Bunny, Edmond. *Of Divorce for Adulterie, and Marrying Again*, 1542.

Bunyan, John. *Christian Behavior*, 1663.

Cleaver, Robert. *A Godlie Form of Household Government*, 1598.

Defoe, Daniel. *The Family Instructor*, 1715; *The Religious Courtship*, 1722; *Use and Abuse of the Marriage Bed*, 1727.

Fordyce, James. *Sermons to Young Women* (two volumes), 1766.

Gataker, Thomas. *Marriage Duties*, 1620.

Gouge, William. *Of Domestical Duties*, 1622.

Griffith, Matthew. *Bethel: Or a Forme for Families*, 1633.

Niecholes, Alexander. *A Discourse of Marriage and Wiving*, 1615.

Perkins, William. *Christian Economie: A Short Survey of the Right Manner of Erecting and Ordering a Familie*, 1609.

Priche, Robert. *The Doctrine of Superioritie, and of Subjection*, 1609.

Rogers, Daniel. *Matrimoniale Honour*, 1642.

Secker, William. *A Wedding Ring for the Finger*, 1658.

Snawsel, Robert. *A Looking Glasse for Married Folkes*, 1610.

Swetnam, J. *The Arraignment of Lewd, Idle, Froward, and Unconstant Women*, 1622.

Taylor, Jeremy. *The Rule and Exercises of Holy Living*, 1650.

Vieves, Juan Luis. *The Instruction of a Christen Woman*, 1640.

Whatley, William. *A Bride-bush: or, A Wedding Ceremony*, 1617; *A Treatise of the Cumbers and Troubles of Marriage*, 1624.

Wing, John. *The Crowne Conjugall; or, The Spouse Royall*, 1620.

In a general discussion of these and other similar writings, Schücking says: "If we are eager to determine the real nature of the Puritan mind, we can find excellent material in the so-called conduct books, which set out to advise the believing Christian in every situation of ordinary life, and particularly in matters that concern the family. In these folios all situations from the cradle to the grave are considered, the specific group of duties which arise out of them being in each case defined."

When any doubt arises in these writings as to what is the Christian position, the Bible is always the final authority. Inevitably, this tends in most cases to be the Old Testament, which happens to contain far more stories of family life than the New Testament. Abraham and Sarah tend to be viewed as the model couple.

We naturally ask: Why did the Puritans devote so much attention to the biblical view of *marriage*, a subject that had been almost ignored, and in fact evaded, in earlier times and again in more recent Protestant churches? Schücking gives the following answer:

The Puritan was very practical in his outlook on life and so came early to realize the vast importance of marriage in the life of the individual. . . . [The Puritan had to] come to terms with one of the most important things in a man's natural life—in this case with the relations between the sexes—in a manner which benefitted the whole moral personality.

In a summary of Puritan teaching, Johnson lists five aspects of marriage that are given special emphasis in the Puritan writings:

1. *Marriage was directly ordained by God.* The emphasis is on the Genesis story where God sees that

Adam, surrounded by creatures different from himself, is lonely and needs a companion. So, God creates Eve to meet this need. In order to be quite sure that she really *is* a fitting companion, she is formed out of a part of Adam's own body—a fact which reassures and greatly pleases Adam. The Puritan view, therefore, is that the primary purpose of marriage is to provide a deep and meaningful *companionship* between man and woman.

This being so, the Puritans rejected the Catholic view that marriage was primarily intended to produce children. They made the point that parenthood became necessary only later, when, as a result of their sin, Adam and Eve were banished from Paradise and doomed to die.

The Puritans likewise rejected the Catholic view that marriage is a sacrament—a doctrine which, as we have seen, was formulated quite late in the history of the church.

2. *Marriage is, therefore, man's normal state and so intended by God from the very beginning.* To the Puritans, the celibate life might be a special calling for an individual Christian, in which case a special gift of grace might enable him or her to endure an unnatural way of life. But to exalt the state of celibacy above that of marriage was to make a secondary way of life superior to what was clearly God's primary purpose for mankind.

3. *Marriage is a social estate and the microcosm of all human society.* It was never God's purpose for human beings to live in isolation, but to enjoy a shared life in community. However, this is a very difficult task to put into practice; so, the small community of marriage and the family provides an opportunity to develop, in a setting of mutual love

and trust, the necessary skills to be practiced in the larger community in which families share burdens and benefits with one another. In the small world of the family, we all need to learn the skills we need in order to live effectively and purposefully in the wider world.

4. *The head of the family is the husband/father, but because of the intimate nature of the marriage relationship, the position of the wife is that she comes very near to being his equal in many areas of family life.* The Puritans saw the family as a community made up of three components—the husband-wife pair, with generally equal status but ultimate authority vested in the husband, the children over whom the parents jointly exercised authority, and the servants, with husband and wife also sharing authority over them.

5. *A major, but secondary, purpose in marriage is that of parenthood, but companionship remains the primary purpose.* Thomas Gataker, a Puritan who taught at Cambridge University in England, considered marriage to be the primary relationship because it was "the first that ever was in the world," and therefore "the fountain from which the rest flow." His point is that, in terms of God's purpose, the established man-woman companionship creates the ideal setting for children's entry into the world.

These are the Puritans' basic beliefs about marriage. We may now consider a few further issues which will help to define their position more clearly.

SOME FURTHER ISSUES

THE POSITION OF WOMEN

As we have seen, the wife enjoyed an almost equal status with her husband, though he was finally in control.

Schücking developed convincingly the view that English women in the seventeenth century were far ahead of their continental European sisters in the freedom and power they enjoyed. He says, "It is quite clear—and the accuracy of our information leaves us in no doubt—that the position of women in England, when compared with that of the rest of Europe, was quite strikingly favorable in just that stratum which was to set the tone for future developments." He provides many instances. Whether this fact helped to develop the Puritan attitudes, or whether the Puritans helped to bring it about in the first place, remains an open question.

THE CHRISTIAN VIEW OF MARITAL SEX

The treatment of this subject is described by Schücking as "Puritanism's greatest and most admirable cultural achievement." He says that Luther and Calvin could never completely rid themselves of conceptions of the medieval church, which took the view that "since marriage has its sensual side, this clearly implied that it could no longer be equated with love in its highest form." In contrast to this, the cool realism of the Puritans recognized marriage as being essentially a sharing of spiritual-sensual experience—a mixture of religion and nature, as Rogers calls it. "The Puritan product was distinguishable from the equally prolific but rather repulsive Jesuit outlook by the cleanness of mind with which delicate matters were handled and above all by the honesty and consistency with which nature was recognized for what it is, accepted as such."

To quote other Puritan writers, Gouge described marital sex as an experience to be entered into "with good will and delight, willingly, readily, and cheerfully." Jeremy Taylor (not a Puritan, but very sympathetic to their views) saw the purpose of marriage as "to lighten and ease the cares and sadness of household affairs, or to endear each other."

THE SHARED SPIRITUAL LIFE OF
THE MARRIED COUPLE

In Puritan marriages, according to Schücking, "the enormously increased importance of the part played by the woman in the lives of her husband and her family can only be explained by the effort . . . to equip the wife in such a fashion that she could accompany her husband faithfully and with understanding on all his journeys in the religious life. . . . The possibility of complete mutual self-revelation which it provides . . . binds the partners of a marriage to one another utterly and completely. . . . Thus the concept of confession underwent a curious change."

This kind of open and honest sharing between the couple is something beyond joint Bible reading and formal prayers. It has a close affinity with the daily sharing that, in our own time, is being rediscovered in the marriage enrichment movement of today.

A spiritual relationship of this kind inevitably excludes any possibility of the husband acting as a superior person in relation to his wife. Gouge, for example, writing in 1622, tells husbands to remember that their wives are very sensitive persons, toward whom critical and arrogant tones of voice should not be used. He adds, however, in a lighter vein that wives can grow accustomed to excessive scolding by their husbands much as jackdaws grow accustomed to the periodical clanging of church bells!

According to Schücking, this spiritual unity in marriage produced its counterpart in what he calls "the advanced nature of the concept of married love." It was something quite different from the medieval concept of conventional "gallantry" which the knight was encouraged to adopt toward ladies, and which, the author observes, "could go hand in hand at times with the grossest brutality." Instead, it is "a transfiguration of the commonplace, resulting from the fact that each partner is conscious of having the support of the other in sustaining dignity and self-respect."

Schücking goes on to add that this kind of thinking about Christian marriage was quite alien to Luther. Nor could it be expected that Luther might, a century earlier, have developed such sensitivity. The Puritan view implied "a most delicate craving for sympathy, a desire to live in an atmosphere that is both comfortable and warm with a sensitive ear for the dissonances in a life of shared feelings and experience and a corresponding delight in its harmonies. . . . Where there is such spiritual accord the whole idea of subjection loses much of its practical significance."

UNJUST JUDGMENTS OF PURITANS

In the light of testimony from outstanding scholars, is it not time for us to correct some of our regrettable misconceptions about Puritanism? The very term *puritanical* has come to mean, in our culture, a negative and judgmental attitude about the enjoyment of life in general and of sex in particular.

James Turner Johnson, in his book *A Society Ordained by God*, speaks out strongly on this question. He says:

> The popular conception of Puritanism today is largely one of a cold, repressive theological and social system dominated by a blue-nosed God who would brook no levity among his saints. . . .
> This popular conception . . . is a misconception. It is nothing short of ironic that studies can be written showing how Puritan thought contributed to the advance of political liberty while at the same time the personal morality of the Puritans is held to be narrowly legalistic and repressive. . . . A composite picture of Puritan marriage doctrine . . . does not support that notion which finds everything bad in modern man-woman relations to emerge from Puritanism.

> ... More at odds with modern conceptions—is the
> liberality and warmth of many Puritan writers in the early
> seventeenth century. They place a high premium on
> mutual love and a high level of intellectual and emotional
> compatibility in marriage ... they give a high rating to the
> orderly life, but a disciplined life is for them the best way of
> expressing the mutual love husband and wife should have
> for each other in a good marriage. Critics of this attitude
> should be reminded that spontaneity is not in itself a
> virtue, and discipline not necessarily a vice.
>
> I do wish to say as forcefully as possible that it is time a
> more balanced understanding of Puritan ethics replaced
> the misconception that all Puritans were sexually and
> socially repressed bluestockings.

Schücking likewise emphasizes the importance to our
world today of the message of the Puritans. He says that for
them "the family became the very center of life to a degree
without parallel in previous ages. It may well be said that
the whole Puritan movement has its roots in the family
and that we cannot even begin to understand it if we leave
the family out of account. Religion is for the Puritan
family religion."

In support of his statement, Schücking then quotes
Richard Baxter's *Christian Directory* (1673): "Most of the
mischiefs that now infest or seize upon mankind
throughout the earth consist in, or are caused by, the
disorders and ill-governedness of families." If Baxter had
lived three hundred years later than he did, he could say
that again with at least equal relevance.

It seems unfortunate indeed that, despite their strong
convictions, the Puritans failed to make a significant
impact on the religious or political system in England.
Moreover, their sensitive understanding of the intimacies
of Christian marriage was not taken up, to any significant
degree, by the developing Protestant churches, and that
remains true up to the present day.

Instead, they were silenced and persecuted in England, and some of them fled to Holland. Perhaps not much more might have been heard of them if some of their number had not then sought sanctuary on the other side of the Atlantic Ocean. A few final comments on that chapter in Puritan history may be in order.

PURITANS IN THE NEW WORLD

Arthur W. Calhoun, in volume one of his massive three-volume work *A Social History of the American Family*, adopts generally negative attitudes toward the Puritans who, leaving home by way of Plymouth, arrived in New England in the early part of the seventeenth century. However, he does acknowledge that they were devoted to their family life.

> These sturdy Englishmen came not as individual adventurers, but as families. If men came alone it was to prepare the way for wife or children or sweethearts by the next ship, and they came to stay. The success of English colonization, as contrasted with the more brilliant but less substantial French and Spanish occupations, is due to its family nature.

> The white colonial population of New England was pure English save for some Scotch-Irish in New Hampshire and Huguenots in Massachusetts and Rhode Island. This homogeneity of the North Atlantic Colonies makes it possible to study them as a group and simplifies the understanding of their cultural lineage.It is particularly to the traditions and standards of the middle class, especially of the Puritan type, that we must look for the genesis of northern Colonial life.

So far, so good. But elsewhere Calhoun's conception of the Puritans reflects a negative and contemptuous attitude that has continued among Americans through the years.

Why is Calhoun's judgment so hostile? He seems to go out of his way to ridicule the Puritans. He conveys the impression that they made life miserable for their neighbors. He seems to take pleasure in citing instances of their firm, and sometimes harsh, treatment of members of the community who didn't share the Puritans' high religious ideals. It is notable that some of his material is taken from court records, which hardly provide a complimentary picture of the life of any community.

Is it true that the Puritans made life miserable for their neighbors? In fairness, we need to remember that they, themselves, scrupulously lived up to the high standards they expected of others; that they had been forced to leave their homes in England because of their ideals; and that, therefore, it mattered very much that they should now, in establishing themselves on a new continent, see those ideals at last put into practice.

Also, we may well ask what kind of community might have developed in New England had the Puritans *not* been there to set high standards for civic life and for family relationships. We should add that they did, in the end, achieve their goal in laying the foundations of a democratic system in which full freedom of religious life and practice was completely guaranteed. As H. H. Kuhn has said: "The culture of Puritan New England had more to do with the shaping of our national culture than did that of any other colonial region, or that of any immigrant group."

That the Puritans were active in condemning and restraining bad behavior among their neighbors is certainly the case. But it is only when we have a better understanding of the make up of those communities that we realize what was happening. Edmund S. Morgan, who contributed a chapter on "The Puritan Attitude to Sex" in

Michael Gordon's scholarly volume *The American Family in Social-Historical Perspective*, gives us an authoritative account of the facts: "In New England there was much sexual abuse—fornication and adultery were by far the most numerous cases in the records." He explains that many of the first settlers had wives back in England, and that these settlers had come in the hope of making a fortune and then returning. However, he points out that "although they had left their wives behind, they had brought their sexual appetites with them." Also, hired servants were usually single, and their masters forbade them to marry. Employed by day, they were free to range through the community at night and have affairs with maid-servants. Even the masters exploited their maid-servants. The result was large numbers of illegitimate children for whose care no provision existed.

Morgan continues:

> The Puritan attitude to sex . . . never neglected human nature. The rules of conduct which the Puritans regarded as divinely ordained had been formulated for men, not for angels or for beasts. God had created man in two sexes. He had ordained marriage as desirable for all, and sexual intercourse as essential to marriage. On the other hand, he had forbidden sexual intercourse outside of marriage. These were the moral principles which the Puritans sought to enforce in New England. But . . . they knew well enough that human beings since the fall of Adam were incapable of obeying perfectly the laws of God. Consequently, in the endeavor to enforce those laws they treated the offenders with patience and understanding, and concentrated their efforts on prevention more than on punishment. . . . It must be admitted that in matters of sex the Puritans showed none of the blind zeal or narrow-minded bigotry which is too often supposed to have been characteristic of them. The more one learns about these people, the less do they appear to have resembled the sad and sour portraits which their modern critics have drawn of them.

181

CONCLUSION

Too long have too many Americans sneered at their Puritan forefathers and made mean jokes at their expense. The Puritans brought two contributions to the shaping of American culture—high standards of efficiency in business and a democratic system of government. Where would America be today if these principles had not been firmly built into its early beginnings?

It may be that the Puritans later departed from some of the high principles with which they began. It may be that they were overzealous in some of their attempts to defend their high principles or to impose them on others. It may be that their new concepts were resented or simply misunderstood. But the fact remains that they developed, and recorded in an abundance of literature, a concept of Christian marriage that was experienced as an appropriate Protestant departure from the rigid and often negative opinions about sex, about women, and about the husband-wife relationship which had dominated Roman Catholicism during the long period of the Middle Ages.

In particular, it seems unfortunate, indeed, that the Puritan development of the concept of Christian marriage as primarily a close companionship between husband and wife should have failed to survive within most Protestant churches. As we shall see later, secular culture has now abandoned other traditional concepts of marriage in favor of an ideal of close companionship, which the churches of today, if they had not failed to follow the lead the early Puritans offered, might have been able to provide. Instead, churches are too often sharing in the spate of marriage failures that is recurring in the secular culture. What is needed above all else is to recover the Puritan concepts and develop them in the setting of the new world we live in today.

Chapter 10

WHAT MAKES A MARRIAGE CHRISTIAN?
(The Development of Post-Reformation Doctrine)

What the Puritans did was to shift the focus in thinking about marriage from the institutional to the interpersonal level. The Catholic procedure in evaluating marriage from the Christian point of view had always been to look at it from the *outside,* with the main emphasis on the conditions to be required of those who wished either to enter into it or to depart from it, on the children it produced, on the public behavior of the couple, and on what action the church should take if that behavior were viewed as improper. The only significant aspect of marriage on the *inside* about which the church made pronouncements was the sexual behavior of the couple, and those pronouncements were formulated mainly by men who were not themselves married, for no other reason than that they believed sex to be an unspiritual aspect of human nature and tolerated only because it led to the production of children—a "necessary evil," as Menander expressed it.

The simple truth is that the church, Catholic and Protestant alike, has given very little consideration to the *quality of the interpersonal relationship* between husband and wife, except when this became so damaging that it began to create external manifestations that had to be dealt with. Otherwise, the personal interaction of the married couple was enclosed in an almost impenetrable veil that purported to "protect their privacy." It is, indeed, proper for society to recognize the right of its members to perform private functions without public interference, but there can be little doubt that in the sphere of the marriage relationship this has had the regrettable result of denying the couple the right to support, guidance, and help in the management of what is now widely recognized to be an extremely complex interpersonal relationship.

What the Puritans did, to their great credit, was to affirm that the companionship of the married couple was a central part of the divine purpose and to treat it as such by teaching husband and wife to manage it in spiritual terms. Never before or since, until today, has the church done this on any significant scale. We shall return to this vital issue in a later part of the book.

However, while the Puritans made an almost unique contribution to defining the nature of Christian marriage on the *inside*, they did not give major attention to its *doctrinal* aspects. The Puritan writers were, for example, at variance among themselves on the issue of divorce. And since the outside aspects of marriage are the ones with which the church has been almost exclusively concerned, the Puritans found themselves misunderstood, and even rejected, in the wider ecclesiastical community. They did not even form an enduring religious denomination as such, but were scattered among those who continued as Anglicans (Episcopalians in North America) and others who were absorbed into various sectarian groups, such as Presbyterians or Quakers.

Another issue is raised by James Turner Johnson in the concluding words of his book on the Puritans. He makes the point that, in the eyes of the other churches, the Puritan teaching about marriage placed too great a focus on the goal of finding happiness *in this life,* and by doing so side-stepped the question of preparing for the life hereafter. Referring to Richard Baxter, who became a leading spokesman for Puritan teaching later in the seventeenth century, Johnson says: "While mutual companionship remains primary among the goods of marriage, there is in Baxter a new stress on that life toward which earthly life is but a preparation. This forward look toward glory is a feature of Puritan marriage doctrine from the first, but Baxter makes it the primary feature."

In this chapter, we shall try to describe the actions of the major Christian organizations as, following the upheaval of the Reformation, they examined and re-examined their teaching about marriage during the centuries from the Reformation and the Counter-Reformation up to the modern era. All that we can do in dealing with such a broad subject is to focus attention on what appear to be the major issues.

We shall begin with the Roman Catholic Church because of its unbroken continuity with the beginnings of Christianity.

ROMAN CATHOLIC POST-REFORMATION TEACHING
ABOUT MARRIAGE

Marriage between a baptized Christian man and woman is, according to the Roman church, one of the seven sacraments. The other six are baptism, confirmation, the eucharist, penance, extreme unction, and holy orders. It was not, however, until the Council of Florence in 1439 that Christian marriage was officially included among the sacraments, and this was confirmed as dogma at the Council of Trent in 1563.

A valid Catholic marriage has to meet various rules and regulations. These are listed in what is called *canon law.* While the Roman Catholic Church recognizes the legal control of marriage by the state, this control applies only to matters that do not contradict Catholic teaching. For example, divorce is *not* permitted for Catholics, even if the state grants it.

There is no scriptural record that Christ instituted marriage as a sacrament, but the Roman Catholic Church assumes this, and the analogy used by Paul of the union of Christ and the church is quoted to affirm that in Christian marriage the husband is the head of the wife.

In order to be considered for Christian marriage in the Catholic tradition, the man and woman must meet three basic conditions:

1. They must clearly understand that marriage is a permanent, lifelong union, intended primarily for the procreation of children.

2. There must be no "marriage impediment."

3. Free and mutual consent to the union must be demonstrated by both parties, and they must be capable of such a choice.

The tests of free consent are primarily that the identity of the persons has been clearly established, that no force or compulsion from an external agent is being brought to bear, and that no limiting future conditions (such as an agreement not to have children) are present.

Impediments are circumstances that would prevent the marriage from being valid. There are two kinds of impediments—diriment, which make the marriage null, and impedient, which make it sinful. Diriment impediments include age under puberty (defined by canon law as fourteen for the woman and sixteen for the man), sexual impotence, an existing prior marriage, being in holy orders (with a few exceptions), having taken vows in a recognized religious order, certain crimes, certain close relationships established by blood or marriage, certain pre-existing spiritual or legal relationships, and any pre-existing relationships that are viewed as violating public decency. There are other impediments that, though they are viewed as sinful, do not invalidate the marriage. Examples are private vows not to marry and close relationships based on adoption.

In some cases, a *dispensation* can be granted to remove an impediment to marriage. This is usually granted by the diocesan bishop, but it might in rare cases go all the way to the pope as the supreme authority.

The parish priest normally presides at the marriage ceremony, and it is his duty to satisfy himself that all the necessary requirements for the sacrament are being met. The main prior conditions are the engagement contract, the prenuptial investigation and instruction, and the publication of banns, normally on three successive Sundays at a service attended by many worshipers.

The engagement requires a contract signed by both parties and the parish priest or bishop. It indicates the serious intention to marry, but is not binding. It is not normally used today.

The instruction by the parish priest makes sure that the engaged couple completely understand the Catholic doctrine of marriage, and also that they have both been baptized and confirmed.

An interesting aspect of Catholic doctrine is that technically it is not the priest who marries the couple—

they confer the sacrament upon each other. In earlier years, they could do this privately, but clandestine marriages, as they were called, caused so much confusion in past centuries that the church, since the Council of Trent, has required a priest to officiate and at least two witnesses to be present. However, what makes the sacrament valid is still the mutual consent of the parties. A surprising feature of Catholic doctrine is that, in the revised canon law of 1918, the sacrament of marriage is valid for baptized Protestant Christians in a ceremony conducted by a pastor or even by a justice of the peace!

ABOUT DIVORCE AND SEPARATION

The Catholic Church, as already explained, does not recognize divorce. A valid Catholic marriage cannot be dissolved as long as both parties continue to live. This was enacted firmly at the Council of Trent in 1563. Under certain circumstances, however, Catholics may obtain an "imperfect" divorce, which is separation *a mensa et thoro* (from bed and board). Of course, this provides no right to remarriage.

The Catholic doctrine forbidding divorce is based on the publicly spoken words of Jesus: "What therefore God has joined together, let not man put asunder" (Mark 10:9). The account in Matthew's Gospel, however, suggests that later, when Jesus was discussing the issue with his disciples alone, he allowed that a man might divorce his wife for "unchastity." The usual Catholic interpretation is that Jesus meant only to allow separation without the right to remarry.

However, even for Catholics there are two situations in which a legal marriage might be cancelled. One is called the "Pauline privilege," and refers to the passage in I Corinthians 7:12-15 where Paul is legislating for a former non-Christian who has now been baptized and become a

Christian, but whose marriage partner refuses to do the same. Paul's judgment is that so long as the non-Christian spouse continues to live peacefully with the now Christian partner, the marriage can continue. But if the non-Christian partner leaves or acts in a way that prevents the Christian from practicing the new faith, it would be possible for the Christian partner to remarry another Christian, and the new marriage would automatically cancel the non-Christian union.

The second possibility for terminating an otherwise valid marriage is that it has not been sexually consummated. The Catholic view is that once the sex act has taken place, no divorce is normally possible. However, in special circumstances an unconsummated marriage can be dissolved by a dispensation from the pope. A typical situation would be one in which the person concerned felt called to enter a religious order in which vows of poverty, chastity, and obedience were required. In that case, the marriage could be terminated at the end of the novitiate, which would not be less than one year. At that point, the other partner in the unconsummated marriage would be free to remarry.

Since divorce as such is not available to a Catholic couple (even if the state grants it), the only possible way out of marriage for Catholics is by the process of *annulment*. What this means is that there is an official recognition that the supposed marriage never really took place, because some necessary condition for the sacrament was not present.

As we have seen, there are several reasons that could make annulment of a Catholic marriage possible—defective consent or the undetected presence of a diriment impediment which was concealed or overlooked at the time, or for which no proper dispensation was obtained. For example, in the Middle Ages people often lived in small rural communities where almost everyone was related to everyone else. It would be quite possible for a particular couple to be related to each other within the forbidden degrees, and for this to be overlooked at the time of the marriage and then discovered afterward. The matrimonial courts set up by the Catholic Church have developed great skill in searching out reasons for which a marriage might be annulled, especially for couples in high social positions who want to end a relationship. If this cannot be done, however, there is no other way out. If a Catholic couple get a divorce in the civil court on grounds not recognized by the church, the divorce is not valid in the eyes of Catholic authorities. The couple may, by mutual consent, live apart, temporarily or permanently, only by securing what is called an *imperfect divorce* from the church. Separation that is desired by one but not the other is permitted if the partner has committed adultery, though not if this was condoned by the other partner. Other reasons are criminal behavior, cruelty, and defection from religious faith.

ABOUT SEX

The Catholic Church has very strict rules regarding sexual behavior for married people and for the unmarried, too. Masturbation, homosexuality, and lesbianism are all considered to be mortal sins. The *Baltimore Catechism* firmly forbids "all impurity and immodesty in words, looks, and actions, whether alone or with others." One theologian, Jone-Adelman, in *Moral Theology*, sums it up by saying, "All directly voluntary sexual pleasure is mortally sinful outside of matrimony."

ABOUT REPRODUCTION

The Roman Catholic Church teaches that the primary purpose of marriage is the procreation and training of children. This means that any attempt to prevent conception is sinful. It repudiates all artificial means of contraception, and the prohibition extends to the interruption of intercourse by withdrawal, to direct sterilization, and to abortion.

Pope Pius XI, in an encyclical letter issued in 1930, declared that "any use whatsoever of matrimony in such a way that the act is deliberately frustrated in its natural power to generate life is an offense against the law of God and nature, and those who indulge in such are branded with the guilt of grave sin." When married Catholics go to confession, they are supposed to be reminded of this.

The scriptural basis for this judgment is the story of Onan in Genesis 38:1-10. After the death of Onan's brother, Er, who had no children, Onan was instructed by his father to fulfill the Levirate custom of producing an heir for Er. But though he did have intercourse with the widow, Tamar, Onan practiced withdrawal—a sinful act for which he was struck dead by God. (In fact, however, the sin of Onan was not withdrawal as such, but avoidance of the possibility of his father's property having to be divided up, so that his own portion of it would be increased. So the Catholic use of the incident as a judgment on Onan's crime is not strictly accurate.)

Although direct birth control devices are not allowed, the Catholic Church permits its couples to confine intercourse to safe periods in the monthly cycle, which is known as the "rhythm method." Pope Pius XII, in 1951, issued his statement that, for serious medical, social, or economic reasons, a wife may restrict her sexual relations with her husband to the periods of natural sterility which are now known to occur in her monthly cycle. This is called natural birth control.

The Catholic Church likewise forbids *induced abortion*, which involves taking the life of an unborn child, as a violation of the Fifth Commandment: "Thou shalt not kill." This applies even if the life of the mother is threatened so that both mother and child might die. The reasoning is that a good end cannot justify the use of morally bad means.

Finally, the Catholic Church is opposed to *artificial insemination,* which Pope Pius XII condemned as immoral. His condemnation included insemination by the husband as well as by an outside donor. His argument was that the procreation of a new human life must take place as a result of normal sexual intercourse by the two partners of a lawful marriage. It has been made clear, however, that provided the natural act takes place, any action to facilitate its normal purpose in a normal manner is permissible.

We have now tried to cover the major issues in the post-Reformation Catholic teaching about marriage, though without going into a great deal of detail. We shall follow this discussion by covering broadly the same general ground in order to examine the Protestant view of the same issues.

PROTESTANT TEACHING
ABOUT MARRIAGE

When we try to match the Roman Catholic doctrine with its Protestant equivalent, we are soon in a confusing situation. Strictly speaking, there is no Protestant church as such, but only a miscellaneous group of religious organizations, exhibiting a variety of types that defy any attempt at coordination. Once the Reformation got started, what broke away from the Catholic stem was a series of splinters, and the splintering process has continued ever since and shows no sign of coming to a halt. There has also been a reuniting process that is in progress at the present time. Someone has remarked that Protestant churches tend to divide when they are prospering and to reunite when they are in trouble! Whether or not this is true, it is certain that if unity is the characteristic of the Catholic system, the opposite is true of Protestantism.

However, there are just a few Protestant groups that, having seceded from the Roman Catholic Church during the upheavals of the Reformation, have retained a fairly clear identity ever since. The Lutherans should head the list, because they carry the name of the man who started it all. Perhaps the Anglicans (Episcopalians in the United States) come next, because the state church of England has changed comparatively little since it severed its connection with Rome. A possible third group would be the Presbyterians, who, under the influence of John Knox, grew out of Calvin's Protestant colony in Geneva.

For our present purpose, we shall consider broadly the attitudes about marriage which seem to represent these Protestant groups, though we shall not confine ourselves strictly to them. We shall look at what they teach in the same general order in which we looked at the Catholic doctrines.

CHRISTIAN MARRIAGE: THE PROTESTANT VIEW

Protestant theologians generally reject the traditional Catholic view that God ordained marriage *after* the fall as a remedy against concupiscence, or sexual sin. Instead, the Protestant theologians tend to take the view that God instituted marriage when Eve was given to Adam as a companion. So while the Catholics see two major purposes for marriage—as a means of producing children to perpetuate the race and as a remedy against concupiscence—the Protestants add a third purpose—the companionship of man and woman; some of them make this the primary purpose. It is easy to see how these different views lead on the one hand to a celibate priesthood and on the other to a married clergy.

This difference leads also to many others. The very negative sexual attitudes that were widespread in the early centuries of Christendom still linger on in the Catholic church today, while the Protestants in general are much more tolerant of human sexuality.

Lutheran teaching, for example, according to the *Augsburg Confession* (Article XIII), defines sex as "that appetite which was to have been in nature in its integrity, which they call physical love. And this love of one sex for the other is truly a divine ordinance."

What this means is that Protestants generally believe that sexual relationships, when kept within the boundaries of lawful marriage, are in line with that divine ordinance of sexual attraction that was in human nature already *before the fall*. As Mario Colacci has expressed it: "Sex is essentially good when rightly used, and sinful only when misused" *(Christian Marriage Today)*.

For Protestants, therefore, marriage is *not* a sacrament. There is no scriptural evidence that Christ assigned this significance to it. That is not to say that it was not divinely ordained, but this was done at its inception, which goes back to the Creation.

However, Protestants recognized that marriage had deteriorated from its original nature as a divine ordinance mainly as a result of polgamy and divorce, both of which were accepted in Old Testament times. What Christ did was to restore it to its original dignity, but that does not make marriage a Christian sacrament.

Protestants also consider that there is inconsistency in the Catholic action of elevating marriage to the level of a sacrament, and then degrading its spiritual status to a level lower than that of the celibate priesthood.

Because they regard marriage not as a sacrament, but as a natural contract, Protestants have been willing to allow the state to take legislative authority over marriage. This action was taken by Martin Luther. However, that does not mean that Christians are bound by the state law if the divine law is in disagreement with it.

The Protestant position makes it entirely legal for Christians to be married by a civil authority, but the practice has been to invest the clergyman with the right to sanction the celebration of marriage as well as to give the couple the blessing of the church.

The Protestant action regarding impediments to marriage has been to accept, in general, the conditions made by the civil authorities, as long as these do not contradict the teaching of scripture. It has, therefore, not been necessary for Protestants to develop any equivalent of the canon law of the Catholic church.

What about impediments to marriage? The Old Testament, in the book of Leviticus, contains a full list of the relationships based on blood (consanguinity) and on marriage (affinity) that make marriage unlawful. These are, in general, part of the civil law in most countries. Such barriers as a previous legal marriage are also part of the legal system. The Protestant churches, in general, are prepared to leave these matters to the state authorities.

ABOUT DIVORCE

Attitudes toward divorce have changed greatly in the Protestant churches in recent years, particularly in the United States, and to a lesser degree in Europe. Writing in 1958 about marriage in the USA, Mario Colacci summarized what he held at that time to be the attitude of Protestants, as follows:

1. Marriage, though essentially a civil contract of public nature, is also a holy institution to be dealt with by Christian people seriously, according to the will and positive law of God, who directly established it.

2. According to the teaching of New Testament Scripture, the bond of a valid and lawful marriage ought, as a general rule, to be considered indissoluble so long as the two partners are alive.

3. Any attitude toward marriage that would overshadow its essentially sacred nature and character is deplorable.

4. The widespread modern abuses in the practice of divorce must be considered as the main factors in lowering and weakening the sacred bonds and responsibilities of the family unit.

(Christian Marriage Today)

Clearly these views, as expressing the attitude toward divorce in Protestant churches generally, have lost much of their force today, when divorce among church members, and even among Christian ministers and their wives, has become almost commonplace. We shall discuss this more fully in a later chapter (chapter 12).

In the light of this great change, it seems almost pointless to discuss the grounds for divorce which are accepted by Protestants, when the state now allows marriage to be terminated almost at will; the churches have made no serious attempt to oppose this action. Even in the Church of England, which retained the traditional Catholic attitude until very recently, the rising rates of easy divorce granted by the state have compelled the church to give ground.

ABOUT REPRODUCTION

The general attitude of Protestants about what is right and wrong in human behavior is decided by what Scripture expressly teaches. The result is that when forms of behavior relate to situations that were unknown in Bible times, the individual Christian is supposed to weigh the issue and make his or her own decision. All too often, Christians in this dilemma lack either the ability or the motivation to arrive at a considered judgment and simply follow the public opinion of the day.

This is very much what has happened as attitudes toward divorce have become more tolerant, and the same can be said of attitudes toward such questions as birth control and even abortion. In the absence of such authoritative judgments as Catholics receive from their church leaders, Protestants drift into unquestioning acceptance of whatever the community generally decides.

However, this was not what really happened in relation to birth control. When it was first denounced by Catholic authorities, Protestants tended to adopt similar attitudes. But over time the convenience of using contraceptives became obvious to Christian married couples, and their hesitation was gradually overcome. This happened also for many Catholics—few issues have made enforcement of the church's policy more difficult.

Protestant teaching, as we have seen, has not supported the Catholic view that the primary purpose of marriage is to produce children. Therefore, the careful spacing of births, by preventing conception when it is not desired, seemed to Protestant couples a good way of maintaining their sex lives, against which the Protestant church has made no negative judgments, since this helped to promote their happy and healthy intimacy.

Abortion raises much more serious questions. There is nothing vague or subtle about it. The developing child in the womb is simply killed. The word *murder* sounds ominous, but it is difficult to prove that it doesn't apply. If the child is known to be grossly abnormal, if the life of the mother is seriously threatened, or if the pregnancy resulted from rape, a case can be made for a justifiable termination of the pregnancy. A devout Protestant can often accept this. But some of today's reasons for abortion are not in those categories.

ABOUT CHRISTIAN PARENTHOOD

Back in 1952, the Commission on Social Relations of the American Lutheran Conference put together a statement about Christian parenthood. The following extracts from it would probably provide an acceptable statement of what most sincere Protestant couples at that time considered to be their Christian duties and privileges:

1. A Christian husband and wife know that children are the natural fruit of their marriage.
2. Married couples have the freedom so to plan and order their sexual relations that each child born will be wanted.
3. The means which a married pair use to determine the number and the spacing of their children are matters for them to decide.
4. Whether the means used [to plan births] be labeled natural or artificial is of far less importance than the spirit in which these means are used.
5. An overabundant production of children without regard for the responsibilities involved may be as selfish as the complete avoidance of parenthood.
6. Abortion must be regarded as the destruction of a living being. A Christian must accept the unintended pregnancy, and willingly welcome the new child.
7. Sex relations outside of marriage are a violation of God's will.
8. The Christian couple unable to have children of their own may choose to adopt children, or engage in community services for the welfare of children.

Other controversial issues relating to Christian marriage in contemporary society will be discussed in later chapters.

PART IV
The Modern Era

Chapter 11

INTERLUDE: BUT THE WORLD KEEPS CHANGING, CHANGING

So far in this book, our emphasis has been primarily on part of the title: *Christian Marriage.* We have tried to trace the history of what has been taught in the Hebrew and Christian traditions, covering a period of nearly four thousand years, about the fundamental human relationship between a man and a woman—marriage, which is the nucleus of the family, which, in turn, is the nucleus of human society.

However, human society has not remained the same during that long span of time. When society began, people saw the world as a large, flat plate under an inverted bowl. Now, we know that it is only a tiny speck in a vast universe that stretches into infinite distance. This realization inevitably changes the way we think about God and the way we think about ourselves.

Even if we consider only the two thousand years of Christianity, the changes have been extensive. In the early days, human life was short. Alexander the Great, the Greek warrior king who conquered the ancient world just before the coming of Christ, was only thirty-three when he died. Today, anyone who aspires to a high-level career will only be beginning a life's work at that age, with the reasonable expectation of living at least twice as long. Today, even dying at sixty-six would be considered falling short of a reasonable life expectation.

In a host of other ways, life today is full of advantages which would have been out of the reach of most people in New Testament times; opportunities for health, education, and travel and a standard of living that we take for granted would have seemed fantastic then.

During the first centuries of Christianity, the church had to operate within the Roman Empire. This had some advantages, especially for spreading the gospel in the region surrounding the Mediterranean basin. But there were periods of persecution in which many lost their lives just for being Christians—a situation unimaginable to us today.

When the Roman Empire fell, the church won over the barbarians and the Middle Ages began. For about a thousand years, Christianity was the major influence in the lives of the common people. But the general standard of living improved very little during that time. Most people were settled on the land, and, as we have seen, the message of the church during the Middle Ages was that life in this world is little more than a testing time for those who wish to qualify for heaven hereafter and avoid the fate of the wicked in hell. The church had no special message for achieving a good marriage; the teaching was that the way to be a *real* Christian was to avoid marriage altogether, because sex had a damaging effect on the spiritual life. Celibacy was the way to true Christian living.

As the years passed, however, there slowly emerged an awareness that life in this world was more than a testing time for the hereafter. With the Renaissance came an awakening to the wonders of the world we live in. Explorers traveled to distant places; astronomers studied the stars; men of science sought a deeper understanding of the physical world; philosophers took up the quest for meaning where earlier scholars had laid it down.

At the same time, people were now moving off the land and into towns and cities. Agricultural workers learned technical skills and helped to shape new life-styles based on a better understanding of scientific methods. Meanwhile, there was a rebirth in the arts—poetry, music, theater, painting, sculpture. Gradually, people came to find this world something much more than a vale of tears. As they became educated enough to read and write, whole new expanses of meaning gave human life much wider and deeper significance.

The church didn't ignore or condemn these changes. It became very much involved in some of them. Sometimes the church took the lead in progress. But as the centuries passed, religion was no longer seen as the only significant influence in the lives of the common people. Local and state government began to play an important part in supporting and directing the way in which citizens thought and behaved. Life in this world became important in itself and offered other goals than preparation for the life hereafter.

Faced with this kind of competition, the church had to make some changes within itself. Its power, hitherto almost supreme, began to be challenged. Some of its leaders had already succumbed to the lure of worldly goals. And finally, a major crisis developed in the form of the Reformation, which was not an attack from outside, but a rebellion from within. Whether the Roman Catholic

Church, enjoying supreme power at the time, handled this crisis wisely is a matter of opinion.

There is no doubt, however, that Martin Luther's initial goal was to reform the church *from within;* no one can seriously question that what he attacked—the exploitation of Christian believers in order to raise money—was far from creditable behavior on the part of the pope. The Catholics *did* in fact take very significant steps in the direction of reform, especially at the Council of Trent. But reform came too late. So the Christian community was split in two, and the rift has not yet been healed.

IMPLICATIONS FOR CHRISTIAN MARRIAGE

Let us now examine some of the changes which have occurred and which are still taking place, and see how they might have influenced the marriage relationship. We shall divide up the broad process of change into six major components:

1. *Industrialization.* As we have seen, since the Middle Ages there has been a progressive movement of population from rural areas to towns and cities. Worldwide, that change continues to the present day. In the Middle Ages, most families lived on the land, which was usually owned by barons who used the labor of their dependents and, in turn, offered them protection. Then, gradually, the more progressive men took their families to the developing towns and became members of the artisan class. At first they worked at home; but later, as factories began to be built, they became employees. This introduced different living styles, with the father away from his family during the working day. Later, with full development of the Industrial Revolution in the eighteenth century, the situation produced some highly undesirable consequences. It was found that wives provided a source of

cheap labor, and they were employed for such long hours that their children suffered. Then the situation went from bad to worse as children proved to be an even cheaper source of labor, and they, too, began to be employed. Finally, both in Britain and in North America, action was taken to bring this situation under control, but not until serious damage had taken place in family life.

In Western societies today, the great majority of people live in urban areas. At first, the pattern of living was for the husband to commute to his workplace and for the wife to stay at home to take care of the children. It became a source of pride for a man not to have his wife work. But now industry has begun to use machines for basic labor. Our society has shifted to an emphasis on services, and again women are becoming increasingly employed, with the result that the family is again being fragmented. This is one of the factors that are contributing to extensive marriage and family breakdown today, a situation that is creating serious concern for the Christian church, both Catholic and Protestant.

2. *Education.* In the Middle Ages, the clergy were usually able to read and write, while the ordinary members of the community were not. This advantage gave the church almost supreme power, and the instruction given to church members (which usually meant the entire community) largely controlled their lives. Other than the clergy, only the privileged aristocracy and the very limited professional classes received any significant education.

With the development of an artisan class in the towns, opportunities for learning increased, and children began to receive at least elementary education. It was not until the coming of the printing press in the fifteenth and sixteenth centuries, however, that the acquiring of knowledge generally became possible. Then, as more and more people learned to read, knowledge of the Bible provided church members with a better understanding of the Christian message.

The Catholic Church relied heavily on direct teaching of the people by the parish priest. Protestants, however, in addition to preaching, favored the use of "conduct" books for home reading. Such classics as *The Pilgrim's Progress* by John Bunyan and *The Whole Duty of Man* were widely read, and we have seen how the Puritans published a considerable literature concerning Christian marriage.

The schools and universities, though at first heavily influenced by religious teaching, later became the means of secular education, and this led to critical reappraisal of what was taught by the churches. Today, in the developed Western countries, the church has to deal with highly educated communities, and its message has to be well reasoned and convincing if it is to be taken seriously.

Now that the mass media have incorporated, in addition to newspapers and magazines, the powerful influence of radio and television, we have a population which is continually being bombarded with new information. The churches must make their message clear and convincing if they are to get a hearing. In the area of Christian marriage, unfortunately, churches have so far had very little to say that is relevant to the needs of married couples in today's world. That is one reason we are writing this book!

3. *Health.* The relative brevity of the human life span during the early years of Christian history is easily explained by the fact that the causes of illness were not at all well understood. Nor was there any real comprehension of the principles of hygiene. The inevitable result was that life was short for most people. Many children died in infancy, and the death rate in every stage of life was appallingly high. It was the constant awareness of death that enabled the church in those early centuries to focus the attention of its members on the need to prepare for the

afterlife, which was considered to be the real goal of Christian living at that time. The combination of the hope of heaven, the dread of hell, and the desire to avoid a long and painful intermediate stay in purgatory added up to a very strong motivation to take religion seriously.

Today, as a result of the amazing achievements of modern medicine, the whole situation has undergone a dramatic change. The death of a child is now a very rare event—so much so that morticians, we are told, no longer maintain a stock of caskets for children, but have one specially made when the occasion arises.

Medical science is now so well advanced that the proportion of people who survive through the normal life-span of seventy years is much greater than it has ever been in human history. What this means is that the great majority of people can confidently plan ahead without giving much attention to the remote possibility of death. And in the later years, after a long and active life, death is not dreaded, but sometimes even welcomed.

4. *Science and Technology.* In the early days of Christianity, the nature of the world was for most people a profound mystery. The Greek philosophers had asked searching questions and had come up with some answers, but the common people knew nothing about that. Superstitious explanations of natural phenomena were widely accepted. Although most people lived close to the world of nature, they had little understandng of the natural laws explaining weather, growth, the universe, the seasons, gravity, temperature, reproduction, the organs of the body, and other familiar processes. And, of course, they would have been dumbfounded, and probably skeptical, to hear about automobiles, telephones, radio and television, steamships, submarines, railroads, and airplanes—not to mention spaceships and computers.

In the absence of any such knowledge, it was inevitable that the people should have developed superstitions about spiritual beings who controlled the processes that otherwise seemed unintelligible, and they, therefore, assumed that good and evil were either the manifestations of God and the angels or of Satan and his devils.

An interesting aspect of this, however, is that people were much more sensitive to the spiritual world around them, whereas we tend to find scientific explanations for everything.

5. *Travel.* In this respect, the world of the Roman Empire was not as backward as many other regions. The Romans had established links all round the Mediterranean, stretching northward across most of Europe and to Britain, south to the African coast, and eastward as far as India. The first Christian missionaries made good use of these opportunities to take the gospel to distant places, and early Christians who had no chance to travel personally had probably heard stories of what life was like in other lands. In the time of the early church, Christians had also probably encountered some of the vast multitude of slaves from conquered countries, because some of these were converted to the Christian faith. In the later Middle Ages many men, and some women, visited Asia Minor in connection with the Crusades. But, of course, people knew nothing of our modern means of transportation. Their ships were moved by the wind or by the toil of oars; sailors had no comprehension of our modern sources of power.

6. *The Status of Women.* During most of human history, women have been regarded as inferior, therefore subservient, to men. Obviously, when survival might depend on the capacity to exert great strength or to be victorious in battle, the critical factor was the amount of physical vigor or skill with weapons that could be summoned to the task. In such situations, women would

inevitably be at a disadvantage. In addition, men seemed by nature to be more aggressive than women. And of course, in the state of nature women had to spend a good deal of their time being pregnant and caring for children, which disqualified them for heavy and very active tasks. So the man was naturally the fighter, the hunter, and the explorer.

In a world where these roles were often essential for survival, therefore, it was inevitable that men took over the leadership and women stayed in the background. This became the pattern by which all female roles, in contrast to those of men, were defined.

There have been outstanding exceptions to this standardized way of role definition throughout history. But not until our own time have the conclusions based on the *physical* differences, leading to false judgments in the wider realms of intelligence, personal competence, and spiritual perception, been seriously challenged. This raises issues of central significance in defining Christian marriage, and we shall return to the subject in a later chapter (chapter 13).

MORE AND MORE CHANGES

The processes we have been describing have not yet slowed down. On the contrary, during the twentieth century they have speeded up at what seems a breathless pace, during what has been called the technological revolution. Those of us who have lived through this century are very much aware of the hectic pace that has often marked its progress.

Inevitably, as the rate of change is maintained, the patterns of life that went before are left further and further behind, becoming progressively out of date. What was once useful is quickly discarded as something much better is found to perform the same task—kerosene lamps were replaced by gas, then gas by electricity; the horse and cart yielded to the automobile, and the railroad to the airplane. In the process, what was once valued and respected goes on the scrapheap. As James Russell Lowell expressed it in "The Present Crisis":

New occasions teach new duties; Time makes ancient
good uncouth;
They must upward still and onward; who would keep
abreast of Truth.

The critical question for us here, as we consider the process of continuing change, is to discover what is happening to Christianity, to marriage, and to Christian marriage, which combines them both.

CONCLUSIONS

We would be presumptuous, indeed, if we attempted in this book such a task as assessing the present state of the Christian religion. This has already been attempted by many who are far better qualified than we are. So far as we are aware, researchers have in general reported that the Christian message continues to spread, as a result of well-organized missionary effort, across the world. Yet there is now evidence in the more developed countries, which were once Christian strongholds, of a waning influence of the churches in the formulation of public policy. And it has been at least hinted that this may be the result of the rapid pace of social change and the inability of the churches to keep up-to-date. We may, however, safely assume that the Christian message is still making its impact in the changing of individual lives, in the maintenance of high ethical values, in the organization of community services, and in some other directions.

What concerns us, however, is Christian marriage. At a

time when marriages and families generally are failing at a very disturbing rate, we find evidence that failure is taking place not only in the secular culture, but also to a distressing degree within the ranks of church membership, and even in the ranks of the ministers who serve the Protestant churches. It is on this issue that we want to focus attention in the remaining chapters of this book. Before doing so, however, we have felt it necessary to go back carefully over the entire history of Christian marriage, in order to make sure that we had the issue in proper perspective. Having now done so, we are ready for our final task.

It is clear that during at least the major part of the history of the Western world, the marriage relationship has in general assumed the outward pattern given to it by the influence of the Christian church. Now, however, the stability of marriages is in doubt, and we need to ask some searching questions as we look to the future.

Are the present evidences of change simply a part of our developing new understanding of human relationships? Are we now caught up in a vast process of readjustment in the private sector of our culture, reflecting the processes of readjustment that have already taken place in the public sector? What are the major factors, positive and negative, involved? Is the present high failure rate of marriages part of an inevitable transition, a temporary result of gigantic forces of change that will do their work and lead, in time, to a new order? If so, what place will marriage have in that new order? Will it count for less, or will it be better than ever before? What action should Christian leaders, and Christian couples, take to guide the present era of transition toward a successful outcome? In other words, what in our Western culture at this time is the outlook for Christian marriage and for Christian family life generally, and what steps should we now be taking to guide the process of change in the right direction?

Chapter 12

CHRISTIAN MARRIAGE AND PARENTHOOD

We now take leave of the past and confront life as we find it in the latter years of the twentieth century, which is already drawing to a close. Having looked at Christian marriage as it has existed in the changing panorama of past centuries, we must also see how it is faring in our own time, in the day-to-day life of the here and now.

Our suggestion is that we do so in three chapters, examining in turn each of the purposes for which marriage has existed in human society. These purposes have been almost universally agreed upon by Christians, and they would not be seriously questioned, for the most part, by other cultures or by behavioral scientists today. So, we can at least start our inquiry with something like unanimity.

The three purposes for marriage are procreation (parenthood), sexual fulfillment, and companionship. In the next three chapters we shall examine these purposes in some detail and try to see how they can best be understood and interpreted in terms of Christian values and standards in the cultural setting of today's world.

THE PARENTAL FUNCTION

We begin, then, with parenthood.

From almost every point of view, marriage is an arrangement that has been developed in human culture to provide the best possible conditions for the continuation of the human species. Edward Westermarck, in his pioneering study of human marriage first published nearly a century ago, found that in some shape or form, the institution of marriage has existed in all settled human societies. His broad definition of marriage still holds true today: "Marriage is a relation of one or more men to one or more women which is recognized by custom or law and involves certain rights and duties both in the case of the parties entering the union and in the case of the children born of it."

Westermarck also, on the basis of his extensive studies, came to the conclusion that the basic purpose of marriage is to maintain the continuity of the human community through the medium of the family. This was well expressed in his often-quoted statement: "Marriage is rooted in the family, and not the family in marriage."

A similar position has been taken by the Catholic church from its beginning, and the other Christian communities have, with very few exceptions, been in agreement. This view would, of course, be an inevitable conclusion for all Christians who accept the theory of evolution. The nature of all forms of life in this world is that without exception they are limited in their duration. It may be true that there are in existence today a few ancient trees whose life-span has covered the entire Christian era, but more active living creatures, including human beings, live for a much more limited period of time. Some insects survive only for a matter of days.

Survival of the *species*, therefore, is achieved through a succession of individuals. Each comes into existence, lives through an allotted span, and dies. Birth and death are part of the same process and are interdependent.

In the more elementary forms of life, cells divide, creating new cells *ad infinitum*. But in sexual reproduction, which provides for much greater differentiation, special cells from two separate units join and form a new cell. Their union is the result of sexual union. In some simple creatures, this is the final act in the life process; the future of the species having been assured, death soon follows.

Throughout the evolutionary system, living creatures have appeared in infinite variety, ascending in complexity up to the human level. With this increasing complexity comes a more extended process of individual development, involving the need for protection and support during the developmental period. Baby herrings come from great numbers of eggs spawned by the mother fish. Many are lost to predators, but enough survive to assure the continuity of the next generation. Baby birds take longer to develop and spend a critical period protected by an eggshell. Higher in the evolutionary scale, the mammal baby spends the critical early period protected inside the mother's body and is delivered in a fairly developed condition, though still requiring a short period of maternal care.

By the time we reach the human level, even after nine months inside the mother's body, the baby is born in a state of relative helplessness and requires a period of years in a supportive relationship. Quite apart from basic physical functioning, the human child does not need only the mother, but *both* parents to provide all the protection, support, and skill training necessary to produce a full adult member of the community. In medieval times, the parental task was often considered complete seven years after birth. In our developed modern culture, however, the child may need support and guidance, jointly from both parents, for as long as twenty years in order to reach responsible and independent adulthood.

Marriage, therefore, is the arrangement guaranteeing that the child will reach the maximum point of development necessary if he or she is to enter the human community fully prepared for future duties and responsibilities. We often use the term *human rights* to indicate the basic conditions to which a person is entitled in order to make life fully meaningful. In those terms, surely the basic human right is the child's entitlement to the care, support, and training of the two parents who gave him life, extended over as long as twenty years of his development to full adulthood.

Parenthood is the fundamental purpose for which marriage exists. Throughout most of human history, the culture has corporately acted to guarantee this basic right to the growing child by insisting that the two prospective parents, when they enter marriage, make a binding commitment to stay together for the fulfillment of this fundamental task. In the past, of course, numerous children were usually born of the marriage, and often the total period of parental care covered the full lifetime of both parents.

The principle that marriage exists to guarantee the proper fulfillment of parenthood is, therefore, a basic and powerful one, and the Christian church has until now firmly insisted upon it by viewing divorce as a gravely irresponsible act and by denying it to all loyal members. The Catholic church still retains firm control over the married couple. However, Luther and Calvin turned control of marriage over to the state, assuming that the principle would be maintained. But with the progressive secularization of the culture, in many Christian countries the state began by allowing divorce for special reasons, and over time the controls were gradually removed until "no-fault divorce" made it easy for married people to abandon their joint parental responsibilities.

If the continuation of human life could have been arranged in some other way, it is pretty clear that marriage as a firmly controlled process in human society would not have been necessary and would presumably never have existed. The state exercises no control over the friendships that people make with one another. However, state control over marriage has been established and maintained for the express purpose of safeguarding children and insuring that they would not be deprived of their human rights.

Christians have always supported this primary purpose of marriage and have tried to insist that it must be taken seriously as a lifetime commitment. If Christians today go back on that fundamental commitment, for whatever reason, they must realize that they are betraying a trust that has been given unquestioning support throughout the history of the church. That is not to say that very special circumstances may not exist for some departure from the basic principle, but to allow such departure must clearly be seen in its proper perspective.

We have arrived at this conclusion by way of the evolutionary view of our human development. Does the Old Testament concept of direct creation, separate from and unconnected with the lower animals, provide another view of Christian parenthood?

Yes, it might appear to do so. The impression is given in the story of Adam and Eve that they were essentially different from the lower creation, and that their sexual function only became relevant following their disobedience and exclusion from Eden. Then, when death became inevitable, it was necessary for them to use their sexuality to produce children, since they themselves were now doomed to die. It was by this reasoning that some Puritans took the view that the *primary* reason for marriage was to provide Adam with *companionship*.

However, that does not alter the fact that parenthood is a basic responsibility for the married couple. Indeed, what later happened between Cain and Abel would seem to suggest that their parents should have done a better job of rearing them, and that we should all take this lesson to heart.

It is, of course, through parenthood that a marriage opens up and becomes a *family*. The importance of family life is of central significance to the Old Testament. The nation was in fact seen as an extended family, because they were called "the children of Israel." Their unity lay in the fact that they all came from the loins of a common father. As we have seen, the biological contribution of the mother was not understood in early times, and the succession through the generations was, therefore, reckoned from father to son. But no people in the world have given a more central place to the concept of family life than did the Hebrews. Of course, at the very center of Christian theology stands the concept of the Fatherhood of God. One of the miracles of human history has been that the Jews, deprived of their homeland and scattered across the earth, have yet preserved their concept of relatedness to one another through all the adversities that have befallen them. There is no doubt that this has happened because of their central emphasis on family life and religion focused in the home. Are Christian parents justified in giving less attention to the sacred duty and the rich rewards of responsible parenthood?

Today we are living at a time, and in a culture, in which parenthood is failing dismally. Not so long ago, in the height of the "Dr. Spock era," American culture had a worldwide reputation for giving special attention to the nurturing of children. Now the situation has greatly changed, and the picture has almost been reversed. Let us examine how this great reversal has happened.

THE DUAL-CAREER MARRIAGE

The full recognition now being won by women has, temporarily at least, turned their attention away from the fulfillment of motherhood, which was formerly their joy and pride. In order to establish themselves as the equals of men in their involvement in public affairs, married women in large numbers have joined the work force and pursued careers outside the home. They have done this with great distinction, and the full recognition now being given to the personhood of woman represents a notable achievement—the final validation of American democracy. The founders of the nation declared that "all *men* are created equal," but it has taken another two centuries to establish the corollary that, as persons, all men and all women are created equal. Naturally enough, women have felt under obligation to establish this beyond further dispute by proving their capability to work alongside men in the workplace. Their progress in the achievement of this goal is highly commendable.

However, in the area of parenthood, a heavy price is being exacted for this achievement. The root of the trouble lies, of course, in the view, long held and acted upon, that the task of parenthood is fundamentally that of the mother, and that the father in the family is simply an authority figure who hovers on the periphery, while the mother assumes the major responsibilities. That can still be said, with some justification, of the early period of infancy. But after that, there is no valid reason why Christian parents should not assume *equal* responsibility for the raising of the children upon whom they have jointly bestowed the gift of life. It is surely the duty of Christians to hasten the day when this will become the accepted practice.

Meanwhile, all possible efforts need to be made to provide proper and adequate arrangements for the care of children when their parents must be involved in needed duties outside the home. We are currently in the midst of a major reorganization of the proper balance between the workplace and the home, and it would be gross irresponsibility and injustice if our failure to move swiftly in this process should victimize the children who are our future citizens. This is a task to which Christians should give all possible help and support.

We are being told that with the increasing use of the computer the time is coming when many people will be able to do their work at home just as well as they could elsewhere, and that the computer may end our need to commute. If this is so, it may help to solve the serious problem with which many responsible parents are now struggling.

However, that is a matter for the future. Meanwhile, we need to give urgent attention to the enormous pressures to which many modern parents—fathers and mothers alike—and their children are subjected in the dual-career marriage.

Amitai Etzioni, a high esteemed sociologist, has made a carefully considered statement about the effect on the children. It is: "We have roughly ten million latchkey children who come home to nothing but a TV set. In many other homes in which both the father and the mother work, both parents come home physically and psychologically exhausted. They are really not very open to dealing with the complicated demands that children make on them. As a result, children are getting short shrift today."

The question to ponder, of course, is how far the well-being of our children can legitimately be sacrificed in return for the full recognition of women's personhood in contemporary society, and for the additional comforts and conveniences that can be made possible for a family with two wage earners. Are these goals worth winning at the cost of depriving children of their birthrights—adequate parental support and training? Do the gains outweigh the losses to either the parents, themselves, or to society in general? To what extent are the churches really grappling with these issues for the guidance of involved Christian families?

A related issue concerns public policy, and the need for Christian voices to be raised. As early as the 1960's, when we spent a summer studying family life in the Soviet Union, we saw this very situation as it confronted Russian parents. In many of those families, both husband and wife had full-time day jobs. But there were no latchkey children. The mother took her young children with her to her workplace, where provision was made for what seemed excellent child care, and where she normally spent her lunch hour with her young children. The schools kept the older children after class hours and provided programs for them until one of the parents arrived to take them home. Can American voices be raised to suggest that in this enlightened country we can surely manage this situation as well as the Soviet Union did nearly a quarter of a century ago?

THE CHILDREN OF DIVORCE

A second, and even more serious, problem for the children of today is the way so many of them are being uprooted by the breakup of their parents' marriages. We are inclined to turn our eyes away from the issue of divorce, which, we are now told by the Bureau of the Census, will involve no less than 50 percent of all couples who are marrying today. Among the couples involved are our colleagues, our friends, our relatives, our fellow church members, and even our pastors. People are suffering as a result of their marital failures, and it is not our wish to add our judgments to the burden they already bear.

Yet, we must face the fact that the children of divorce suffer as much as do their parents. A major study in California, by Dr. Judith Wallerstein, came up with the finding, based on continuing observation over a five-year period, that one-third of the children of divorce turned out to be permanently emotionally damaged. But even if the others recovered from the upheavals they went through, what will be their feelings about the experience of marriage and the obligations of parenthood when they later become adults?

As already indicated, Christian churches are placed in a very complex situation regarding divorce. During most of Christian history, the Catholic church exercised an almost total control over the question of marriage—under what conditions a couple might enter the marriage state and under what conditions (there were very few indeed) they might terminate their relationship. The task of the ecclesiastical organizations that undertook this function was a very difficult one, but they did their best.

Following the Reformation, however, the management of marriage was handed over to the state. Luther did so because he thought that state officials were in a better position to make the complex decisions involved, and he fully expected the state to uphold Christian principles. In Geneva, Calvin established a civil community to be controlled in all its aspects by Christian principles. These included the regulation of marriages. In England, the situation was more complex, but to this day the Church of

England is an integral part of the state, with bishops serving in the House of Lords.

Over time, however, secular cultures have increasingly departed from Christian standards. At first, divorce was very difficult to get. There had to be evidence of serious departure from acceptable behavior; the evidence had to be examined in a court of law, which might involve considerable expense; and public opinion was strongly opposed to people who violated their marriage vows. So divorce rates were, by present standards, low enough to leave most marriages intact. Expectations of marriage were in any case not very high, so far as men were concerned, and women faced real hardship if they gave up the support marriage provided.

However, the situation has greatly changed. Singlehood has become an accepted behavior pattern, and even a desirable life-style. Sexual freedom has made it possible to have access to partners without the need to marry them and has provided plenty of variety. Living with a person of the other sex without being married has now become acceptable in some circles, and you can walk out at any time without penalty. Sexual relationships before marriage, and outside marriage, have becomes so commonplace that an increasing number of couples have no motivation to enter into a legal union.

These changes have so altered the situation that many young people growing up in our culture today see no particular advantage to be gained by being married. At the same time, the legal system has responded by giving up the effort to restrain those who want out of marriage by introducing "no fault divorce," which has made divorce little more than a formality.

The question of parenthood, however, remains. And of course having children, according to the teaching of the church, is the primary reason for marriage. What about the obligation of parents to the children they have produced? What about the basic human rights of the child? What usually happens is that the mother is left with the children and has to take all responsibility for their upbringing. The father may contribute something toward the cost of maintaining a family, but there are plenty of defaulters. The father may continue to see the children from time to time, but often he loses interest, moves away, or remarries and finds himself rearing another man's children. For the children, this lack of constancy may well undermine emotional security and give them no continuing experience of the life of a happy and stable family—which is poor preparation for their own prospects as future family members.

There are parents who, under these difficult conditions, manage to cope remarkably well. But when all the facts are added up, it is difficult to evade the impression that marriage and its primary function of joint parenthood are in grave peril. Some people simply take the view that the whole system has collapsed, and that some other way of handling the issue of the continuing life cycle will have to be found. One plan that has been seriously suggested is to allow children to be born only if certain requirements are met, and then to arrange for them to be raised by suitable adults, selected and trained at state expense. In other words, abandon the family system entirely.

Can Christians, who are by no means a minority group in our society, stand by and allow this to happen? Already many Christian marriages, and Christian parents, are being involved in the trends pointing in that direction. At what point do churches begin to take a firm stand and make it clear that their principles are different from those of the secular society?

CHRISTIAN PARENTHOOD IN PRACTICE

Let us now turn to those Christian couples who stay together and seek to raise their children in a truly Christian home. What should this involve?

Their first task is to decide how many children they should have. In the past, this was not an issue for most couples. Christian marriage gave the husband the "right" to sexual access to his wife, and she was expected to allow this and to accept the consequences. To devout Catholics, the only way a fertile couple had of avoiding the possibility of an annual birth was to abandon sexual intercouse completely—a very unlikely decision. The result was that a wife, worn out by successive pregnancies, might die relatively young, leaving a brood of children to be cared for by somebody else.

Then came contraception. Catholic teaching opposed this strongly and continues to do so. We shall examine this in the next chapter (chapter 13). But for Protestant Christians, birth control is now permitted, so the couple are free to continue their sex life and, with a small possibility of error, to have the number of children they feel to be appropriate. If they are not able to have children of their own, they may adopt those who lack proper parental care.

Traditionally, having children was a welcome and happy experience. We have seen how this was especially so in Hebrew society, but it was also true among most early Christians. Life was relatively brief in those days, and children meant security for the future. They would in time help with the work, look after their parents in their latter years, and continue the family line and cultural values. The death of a child was, alas, a common event in those days, and in some situations it was wise to reckon that only half of all children would survive to adulthood.

It was easy, then, to assume that the values Christian parents cherished would be passed on. Of course, there might be individual children who brought sorrow or disgrace to the family, but when this happened, it was a burden to be born with resignation. The immediate community in which Christian families lived was usually Christian in its principles and practices, and was under the continuous influence of the church.

By contrast, raising children in a Christian home today can be a formidable task. Even if young people get some teaching of Christian principles, they are also exposed to other influences—and often contrary influences. In the public schools of today, youth are likely to meet other children who are not being raised in Christian homes as we understand them. On radio and television they are exposed—often for as many hours as they spend in school—to the teaching and demonstration of very different standards of behavior from those in which their parents believe. David Benson, a campus minister in Wisconsin, says, "If most parents picked up the album cover that holds their child's favorite rock record and read the lyrics often printed on the back, they would be shocked." The inevitable result is that as the children move into their teen years, they can very easily develop behaviors that bring grief and disappointment to those who are trying to give them a Christian upbringing.

A number of studies have tried to measure the happiness of average marriages over the life cycle. All but a very few of them have come to the same conclusion: that happiness follows a *curvilinear* pattern. The married couple who stay together feel reasonably happy at the beginning. When children arrive, however, their happiness begins to decline. When the children enter the teen years, the parental happiness drops down further still, to its lowest level. Finally, when the children leave home, the parental happiness rate begins to rise again, and stays that way if the couple remain together.

CONCLUSION

These facts raise many questions for Christian parents and for the churches. Despite all the difficulties, deeply committed Christian young people are being reared in today's culture. But our impression is that this is much more likely to happen in churches where programs to help and support families are active, and where young people from Christian homes can find real support and become committed Christians as a result of the fellowship they enjoy through the church. Ours may be a Christian country in name, but many of the influences that are brought to bear on youth are not strongly supportive of Christian family life. Christian married couples and the churches to which they belong have many challenges to meet as they try to fulfill the duties and responsibilities of Christian parenthood. We may be proud and thankful that so many families are managing to do so.

It would help greatly if young people from Christian homes had every encouragement to find their future marriage partners through the fellowship of the church, so that they might start their married life together on the basis of a shared commitment to Christian standards and the Christian way of life.

Chapter 13

CHRISTIAN MARRIAGE
AND SEXUALITY

The role of sex in human life, in and out of marriage, might well be rated as the most controversial aspect of human behavior in the history of the Christian church. Let us examine this.

SEX IN THE HEBREW CULTURE

We need to begin with the Hebrew culture out of which Christianity emerged. As we have seen, the Hebrews saw the sexual function as something of profound religious significance. God had created man in his own image. After the animal and vegetable world had been established, Adam appeared. He was in some respects like the animals; yet he was fundamentally different. He carried in his being something of the divine image.

Then things went wrong. After each day of creation, God saw that what he had created was "very good." The plan was developing. Then man, the crown of creation, took a false step, upset the entire program, and had to be banished from the garden with the loss of his immortality. Yet Adam and Eve were not destroyed. There was still hope that, as they faced the punishment toil and death meant for them, they and their descendants could make good.

Fundamental to the plan of salvation was the fact that Adam and Eve had the power, acting together, to reproduce themselves and thus to perpetuate the human family. Out of that first family, with all its faults, including murder, the line *was* continued. Later, in the time of Noah, it seemed again that God was about to give up on the human race, but again one righteous man and his family were allowed to survive and to continue the line of succession.

Central to the divine purpose, therefore, was the power of reproduction. To the Hebrews, sex had a vital function to fulfill. The human father was endowed by God with the power to create new beings in whom were implanted something of the divine nature. The awesome power that sex gave to Adam, and to all who followed him, enabled God's chosen people to continue to fulfill the divine purpose generation after generation.

This may not be a precise account of how the Hebrews interpreted the sexual function. But there can be no doubt that they looked upon it with veneration, and even awe. We have seen how, when Abraham wanted his servant to make a very solemn promise, as in our own time an oath sworn with one hand on the Bible has binding force, the servant was asked to place his hand on his master's sex organ (Genesis 24:2).

Put it all together, and the resounding message is that sex is good. It is man's sharing with God in the continuing work of creation. This is the major purpose of marriage, an experience of religious significance that brings joy and pride, earns God's blessing and reward in the gift of children, and ensures the continuity of the eternal purpose. Used as God ordained, for the Hebrews, there was nothing in sex that was in any way unclean, shameful, sinful, or unspiritual.

SEX IN CHRISTIAN HISTORY

A very different picture appears as we consider how sex was viewed in the long stretches of Christian history. Even in the early New Testament period, negative attitudes from the philosophy of the Oriental religions were challenging the positive Hebrew view of sex. The new focus was dualism, which saw man as a conflicting combination of body and spirit, each striving for supremacy over the other. From this viewpoint, the goal of religion was to bring the physical under the subjection of the spiritual. Control over bodily functions could only be partial in most areas. If life was to continue at all, it was necessary to go on breathing, eating, and drinking, at least to a modest degree. You could cut back on sleep to some extent, but you had to give in to it finally. The functions of elimination had to go on. The one area where bodily functioning could be brought to a complete halt was sexual desire.

This, then, became the acid test of bringing the body under subjection to the spirit. Consequently, surrender to the sex urge became the point at which a person manifestly failed to cultivate the spiritual life.

The cult of asceticism has always been an important element in the practice of religion. Being in control of one's bodily functions is an essential part of responsible living, and it is perhaps not surprising that the most ardent cultivation of the spiritual life should be seen as carrying this to the point of striving for perfection. If we feel that it is pleasing to God to suppress as far as possible all natural desires, the one that offers the best opportunity of complete suppression is obviously the sexual urge. So the power to bring sexual desire totally under control could be seen as the final test of spiritual achievement. This, of course, is the meaning of celibacy.

We have seen how extensively this concept dominated long stretches of Christian history. Indeed, the cult of asceticism had already penetrated the Hebrew culture in the time of Jesus. Later, when excessive sexual indulgence became a continuing feature of the life of the Roman Empire, the denial of sex offered, by contrast, a striking witness to the cultivation of the spiritual life, and therefore became the acid test of Christian living.

SEX IN TODAY'S WORLD

One lingering manifestation of the suppression of sex in the later Christian community was that it became an avoided subject among Christians. As so often happens, avoidance of direct reference to sex made it the subject of curious inquiry and subtle jokes, resulting in a situation in which it was rarely open to serious examination and investigation. In medical literature, for example, there was a time when specific references to sex tended to be made only in Latin.

However, in today's world, the era of silence has ended. The fields of sexuality and reproduction have now been extensively investigated by a long line of highly qualified experts. Havelock Ellis, in describing his early years in Australia, said "A resolve grew up within me; one main part of my lifework should be to make clear the problems of sex." This intention was fully carried out—the first of his seven published volumes on *Studies in the Psychology of Sex* appeared in Britain, to which he had moved in the year 1900, and the last in 1928. In America, Ellis was followed by Alfred Kinsey, whose attention focused on the facts about sexual behavior—his massive volume on male behavior appeared in 1948, followed by the one on female behavior in 1953. William Masters and Virginia Johnson (who later married each other), then took up the theme of *Human Sexual Response* and published their first report in 1966, followed by *Human Sexual Inadequacy* in 1970.

Many other studies have followed, and a vast literature on sexual behavior has now been accumulated. A book was even published in 1973 by William E. Phipps about *The Sexuality of Jesus*. Widespread interest was aroused by all these publications, and it could almost be said, so far as our understanding of sexual behavior is concerned, that the subject has now been exhausted. We should, therefore, now be in a good position to examine what should be our Christian attitude about human sexuality.

SEX IN MARRIAGE

Most Christian couples today think of sexual intercourse as an entirely good experience that is an expression of their love for each other to be enjoyed by both of them. The investigations already referred to have established what is called a "normal" frequency of twice a week, though there are great variations in individual cases.

The modern Catholic position, in theory at least, does not significantly depart from the strict traditional view. Sexual intercourse may occur, of course, only in marriage. It must be directed toward its basic object, parenthood. No contraceptives may be used, but it is not forbidden to choose a time when pregnancy is much less likely to occur. The traditional instruction that it must not be enjoyed for its own sake, but only with the conscious object of producing a child, seems no longer to be stressed. Indeed, parish priests acknowledge that they have great difficulty in preventing the use of birth control methods other than those permitted by the church.

Many Protestants at first joined the Catholics in opposing birth control. The Church of England, for example, supported this position for some time, but gradually abandoned it. The view of most Protestant couples today is that sexual intercourse, quite apart from procreation, is a symbol of their love for each other, and at its best is an almost sacramental experience.

In fact, it is now widely recognized by Christian couples that the injunction to multiply has to be interpreted with restraint in a world fast becoming overpopulated, and that small families are appropriate today. So the Hebrew view that the seminal fluid (the *seed*) must not be wasted and the similar Catholic attitude that the size of Christian families need not be limited are being modified. Christian couples today even feel justified, in special circumstances, in deciding to have no children at all when it seems likely that children will be severely handicapped, or that the wife's life might be endangered by pregnancy. On the other hand, Christian couples who seem unable to have children do not hesitate to seek medical help in the hope of finding a remedy for their infertility.

These changing attitudes are not a departure from religious faith. They are rather the results of our increasing understanding of what takes place in the reproductive process, and the change from unquestioned observance of general rules to the exercise of personal choice based on an expanding range of possible alternatives. More than ever before, Christian couples today have the right to seek God's will concerning the proper time and the best circumstances to bring a child into the world, instead of a blind obedience that accepts whatever comes. This can, of course, be carried too far when a pregnancy is terminated if it occurs at an inconvenient time. But in general the right of choice about offspring, when exercised sensitively and in line with a sincere seeking for divine guidance, is surely not an evidence of lack of faith.

Christians today are, therefore, learning to plan their families on the basis of enlightened understanding of the sexual function, on their own readiness to make wise and responsible choices, and on the social factors which need to be considered in establishing new family units. The churches, though as yet on a limited scale, are providing for their members welcome services in family ministry and in pastoral care and counseling. The era in which the church issued orders to its members about their parental obligations is giving place to a readiness to help them make their own responsible decisions.

One particular area in which making a choice is especially difficult is when *abortion* may have to be considered. This is one of the most critical issues of our time. Though the right of choice was granted to American women by the United States Supreme Court in 1973, the issue keeps being challenged by religious groups.

The Catholic Church takes a firm stand and strongly opposes any resort to abortion on the ground that abortion is the murder of a human being whose life has already begun. The tendency of most other Christians is to support this view, but in particularly critical situations, as when the evidence suggests that the child will be grossly abnormal, the parents may decide to terminate the pregnancy. At the time of this writing, the issue is still a highly controversial one.

SEX OUTSIDE MARRIAGE

Along with the contemporary investigation, research, and study of sexual behavior, we have seen some dramatic changes in our cultural attitudes. It is as if the lid has been lifted from a closed receptacle, and its hitherto concealed contents have come tumbling out. What has come to light has been in part a revelation of what had before been going on beneath the surface of our society, and in part an opportunity to re-examine our traditional attitudes and to formulate new plans for the future. All this has added up to what has been called the "sexual revolution."

The revolution has consisted partly in new knowledge, in changes of attitude, and in resulting changes of behavior. Although most of the changes have not directly affected marriages, their indirect effects have been profound and far-reaching. While we cannot here examine them in great detail, we need to assess the situation generally in the light of our Christian standards and values. Here are four of the issues concerned:

1. *Sex Before Marriage.* While there have always been recurring instances of sexual activity among young people who are not yet ready for marriage, these have in the past been treated as individual lapses from the generally accepted standard—usually revealed by a premarital pregnancy. Too often, the Christian way of dealing with such a situation has been to seek, as far as possible, to cover pregnancy up by urging the young people to marry. These marriages have, as a rule, been conspicuously unhappy and unsuccessful.

Today, however, the restraints of the past have collapsed extensively, and the large number of pregnant teen-aged girls now confronts our culture with an impending crisis. The girls themselves have been less and less willing to marry the boys who made them pregnant or to give up their children for adoption. The children are being raised partly by the girls themselves, whose education is being interrupted in the process, and in many instances the mothers and grandmothers of the girls, often reluctantly, are taking over. The outlook for future marriage for the young people concerned is far from bright.

Important new information on this issue has recently become available. The Alan Guttmacher Institute in New York has completed a study of the numbers of unmarried teen-aged girls becoming pregnant in the United States and in seven other Western countries. It is reported that the pregnancy rate for girls of fifteen to nineteen years old in the United States is now 96 per 1,000, as compared with 45 in England, 44 in Canada, 43 in France, 35 in Sweden, and 14 in the Netherlands. Even fourteen-year-olds in the United States have a rate of 14 pregnancies per 1,000. The general implication of the report is that little or nothing can be done to change the behavior patterns of teen-agers, and that the solution is to make sophisticated contraceptives widely available, with parental support, to all teen-agers.

Another aspect of sex before marriage is found in the young couples who, unwilling to make the required social commitment, resort instead to what is being called *cohabitation*—setting up a relationship of living together which appears to be marriage, but is not registered as such. Some of these alliances become registered marriages in time, but many do not. Of course, no religious commitment is usually present.

These patterns are based on sexual experiences that are separated from the commitment, and the public recognition, that go with marriage. They present very difficult challenges to the churches, because often the young people involved are associates and friends, if not actual members, of Christian families.

2. *Extramarital Sex.* It has been recently estimated that of all married couples in the United States today, one-half of the husbands and one-third of the wives have, on at least one occasion, been involved in a sexual relationship with a person other than the marriage partner. This, of course, also reflects the liberal attitudes that have resulted in the so-called sexual revolution. Such behavior is often highly damaging to the atmosphere of mutual trust and exclusivity that is part of the Christian marriage standard. Sometimes these couples can be reconciled, though never

painlessly, by repentance and forgiveness, which are Christian virtues. But in many other cases, the trust and unity of the marriage are so severely ruptured that divorce follows.

3. *Solitary Sex.* Earlier in this century, the practice of masturbation was often very severely judged as a violation of Christian standards. It was at first thought to exist only among boys. Booklets describing the supposed serious consequences of this so-called "secret sin" were widely circulated. The view was that the precious fluid that had the power to create new life was being willfully wasted. Possible disastrous results, including insanity, were hinted at.

A good example of the lengths to which these judgmental statements went is provided by Dr. Adam Clarke, a famous divine, in his commentary on Genesis 38. He describes masturbation as

one of the most destructive evils ever practised by fallen man. . . . It excites the powers of nature to *undue action*, and produces *violent secretions*, which necessarily and speedily *exhaust the vital principles* and energy; hence the muscles become flaccid and feeble, the tone and natural action of the nerves relaxed and impeded, and understanding confused, the memory oblivious, the judgment perverted; the will indeterminate and wholly without energy to resist; the eyes appear languishing and without expression, and the countenance vacant; the *appetite ceases*, for the stomach is incapable of performing its proper office; *nutrition fails*, tremors, fears, and terrors are generated; and thus the wretched victim drags out a most miserable existence, till . . . with a mind often debilitated even to a state of idiotism, his worthless body tumbles into the grave, and his guilty soul (guilty of self-murder) is hurried into the awful presence of its Judge! Reader, this is no caricature, nor are the colourings overcharged in this shocking picture. Worse woes than my pen can relate I have witnessed in those addicted to this fascinating, unnatural, and most destructive of crimes. . . . The intelligent reader will see that prudence forbids me to enter any farther into this business.

This description was published in a Bible commentary in 1836. About a century later, Carl Jung, the famous Swiss psychiatrist, also in describing masturbation, said, "Under circumstances where either for physical or psychical causes normal intercourse is impossible, and it is used merely as a safety valve, masturbation has no ill-effects."

We now know that the average male produces a fabulous amount of sperms in one discharge of seminal fluid, and that almost all are wasted. We know, too, that girls as well as boys masturbate. The modern view is that no known serious consequences can result from the practice. It can even help a married couple to balance inequities in their frequency of sexual desire, or to tide them over periods of involuntary separation.

4. *Homosexuality.* The puzzling fact that some people, both men and women, find themselves sexually attracted only, or mainly, to persons of their own gender has been fully established by investigation. Clearly, dislocation of the normal process has occurred, and while some people seem to be bisexual, therefore flexible, for others it is not so. The general conclusion is that no readjustment is possible for most of these persons, and our society today is tending to accept this situation, though often reluctantly. There seem to be some differences, in terms of interpersonal attraction, among particular homosexuals, and between male and female homosexuality generally. The question of recognizing so-called "homosexual marriages," which in some cases can be marked by true love and devotion, has been raised in some liberal Christian circles, but the general stance at present seems to be one of strong disapproval.

THE ERA OF SEXUAL FREEDOM

Our new understanding of human sexuality has had some good results and some bad ones. The sex drive has always had to be a powerful one, because upon its operation, for the animals as well as for man, depends the continuity of the species. It happens that in most living creatures sex functions only at certain times, but at those times, it is very powerful. When the female is open to the sexual approach, the male disregards almost every other claim to his attention and seeks her out in order to mate with her. His approach is an insistent one and may assume the nature of a brutal assault.

In the human race, although the woman goes through a succession of menstrual cycles, she is sexually approachable most of the time. This means that sexual opportunities are widely available, and if the needed stimulation is provided by the culture, sex can become an almost ever-present enticement. With the mass media existing everywhere today, and the seductive behavior that is assigned to physically attractive women, our culture tends to be saturated with real or imagined sexual opportunities. The result is that sexual experiences, which in the past were available only by seeking out prostitutes, seem now to have penetrated much of our social life and much of the field of entertainment.

This trend applies particularly to the nation's youth. Today, high school students often view "dates" as opportunities for sexual adventures. Social events bring young men and women together in an atmosphere that assumes that "pairing off" is part of the procedure. Mixing of the sexes at evening events elicits no special comment if men and women "pick-ups" end by going off together for a "one-night stand." The idea that you don't "pair-off" until you have gone through a period of mutual acquaintance is now considered old-fashioned. It all comes down to "casual sex" for the unmarried. And even married people may join in from time to time—either by mutual consent, or without disclosure to each other.

One result we all hear about is the ease with which venereal diseases are spread. A lesser known effect may be the increasing rates of infertility among both men and women. Here is an account from "The Futurist" of February 1985 by Dr. Robert Blank:

> The United States is experiencing what some experts are calling an epidemic of infertility. About one in six married couples in their childbearing years now have fertility problems and the proportion is on the rise. . . . The sperm count of American males has fallen more than 30 percent in the last half century, and it is continuing to fall. . . . Whatever the cause, nearly 25 percent of all American men now have sperm counts so low as to be considered by some researchers to be functionally sterile. . . . The proportion of American women finding it difficult to conceive is also on the rise. Of the approximately 1.5 million American women who suffer from involuntary sterility, about 40 percent are sterile because of diseased fallopian tubes. These highly sensitive oviducts are easily scarred by disease or infection, thus blocking passage of the ovum to the sperm. Scarring can result from pelvic inflammatory diseases or other low-level gynecological infections. . . . Contemporary social problems, including increased sexual contact of young women with a variety of partners, appear to be linked with increased infertility in women. The epidemic proportions of venereal disease among young women promise to accentuate this problem.

However, behind these immediate effects is one that is much more serious. It is the impact of sexual freedom on parenthood.

We saw in an earlier chapter that marriage exists primarily for the fulfillment of our duty toward the next generation. With sexual freedom comes a process of shifting from partner to partner which undermines the fidelity principle, and with it the possibility of developing steadfast family units.

It could be said that marriage is a human institution that raises men and women above the level of animals. The male animal, having impregnated the female, usually walks away and leaves her to carry out the total task of parenting. Since she is fully equipped for this task, nothing more is required.

But, as we have seen, the fact that humans are far higher in the evolutionary scale lays upon them decidedly heavier parental duties. Humans must devote a period of many years to the critical task of bringing their children to maturity. If this is not done, human superiority to the animal level could be forfeited.

The critical factor here, as we have seen, is to engage the father in a continuing and supportive relationship with the mother in the joint task of parenting. The achievement of this goal has been one of the triumphs of human development. It has taken long centuries to bring about, and the key to its success has been the development of an accepted standard of marital fidelity. Religion, law, and a supportive public opinion have together maintained the conditions guaranteeing the human rights of our children, the future citizens.

We now face the real possibility that this cultural achievement may be on the way to collapse. Sexual freedom takes the man back to the stage of the male animal, who meets his sexual needs without assuming any responsibility. The woman is then left with the task of child rearing alone. And since, at this moment in history, she is already fully preoccupied with the task of justifying her claims to be equal with the man in the competitive field of the workplace, she must desperately struggle to combine her duty as a parent, sometimes with no co-parent to support her, and her competition with men in the sphere in which they have hitherto reigned supreme.

This situation has the potential to become a very serious crisis in our cultural development. There are those who say the family is becoming obsolete, and that we shall have to devise a new system to carry the nation's children through those critical twenty years when they must somehow make the journey from helpless infancy to the high level of mature adult responsibility that will be needed to maintain the values and standards of an advanced civilization.

There is also an important *religious* issue involved here. Both in Hebrew and Christian thought, the concept of God as the loving heavenly Father is central to theological teaching. What is this concept going to mean to a generation of young people, many of whom have never experienced a loving earthly father?

As we see it, these are issues of paramount importance, which should be a priority concern for all Christians. "What shall it profit a man," we quote, "if he should gain the whole world, and lose his own soul?" (Mark 8:36 KJV). Likewise, we may say, "What shall it profit a nation, if it should reach dazzling heights in the development of technology and lose the warmth, love, and mutual happiness of home and family life?"

Our future is in danger—but all is not lost. In the next chapter, we shall look for some answers in a field in which there is the promise of better things to come.

Chapter 14

CHRISTIAN MARRIAGE
AS COMPANIONSHIP

We have seen that in the opinion of some Puritan writers any listing of the three widely accepted purposes of Christian marriage will place companionship first and not last. In the Creation story, we are reminded, God made Eve and gave her to Adam, because "it was not good for him to be alone." At that time, the questions of sex and of children were not under consideration. It was Adam's sense of isolation, because he was different from the animals and separated from them, that created the need God met in giving Eve to him as a partner. And the fact that Eve was developed from a part of Adam's body provided a pleasing sense that both of them were from a common source and, therefore, truly shared a sense of unity.

Why, then, did we leave the issue of companionship for discussion now? If reasons are needed, we would offer two—because the Christian church, in interpreting marriage, has placed nearly all the emphasis on the other two, and we, therefore, felt they should be dealt with first, and because in our opinion this is the reason for marriage that offers the highest promise for our future, and it therefore seemed appropriate to leave the best until the last!

We are not saying that in Christian history the issue of companionship in Christian marriage has been ignored. In every period covered by our survey there have been instances of mutually happy and cooperative relationships between Christian husbands and wives. Abraham and Sarah were prominent Old Testament models, and the couple described in Proverbs 31 are paragons of virtue. In the New Testament, Aquila and Priscilla, who shared in a joint ministry, must have been typical of many other couples whose names are long forgotten. Throughout the history of the church, there must have been many couples who, humbly and without recognition except among their friends, enjoyed Christian marriages at a deep and satisfying level as close companions.

However, what we are saying, and what must be faced, is that the "companionship marriage" has seldom, until our own time, been widely identified as the true Christian marriage. There is a reason for this. It has to do with the nature of human society before the democratic era, and also with the traditional view of womanhood. Let us explain.

THE HIERARCHICAL SYSTEM

Although traditional human societies, large and small, differed very widely, they were all based on a concept we call *hierarchy*, which is defined as "the body of persons organized or classified according to rank, capacity, or authority." In any group of persons who try to operate together, there inevitably arise situations of differences of opinion about what to do next. This creates a situation in which the persons either do nothing at all, which may be inappropriate or even disastrous; in which they split up and go off in different directions, sacrificing their unity; or in which one of the persons overrules the wishes of others and compels them to take a course of action of which the group does not approve. Recurring situations of this kind would in time destroy the unity of the group, so some solution must be found.

The solution that has become standard in human history is to give to a particular person, or to a small group of persons, the authority and power to decide for, and overrule the wishes of, the others. In a primitive society, the usual practice is to allocate supreme power to the chief, who is appointed because, by birth or by demonstrated prowess, he has gained authority over the others. By exercising the power given to him, he makes all the decisions, and the others have to accept these decisions whether or not they think they are the best.

In most human societies, and among associated animals and birds, this system runs through the whole body of members. Apart from the persons at the top or bottom of the list, all the others come to know to whom they can issue commands and who they must obey. This is sometimes described as the "pecking order." Only by this means can the group maintain cohesion.

The hierarchical system has operated in almost all traditional human families. Built into it there has been another basic principle—a man takes precedence over a woman. As we saw in the Hebrew culture, the husband was the dominant member of the family, and the wife was expected to be subservient. Two underlying principles were in operation here. First, in the struggle for survival, men were superior as fighters and in physical strength, both important qualities. Second, in the vital task of continuing the tribal group, it was widely believed that children were formed from the man's seminal fluid which coagulated in the womb of the woman, who provided only the receptacle for its prenatal growth.

At both of these important levels, therefore, women were considered inferior to men. Since in those days there were no contraceptives, it also turned out that most married women, usually from their teen years, went through a series of pregnancies that occupied their time and attention and gave them little chance of taking part in the wider life of the community. Many women died, or were incapacitated, as a result of excessive pregnancies.

Consequently, women were treated as inferiors. One result was that they were given no chance to be educated, and as a result of being ignorant, they appeared to be stupid, which seemed to confirm the view that they actually *were* stupid.

Whether we like it or not, the fact is that Christian marriage was for a long time based on these concepts, and the result was that marriage was seen as a one-vote system. The husband made all major decisions, and in the event of a disagreement he had the casting vote. Any other arrangement in those earlier times would have introduced serious and damaging conflicts into the relationship. Paul supported this view that had been, and still was, a generally accepted opinion of marriage in all the ancient cultures and in all the world religions. Nothing in the teaching or life of Jesus seems to treat women as spiritually inferior to men, but Jesus was not primarily concerned with changing the social customs of his time.

So, the view of Paul has been accepted throughout Christian history until today, when there has arisen a great deal of controversy. It was Paul's use of the relationship between Christ and the church as a model for Christian marriage that was used by the Catholics as biblical support for making marriage a sacrament.

Some, however, have used this analogy as a means to relegate the Christian wife to a position of low status in comparison to her husband. Though Paul was only using an analogy, it was perhaps unfortunate that the husband was equated with Christ, who, of course, was seen as sinless, and that the wife was identified with the church, wayward and with many faults.

THE IMPACT OF DEMOCRACY

We are now living at a time in history when the traditional concepts of human society are being critically re-examined. The advent of the democratic ideal, challenging the universal acceptance of hierarchy in the past, is hardly new. The flag was first unfurled with the Magna Charta (the Great Charter), when English barons presented to their king, at Runnymede in 1215, their demand for a share of his previously exclusive hierarchical powers. Much later, democracy was a basic principle for the founding of the American nation in the statement of the early fathers that "all men are created equal." The establishment of democracy is, however, a slow and painful process—even today, only a minimum of the nations of the world have as yet accepted it. However, democracy is seen as a Christian principle—the founding of the American nation is described as being "under God."

In the two hundred years that have passed since the founders of America declared that all men are created equal, a groundswell has developed insisting on adding the corollary that, as persons, all men *and women* are created equal. The first implementation of this principle took place in New Zealand in 1893, when women were given the right to vote. Other nations followed this example, including England in 1917 and the United States in 1920. Throughout the world, the full personhood of women is now being progressively recognized. It may well be that future historians will see this as the most significant development in human society in the twentieth century.

What we are concerned about here, of course, is the impact of this significant change on our view of *marriage*. So far, it has been dramatic and disturbing. But there seems to be little doubt that the concept of husband and wife as members of an equal partnership has now come to stay. It is already having profound and far-reaching effects worldwide.

Women today, granted the power to vote and being seen as equal partners in marriage, have precipitated a major crisis in family life, which is sweeping away some of the conventional ideas that have been in operation during the whole span of previous human history. Women are shattering the early misconceptions that saw them as weak, stupid, and dependent. With grim determination, they are invading fields previously dominated exclusively by men and proving themselves to be as competent, and often superior. This process is now so well under way that we cannot expect it to halt until the battle for equality has been fully won—a process likely to carry us into the twenty-first century, and to be a turning point in human history.

The impact of this dramatic change on contemporary marriages has so far been disturbing. Divorce rates have risen alarmingly in Britain, the United States, and elsewhere. Children, as we have seen, have suffered grievously under the impact of broken homes. The continuity of families has been shattered by an influx of step-relatives. In the resulting destabilization of human relationships, established conventions have been violated and community life has been thrown into confusion. There is enough happening to suggest to some onlookers that the foundations of society as we have known it are being rudely shaken and may collapse in uncontrollable disorder.

That, at least, is one way of looking at the situation. We, personally, can understand that some people may well view it as disastrous. However, we see another side to the picture, and it is to this that we must now give our attention.

HOW MARRIAGE IS CHANGING

Most people today recognize that marriage is changing, but few of them really understand the nature of the change. Marriage is a subject surrounded by veils of strict privacy, and is, therefore, seldom seriously discussed at the personal level when people get together. The subject of marriage lurks under a taboo, and the result is that popular thinking about it is full of almost incredible myths and misconceptions. One concept that lives on is that, in some esoteric manner, a man and a woman "fall in love" with each other, as a result of which they get married, settle down together, and "live happily ever after." When this sequence fails to occur, which is often the case today, the conclusion is that either the two people concerned have been mistaken about each other, or that some malignant influence has interfered with the process. Why, it is asked, are so many marriages failing today, when they would presumably have worked all right in the past?

The answer, of course, is that, by our modern standards, they *didn't* work all right in the past. Then, our society was so structured that, once married, the couple were "locked in" for keeps. There was no way out. In other words, divorce was either not available at all, or it could be obtained only by very wealthy or influential people. Until the latter part of the nineteenth century, for example, each separate divorce in Britain could be obtained only by a special act of Parliament!

Consequently, many people simply had to tolerate what happened to them, because there was no alternative. And because the "happily ever after" legend was widely promoted, it was best not to disclose to your relatives and friends that you were not happy, lest they come to the conclusion that you were an abnormal or irresponsible person. So you stifled your disappointments and made the best of the situation. Sometimes, that alone was enough to make it more tolerable.

However, the time has now come to recognize that gloriously happy marriages were few and far between. A husband who was sensitive enough not to want his own way all the time, and a wife who felt emotionally secure in a servile situation, could jog along together quite happily. But feelings of frustration and anger just had to be bottled up; it was best not to nurture too ambitious expectations.

But what about being "in love"? Isn't that the basic ingredient of a happy marriage? The truth we must accept is that in the process of being married there are two different and distinct kinds of love, and they have very little in common with each other.

The first is romantic love. We have seen that in the Middle Ages this received a great deal of attention, but that the accepted view was that romance couldn't happen or be sustained in marriage. Freud once defined this love as "aim-inhibited sex." The sexual drive draws two people together in order that they may unite physically—this has to be one of our most powerful drives, because the perpetuation of the species is involved. But since, in most human cultures, coming together sexually is strictly controlled, the urge cannot be fulfilled as soon as it is felt. What then happens is that, denied immediate expression, it builds up to a sustained state of emotional excitement that idealizes the other person and generates dreams of perfection, which become obsessive. All normal young people have been through this experience, which includes rapturous dreams. In the Middle Ages, this behavior was clearly understood, but it was also understood that the emotional state of romantic love, if it *can* be sexually expressed, soon dies away, and the loved person then emerges at the level of reality. In marriage, the record shows that there is almost universally a falling away in sexual frequency during the first year. This was fully explored by Carol Botwin in her book *Is There Sex After Marriage?* Once the sex object is within easy reach, the obsessive images fade, and the two people as they really are have to come to terms with each other. All too often this can be an experience of disillusionment.

However, now the other kind of love must take over, or disaster may follow. Mature love is based on genuine appreciation of the worth of your partner. This may have been there all the time mingled with the romantic love. But if not, it must now be developed, or there will be no "glue" to hold the marriage together. We would, however, emphasize that it must be *developed*. This is done by a complex process of mutual adjustment of the two persons to each other. The dreaming is now over, and the task of building a marriage must begin.

As we have already seen, this task was not too difficult in the past, because what was involved then was for the husband to catalog his wishes for the relationship and for the wife to respond that she would do anything in her power to meets them. We have referred to the French book by le Ménagier de Paris, dating back to the fourteenth century, in which this process is actually described in detail. It was, as we have pointed out, a one-vote system. The wife simply did not list *her* wishes, because her task was to please her husband in all possible ways, thus to earn his love and devotion. If this was to be in any sense a companionship marriage, it was the companionship between a master and a servant. In fact, in the French story, the husband describes the obedience of a well-trained dog as a model for his wife to follow!

A spirited girl of today would, of course, find a situation like this quite intolerable. She would insist on stating *her* wishes for the new life she had entered and would fight back if her husband tried to give her orders. This would make them both angry, and a process of alienation would follow. The idea of a relationship based on subservience on her part would be totally unacceptable.

COMPANIONSHIP MARRIAGE TODAY

What is clear is that the achievement of a companionship relationship between two people with minds of their own is a tough assignment. That is the plain truth, and there can be no understanding of the task of building a marriage today until we accept that fact. Most of the couples who are failing in marriage, in such large numbers, simply have not taken the measure of what they are attempting to do. They misunderstand the objectives. They lack the necessary skills. They become progressively alienated and often decide that they are simply not suited to each other. Then, because it is now so easy to walk out of marriage, they get a divorce and hope later to find a more suitable partner. But as often as not this doesn't happen. The failure rate of second marriages was until recently actually higher than that of first marriages.

What can be done about this? The answer is simply that modern marriage has become a quite different proposition from the now discarded older model. All those failures are not to be explained by saying that the people involved are irresponsible or wicked. The explanation is that achieving a companionship marriage, the goal of today's couple, is a very different process from that of the past; most of the people who are marrying today simply don't understand the difference, and go into the experience lacking the necessary skills to complete the task. It would not be inappropriate to say that succeeding in marriage today requires as much knowledge of the process, and as many learned skills, as does success in a fairly high-level career. But as long as couples don't know this, and don't understand that they have to learn how to do it, the failures will go on occurring.

However, there is an answer, and we would only be harbingers of doom if we had nothing more to offer. Fortunately, to those who will listen, *there is an answer.* New experimental programs, supported by research projects, are bringing us increasing insight into the ways companionship marriages can be enabled to succeed.

These new developments are part of an exciting growth of the behavioral sciences, which we believe are destined to play a central role in the twenty-first century. Just as the coming of age of the biological sciences enabled them to team up with pragmatic medicine in the earlier part of the present century, and to achieve miracles in the maintenance of physical health and extension of the human life span, so it is our hope that the behavioral sciences will increasingly point the way to the improvement of human relationships, an area of major importance for our human future that has been tragically neglected, but that is the vital key to the ultimate achievement of world peace.

We, therefore, now have considerable hope that new insights and new resources have already arrived and will be increasingly available to those who are seeking to foster the development of companionship marriages in the world of today. This is of particular importance to the churches, for whom the achievement of true Christian marriage is now a major concern.

THE PROMISE OF MARRIAGE ENRICHMENT

Let us conclude this chapter with an account of what is now possible for Christian marriage. The great advantage of the Christian position is that it has always insisted that members of the churches must take marriage seriously and make all possible efforts to enable their relationships to work successfully. This fact, together with the exciting new resources that are now available, should hold out high promise for dedicated Christian couples, and should enable the churches to demonstrate to our society that, far from being outmoded, marriage provides the essential foundation for high quality families, which in turn can make possible the development of a society based on high quality human relationships. The task will not be an easy one, but if the churches are ready to devote themselves to it, they should have a vital witness to bear to the secular society in our day and age.

It is not our intention in this book to go into detail on the subject of marriage enrichment. We have written half a dozen other books on that subject. However, for those not well informed, it may be helpful to summarize the basic facts.

We have found, by working at first hand with hundreds of married couples over a period of many years, that what is needed for the achievement of the "relational potential" in a companionship marriage can be summed up in what have become known as the "three essentials."

1. The couple must make *a serious commitment to the building of a marriage.* A wedding is *not* a marriage. It is only the beginning of a long-term process that must be undertaken by the couple. The building of a house is a good illustration. When the builders have unloaded their piles of bricks, lumber, and other materials on a vacant lot, they do not have a house. The house comes later, when all the pieces have been fitted together by people who undertake the task and have the necessary skills to carry it out.

Likewise, at the wedding, the man and the woman each bring their raw materials, which are raked together so that the work of unifying them can begin. In the past, the wedding vow was that whatever happened, the couple would accept it—"for better or for worse." But now we see clearly that the issue of better or worse is not accidental, but depends on how effectively the couple, themselves, manage the building operation. It would be bettrr, rather than making a vow to accept whatever happens, for the modern couple to vow to commit themselves to work together for the necessary growth and change to establish a life-long companionship. Good marriages don't just happen. They are built by cooperative and enlightened effort over time, as good houses are. Couples are not ready for marriage until they understand this clearly and are fully prepared to make the necessary commitment.

2. The couple must develop, first and foremost, *an effectively functioning communication system.* The uniting of two persons in a relationship of close companionship is impossible if only certain parts of the persons get involved. The old fairy tales were right. After the prince rescued the fair lady from the dragon, the prince and his lady sat down together and "he told her all his heart." A satisfying marriage cannot be built from selected areas of the lives of those concerned any more than a sound house can be built by excluding some of the basic materials.

Endless studies in recent years have shown that without opening up their inner selves to each other, and without maintaining open communication at all levels, a deeply shared life cannot be achieved and sustained by the couple. People who don't know each other in depth can't understand each other and can't interpret each other's behavior, and the resulting situation leads inevitably to conflict and alienation. Couples can now be trained in communication skills, and this can often bring new vitality to a languishing marriage.

3. The couple must also *acquire the necessary skills to make creative use of anger and conflict*, which will inevitably develop in their relationship. This is the most widely misunderstood of all the new insights we have developed about modern marriage. The sentimental attitudes generated by the romantic approach include an idea that anger and conflict shouldn't exist in a loving relationship, and that when they do occur they should be avoided or suppressed. We now know that this is a dangerously mistaken idea.

What is happening in marriage is that we are trying to achieve a close relationship between two people. In order to do so, we must cut down on individual living spaces and on the freedom to act separately and independently. This inevitably puts the couple on the defensive. The best definition of anger is that it is "the defense system of the ego"—anger is a healthy emotion that protects our personhood. In a good marriage, love and anger work together in the delicate task of achieving, but also limiting, intimacy. Love draws the couple closer together, but anger halts the process when it threatens to go too far and, therefore, produces a state we call "enmeshment." By learning to get behind anger and conflict, the couple can identify what is preventing the proper expression of their love and can keep a healthy balance between unity and independence in their relationship.

These, then, are the essentials for the achievement of a companionship marriage. All three are necessary; without them, a modern marriage has a very poor chance of success. If, however, they are fully used and in good balance, a marriage between reasonably normal people has every chance of achieving, in time, its full relational potential.

Unfortunately, tens of thousands of couples continue to marry with little understanding of these concepts, and these couples make no attempt to find out. The companionship marriage represents a great advance in our understanding of close relationships, and we now know how to make it work. This calls for replacing the mythology of the past with the sound knowledge of a more enlightened age. That proves to be a very slow process that is costing us a terrible price. But, thanks to our new knowledge, the outlook for the future of Christian marriage is bright and full of promise.

As we have seen, the Puritans had begun to understand this centuries ago, but their message was not heard by the churches.

Chapter 15

A CHALLENGE TO THE CHURCHES

In the light of all the issues involved, what contribution can we make toward the future of Christian marriage?

Look at the facts. The United States has the highest divorce rate of any major country in the world. It has now reached the 50 percent level—half of all couples getting married this year will, sooner or later, end their relationship in divorce. True, many of them will find another partner and marry again. But the failure rate for second marriages is not much lower than for first marriages.

The best estimates today suggest that the divorce rate isn't likely to go higher in the near future. But even if we halt at the halfway mark, that is a terribly high rate of failure. What would we say if half of all our airplane flights crashed, or half of all new business enterprises ended in bankruptcy, or half of all children in our schools or universities failed to graduate?

Anyway, if the idea of divorcing as soon as trouble shows up brings wider acceptance, we have no assurance that the rate won't go higher still. As an alternative, couples may not bother to marry any more. Already many just move in together and substitute cohabitation for marriage, with no legal obligation or social commitment to stay together. In fact, in the absence of any lasting commitment, most of these couples seem in time to drift apart.

Meanwhile, the legal system has given up on requiring people to provide acceptable reasons for breaking up their marriages. As we have seen, the Reformers handed over the control of marriages to the state, and for a time this worked reasonably well. But divorce courts today have not seen it to be their task to uphold traditional marriage standards, and they have settled for a no-fault system.

The Catholic church never did hand over the control of marriage to the state, and the church is struggling still to maintain high standards in order to keep couples committed to their relationships. Protestant churches, having allowed the state to take over, have in effect lost all control over the situation. They still conduct weddings and require the couples to make a solemn pledge to stay together "till death do us part"; but for many couples this has become a tongue-in-cheek formality and is not treated seriously. Anyway, the number of couples who are married in church is now steadily declining, and many who still arrange it this way do so mainly to please their parents and relatives, or because they want a "pretty wedding." The lifelong commitment is not taken seriously any more.

Meanwhile, sexual freedom among our young people is becoming more and more widely accepted. At one time, the understanding that the sexual relationship would not begin until after the wedding was widely honored, if only because it provided some assurance that the future bridegroom would have something vital to wait for. Today, when couples planning to marry are asked the question directly, they almost invariably admit that they are already having sexual relations.

It may be a little unfair to say that the promise of a readily available sexual partner was a major motivation to induce a young man to enter marriage, but there is no doubt that it played a significant part. And the young woman realized that it was in her own best interests not to yield sexuality in advance. So, for a good many young couples, their first sexual experience took place after the wedding. If this implies that men were lured into marriage by the promise of sex, we had better admit that there is some truth in that statement. The basic logic behind this fact is that in order to guarantee the rights of children, prospective fathers had to be given every possible inducement to enter marriage and to stay in it.

Today this has been largely given up, and the result, to put it plainly, is that since men can now easily find sexual partners without having to marry, some of them are slipping back on the evolutionary scale to the animal level, at which all that is required of the male is to impregnate the female, and he can then walk away. We see an illustration of this in the former slave population in the Caribbean, where the owners abolished marriage and thereby undermined the duties and continuing obligations of fatherhood—an arrangement that continued after slavery was ended.

The result of these changes is that marriage is becoming an outmoded institution, and some people are not hesitating to say so. They are, however, losing sight of the basic fact, which we have kept reiterating in this book, that is rooted in Christian teaching: *Marriage exists to provide a guarantee that the duties of parenthood will be faithfully discharged by both partners.* Women who make themselves sexually available outside marriage probably have no idea that they are betraying one of the most fundamental rights a woman possesses—to ensure that the man who fathers her child will faithfully share with her the arduous and responsible task of rearing that child from infancy to adulthood.

WHAT SHOULD THE CHURCHES DO?

It must be stressed that all this precipitates a crisis for Christian policy. There are two major issues. First, since the state has now made no-fault divorce an integral part of the marriage system, has the time come for the church to respond by declaring that Christian marriage and civil marriage are fundamentally different, in that Christian marriage requires the sincere commitment of both partners to Christian living standards, and particularly to shared responsibility for the raising of the children who are born to them? There may be rare exceptions to this basic rule, but where the rule is not established, exceptions just keep multiplying. What this decision would imply is that henceforth the churches would "take back" Christian marriage, set the standards for the couples concerned, and provide a clear set of rules for those who were really committed to all that Christian marriage means.

Second, the churches would have to implement this action by providing all the guidance and support that should be available to couples who make such a solemn commitment—living the Christian life together, developing all the skills needed for an enriched marriage, and taking a stand against the subtle secular values that are everywhere invading the lives of Christian homes, and to some extent, of Christian churches. There have often been times in Christian history when sincere church members have had to separate themselves from the lower non-Christian values of the community. There are Christians who take their religion seriously enough to do that today. But large numbers of church members simply make the assumption that this is a Christian country and turn a blind eye to widely accepted practices in our community life that are far from being Christian.

It would be a very serious step for the churches in the United States to carry out a policy of this kind, and it would require very careful consideration. But the alternative is not pleasant to contemplate. If churches continue to be infiltrated by the prevailing secular values, the high standards of Christian marriage, Christian parenthood, and Christian family life seem likely to deteriorate progressively until they reach the present secular levels. If this were to happen, what would be left?

We must leave this question unanswered and move on to some specific suggestions for action the churches could begin to take right now.

ACTION BY THE LOCAL CHURCH

While major national issues are debated, there is much that can be done at the level of the local churches. We must, however, face the fact that most of them, to some extent at least, are divided among themselves. In our lifetime we have personally worked and worshiped with Christians of many different persuasions—Catholic and Protestant and all kinds of denominational sects. Perhaps the vast variety of interpretations of the gospel helps the message to reach people of all sorts and conditions. As we have seen in chapter 2 of this book, even the New Testament can offer three different interpretations of the gospel message. We have also seen, across the vast sweep of Christian history, that the message has been interpreted in a great variety of ways.

At this particular period in history, it is our impression that the main concern of the churches is with what we have called "Kingdom-building" Christianity. Despite our denominational divisions, and even our national divisions, the world today is increasingly being seen as one unit—a vast company of human beings, numbering many billions, and yet all dependent on one another. We are all bound together by trade, by exchanges of knowledge, by our sharing of the products of the earth, and by the hopes and fears we share as members of the human race. We are also, as we Christians believe, all united in sharing the divine image and in an urgent need to avert the horrors of war and to live together in harmony and peace.

Our purpose in this book has been to focus on the basic unit of human society, the marriage relationship, in order to see how the churches have understood and treated this relationship across the broad sweep of the centuries. What emerges is a very mixed picture, but as we have tried to show in the closing chapters, the need for some principles in promoting the closest of all adult human relationships is today more important than ever. It is increasingly clear that our statesmen cannot build world peace from the top down, unless we, the people, also establish it from the bottom up. Our human world is a series of expanding circles, with their focus set in the man-woman relationship we call marriage, opening out from that core to the family, to the local community, to the nation, and to the human race.

We, therefore, find it difficult to think of any task confronting the churches in this day and age that is of more central importance than the promotion of growing numbers of effectively functioning Christian families. Of course, this must begin by the bringing of individuals to a right relationship with God, but once that happens, the next step is to put the Christian message into action in the daily life of the man or woman concerned, and for most of us that means in the relationships in our homes. When the church wins converts to the Christian way of life, that should surely be the first step for them to take. And the church, the fellowship of believers, should provide all possible support for the development of yet another Christian home.

However, this has not always been seen as the primary Christian task. Some years ago, when we worked as consultants in family life for the World Council of Churches in Geneva, we carried out programs and projects for churches throughout the world. Emphasis on promoting Christian family life was often sadly lacking, while time and attention were given to all kinds of other causes. We can remember a distinguished German theologian who took us aside and earnestly entreated us not to raise family issues in the churches. "To talk to church members about their families," he said, "is an invasion of their privacy. Such matters should not be discussed among Christians." And in Africa a high Christian official, when we raised the issue of Christian family relationships, responded angrily: "What on earth has my family life to do with my religion?" In those days we used to say that as we worked with the churches in many lands, it almost seemed that Christian family life was at the bottom of their lists of priorities.

That is no longer true today. The need to face the facts is now obvious. But the churches have, in our experience, been very slow to involve themselves in the field of family relationships. That is one reason why, now that the subject has become a major issue and secular standards have invaded our religious communities to such a large extent, the churches have seemed at first poorly equipped to respond with a clear sense of what they needed to do.

We, therefore, want to sound a challenge to the churches by offering the following recommendations:

1. Recognize the Central Importance of Christian Marriage to Our Christian Witness Today.

Already, disturbing numbers of church members are failing to make their marriages function and are getting divorced. Billy Graham, in *Approaching Hoofbeats*, says:

"Look at the condition of marriage within the context of today's Christian homes and churches. The staggering high divorce rate is almost the same among believers as among unbelievers. Every day a new rumor crosses my path of another leader in the church whose marriage is in shambles." Yet, this is the very time when the witness of happy and creative Christian marriages is needed as never before to demonstrate that we have the answer to the needs of the secular world. If Christian couples, who have taken the solemn vow of lifetime devotion to each other, are in increasing numbers demonstrating that they are doing no better than their non-Christian neighbors, then the witness of the church is sadly diminished at a vital point. Of course, it is distressing to find that church members, and even pastors, have experienced failure in life's most intimate adult relationship. Instead of judging them, however, we need to ask whether the churches have been giving their married couples the guidance and support that might have enabled them to avoid marital failures.

The subject of divorce is a very difficult one for Christians. In some periods of history, the stance of the church has been so rigid and inflexible that it has shown little sensitivity to tragic human situations by adopting strict regulations based on purely legal issues. But more often, the trouble has been that the church has lacked the caring concern to intervene and offer help to its members who were in marital trouble—which brings us to our second recommendation.

2. Lift the Taboo on Talking about Marriage and Face the Facts.

The sad truth is that the local church can at present do very little to help its married members who have trouble in their relationships, because far too often the church has no idea of what is happening to these couples until the situation is beyond recovery.

This state of affairs is the direct result of what we call the "intermarital taboo." Our theory is that the taboo goes back to an early period when people lived in small rural villages and it was necessary to safeguard married couples from the idle curiosity of their near neighbors. Today, however, in our very different urban communities, we have preserved the taboo in a situation in which it is doing much more harm than good and is preventing married couples from getting the kind of help and support from each other that they would not hesitate to seek and use in other areas of their lives. A vast amount of useful learning comes from the simple process by which friends and neighbors seek one another's advice in all kinds of life situations. It is tragic that the one exception to this very valuable process is the marriage relationship, where an outmoded and useless taboo lives on and prevents couples from helping each other by sharing their experiences.

It was this taboo, of course, that the German theologian was defending. According to our observation, the intermarital taboo is more rigidly observed in the churches than in any other section of the community. We have often said that it would not be difficult to get a group of Christian married couples to stand up and say in church: We are sinners in need of repentance. "But it would be quite a different matter to get those same people to stand up and say: "We are married couples, and our relationships are far short of what they ought to be." This defensive attitude has appeared again and again when Christian couples have been invited to attend a marriage enrichment event. Sometimes their defensive attitudes are embarrassingly hostile.

The explanation, of course, is that the church atmosphere is often so formal that it seems essential to put up a good appearance—especially for a married couple. In that kind of defensive atmosphere, there is little chance that marriages can be helped to grow. Instead, deterioration of the relationship can go on progressively until it is past saving, and then everybody is horrified to learn that the couple are getting divorced. The usual comment is, "We had no idea they were having trouble." Of course not—the taboo prevented the couple from reaching out for help.

We think churches can change all this and allow their members to acknowledge that they are human beings struggling with the complications of human life, and that one of their major purposes for being together is to help each other to grow in every aspect of life, including marriage. The development of marriage enrichment programs in the churches seems now to be making this easier, but there is still need for further progress.

3. Encourage and Train Pastors to Make Themselves Available to Help Married Couples.

This statement is almost sure to be interpreted in terms of training pastors to become qualified marriage counselors, but that is not what we mean. On the whole we are not in favor of parish ministers functioning as marital therapists, for this is a very time-consuming occupation and can divert them from their primary task. Also, when pastors get into counseling they may convey the impression that couples should seek their aid only if they are in serious trouble. Every pastor should be able to refer any couple who need therapy to competent professional help. But what is much more important is that the church members, knowing this, should also know that they can be free to talk about their marital growth, or lack of it, to their pastor without any implication that they are in serious trouble. The work of the pastor, so far as marriages are concerned, should be entirely preventive and supportive. We like the rule in some churches that a pastor may normally spend no more than two scheduled counseling interviews with a particular married couple. After that, if they need further help in the situation involved, they should be referred to a private clinician.

We consider it particularly helpful for the pastor to be available with his wife (or her husband) in situations in which they can bear witness together to what their own Christian marriage means to them. By informal modeling, they can identify with other married couples in the congregation. We have known cases of pastors who, on special occasions, spoke with their wives from the pulpit in order to bear a united witness to their roles as members of a Christian family. The cause of marriage enrichment can be very effectively promoted when the clergy couple make it known that they, themselves, have been involved in a couples' retreat, and better still if they can lead one together.

Now that we are seeing an increase in the number of two-clergy couples, it seems that some of them could make a special contribution to the churches they serve by doing some teamwork in modeling Christian marriage. To acknowledge that it takes effort, and even pain, to win through to all that marriage can offer would get over very powerfully to lay couples the need to work seriously on their relationships. In this connection, it is significant that the only professional study so far published of two-clergy marriages (by E. M. Rallings and David Pratto) reports that 80 percent of the group of fifty-four couples studied had "felt the need for human help" in their marriages, and almost all of them had been wise enough to seek counseling.

Of course, this kind of ministry is not confined to two-clergy couples. It is open to any married pastor, with wife or husband, to be available to the congregation to share what they are learning in their life together. By doing so, they can free couples in the congregation from the impression that such sharing is "not done" in the Christian community.

When therapy is really needed, there are obvious advantages to making a referral to a counselor who works from a background of Christian values. A good plan is for a group of churches in a community to make use of a designated local practitioner, if possible with Christian convictions, who can, where necessary, cooperate with the clergy in the churches concerned.

4. Make Adequate Provision to Guide Couples Who Are Moving into Marriage.

The tradition of marriage preparation has already been established in most churches, but it needs to be extended in both directions—earlier and later. Teen-agers today tend to hear much more about sex than about marriage, and preparation for marriage should begin by seeing that their knowledge is sound and accurate. We are not necessarily thinking of a formal course on the subject, though that could serve a useful purpose. What young people need much more, however, is to hear directly from happily married couples who can make married life attractive and at the same time correct some of the superficial views that are so widely current in our culture. We, ourselves, have organized small groups of teen-agers to meet informally with happily married couples who are ready to respond to any questions, however personal, the teen-agers wish to ask; this has made a deep impression on the young people concerned.

When it comes to working with the engaged couple, follow-up studies have shown that talks by the pastor don't have much effect, and sometimes the effect is actually negative. We are coming to realize that just before marriage is not the best time to help couples, other than by winning their confidence and friendship. It is the first year of marriage that is the critical time, when the couple establish their interaction patterns, and we are seeing more and more clearly that it is newlyweds who really need help and can benefit greatly from suitably planned programs. To team up newlyweds with couples who can be completely open with them and develop deep and enduring friendships is probably best of all. To use the term coined by psychologist Robert Havighurst, we must offer needed help at the "teachable moment." We are now strongly convinced that this occurs not in the premarital period, but in the time after the wedding when the couple are making the difficult, but vitally important, adjustments to each other that will lead either to success or failure as the relationship takes shape. The programs for newlyweds now being developed by the Association of Couples for Marriage Enrichment (ACME) show great promise and need to be made much more widely available.

5. The Church as a Family of Families.

There are aspects of church life in which formal behavior is appropriate and desirable, but our impression, based on extensive experience, is that what makes the life of any church vital and creative is a pervading sense of warm friendliness and loving care. After all, what is the primary purpose of a body of Christian believers? Surely it is to provide a setting in which they can all grow together in Christian living and learn to bear a vital witness to their faith in the surrounding community. That was what happened in the early churches described in the New Testament. Most of them began in the homes of Christian believers and expanded later as larger buildings became necessary. The spirit and atmosphere was that of a family, lovingly concerned for each other's welfare, growing in grace together. So a Christian church should be at once an expanded version of a Christian family unit and at the same time a microcosm of a Christian world.

Highly organized churches have at times divided up their members by age and sex—departments in the Sunday school, separate men's and women's organizations, separate age groups. Within reason, this separation can serve some useful purposes. But if this is done in such a way that these groups become segregated and the sense of central unity is lost, the local church is no longer a family, but an institution. Certainly singles need a chance to get together, as do married couples, teen-agers, and retirees. But the great value of a family is that all its members, at various stages in the life cycle, may reach a loving and caring understanding of one another's joys and sorrows, hopes and fears. Surely this is what a church should make possible. And if this atmosphere and spirit could become that of people the world over, we would have taken the first major step toward the establishment of world peace. Whatever other goals the Christian church is trying to achieve, this surely is a central one.

CONCLUSION

In this book we have looked back over the long centuries during which the Christian message, first heralded in the Hebrew culture, found its focus in the life and teaching of Jesus of Nazareth. Then, amid hardships and perils innumerable, an endless line of dedicated disciple formed a fellowship of believers who have bridged the centuries and taken the message to the ends of the earth. Still today the unfinished task is being taken up by men and women who have found in the Christian message the way, the truth, and the life.

Against this broad background, we have tried to understand how the ongoing fellowship of Christian believers has struggled to understand and to interpret the meaning of marriage, that fundamental union of a man and a woman through which humanity is renewed from generation to generation.

What have we found? Let's list our main conclusions:

1. Marriage is a central part of the divine purpose for humanity.

2. At its highest and best, marriage is a close lifelong companionship, jointly shared by a man and a woman as equal partners.

3. Through sexual union, marriage provides the means to assure the continuity of the human race by passing on the gift of life from generation to generation.

4. The sexual union also provides a source of mutual fulfillment that expresses the love between marriage partners.

5. Marriage lays upon the couple the solemn responsibility of jointly supporting and training, through the years from infancy to maturity, the children born to them.

6. The task of parenthood is best accomplished by building together a Christian family which develops in all its members a fellowship of caring love and mutual support.

7. Such a Christian family provides a working model for the wider human community and for a peaceful world.

8. The shared life of husband and wife, continued through the life cycle, provides an ideal means for their full personal and relational development.

9. A successful Christian family is the most convincing manifestation of the Chistian message.

10. A continuing ministry to Christian marriages and families is the primary pastoral duty of the local church.

We may bring this book to a fitting conclusion by quoting some words of H. Hensley Henson in *Christian Marriage:*

> "From the hallowed enclosure of the Church the sacred fire of domestic love, kindled from the altar of divine love, shall be carried far and wide into the world of human life, and shall create everywhere the light and warmth of home."

A Personal Postscript:
WHY WE WROTE THIS BOOK

As your authors, we have worked on this book over a period of about three years, taking time off at intervals to go to libraries where we could find the necessary sources of information. As a result, our knowledge of history has been greatly enlarged and clarified, and issues that had previously confused us have become much clearer.

We have spent most of our time, since our marriage fifty-three years ago, working together to make the world a better and a happier place. We soon decided that the best way to achieve this goal was to focus on the quality of human relationships. In order to do this, we saw that the place where nearly all of us learn, for good or for ill, how to relate to others is in the family where we spend our earliest years. We also saw clearly that what we learn in that family may depend a great deal on the quality of the marriage relationship on which that family was originally founded. So it seemed logical that if we wanted to attain our goal, we should focus on working for better marriages, beginning with our own. That became the definition of our purpose in life.

Over the years, therefore, we have tried to do just that. It seemed logical to begin by helping couples whose marriages were in trouble; so we became pioneers in the field of marriage counseling. We played a leading part in establishing programs for marriage and family counseling in Britain, in the United States, and in several other countries.

However, having played our part in providing these services, we saw that this was not of itself enough. Despite the widespread availability of marriage counseling today, the divorce rates in most countries have been rapidly increasing—indicating that, though counseling could help some couples, for many others the damage had already been done beyond repair, and it was now too late to change.

So we shifted our focus. We saw that what was needed was to match our remedial services with *preventive* services to enable couples to gain new insights and to learn new skills before the destructive forces begin to produce alienation and breakdown. Working with groups of couples whose marriages were not in need of therapy, however, we often found that the seeds of later problems were already there, but that they could be cleared up by a process we called *marriage enrichment*. This was an exciting discovery, and in 1973 we formed the Association of Couples for Marriage Enrichment (ACME), a new organization that has now become international. By getting groups of couples together for intensive learning experiences and then putting them into follow-up "support groups" over a period of time, we found that dull, superficial marriages could often grow into deeply satisfying relationships. You may write to the headquarters office at P.O. Box 10596, Winston-Salem, NC 27108.

We discovered, however, that this was not an easy program to operate. The difficulty is a massive obstacle in our culture—we have called it the "intermarital taboo." In the past, in simple rural communities, it was obviously necessary to protect the privacy of the married couple from curious and prying neighbors, and this placed an exaggerated importance on privacy which has continued in our very different culture of today.

The result of the taboo is that while married couples feel entirely free to help and support each other in most areas of living, a seemingly inpenetrable barrier blocks this process when the *relationship* of the couple is involved. John and Mary usually feel quite ready to seek the advice and help of other couples who live in their neighborhood or go to their church, if their roses aren't growing successfully, if the dog is sick, even if a child is being troublesome. But if their *marriage relationship* isn't working right, their lips must be tightly sealed and they must suffer in silence—until the situation has deteriorated so far that in desperation they separate or begin divorce proceedings.

The irony is that today we understand the dynamics of marital interaction much more clearly than ever before. We now have the knowledge to make marriages generally far happier and more creative. But we can't get that knowledge out, or teach the new skills that result from it, because when we try to do so, we meet a wall of silent resistance. Offer marriage enrichment to a great number of couples, and the response is in effect: "Go away! We don't need help. Our marriage is all right!"

HOW THE CHURCH IS INVOLVED

When we moved into the field of working for better marriages, we saw our work as a new form of Christian service. That was more than forty years ago. David was then the minister of a large Methodist church in London,

England, and Vera had been the executive director of a national organization for young women in the Methodist Church.

We found, however, that our attempts to work for better marriages were not welcomed in the Christian community. Some of our religious friends supported us, but others gave our efforts a very cool reception. We were told that getting into marriage counseling was quite inappropriate for a Christian minister. It was even described as "interfering in the private lives of other people." And when David began to play a leading role in developing the National Marriage Guidance Council in Britain, he found himself finally in a situation in which he had to resign from the ministry. He has no feeling of resentment about that today. It does, however, provide a dramatic picture of the thinking of that time. Fortunately, the churches now see the matter in a very different perspective.

WHAT HISTORY CAN TEACH US

During the years when we were heavily involved in programs and projects in the field of marriage and the family, we had little chance to study how the churches had treated Christian marriage in earlier times. But provocative questions kept coming up, and we often just didn't know the answers.

So, when we finally retired, we decided that we must confront our ignorance about the history of Christian marriage. We found no one book that tried to view the whole picture objectively, so we decided to write one. As the complexity of the task began to confront us, we found ourselves getting discouraged. And although we were now technically living in retirement, we were again and again called upon to speak at conferences, to take part in committees, to lead programs and workshops, and to write smaller books and articles.

However, we persevered. Although the task was immense, was also found it stimulating. We ended up, inevitably, with far more material than we could possibly include in one book. Any reader with a knowledge of Christian history will find obvious gaps. But the dearth of literature that tries to look at the broad picture in some kind of perspective encourages us to think that our book may be as helpful to some of its readers as producing it has been to its writers.

Would it be a fair question to ask what, among all the information we assembled, made the most significant impression on us personally? We think it would, and we have a clear and simple answer.

In a general sense, we had already been aware of most of the facts we encountered in our reading. However, one piece of information impressed us deeply, because it was entirely new to us. It was what we learned about the Puritan interest in, and interpretation of, Christian marriage.

In the first place, we were puzzled that we had never known about this before. Almost everything we had heard about the Puritans was negative—they were unbalanced extremists, infusing into the early beginnings of American culture a priggish, spoilsport, judgmental attitude and a moralistic and anti-sexual philosophy. Our first reading of the Schücking book left us incredulous, and we concluded that, as a German scholar, he must have developed a distorted view of the matter. But as we probed more deeply, we could no longer dismiss him as misinformed. The evidence from other sources was too convincing. In book after book written by the early Puritans, and even by non-Puritans who were influenced by them, the evidence was convincing.

What impressed us, therefore, was that some of the new attitudes toward marriage which are slowly emerging today, and particularly the new concepts of marriage enrichment that we are now developing, are not really new at all! They were understood and developed by Christian inquirers in the seventeenth century—three hundred years ago! They were not only known, but also they were talked about, taught, and put into practice by Christian couples, and they were put into writing in a series of books by different authors!

Well, what happened next? The Puritans were just one section of the Protestant Reformation. Even if their attempt to change the Church of England was a total failure, they made a lasting contribution to the development of the new culture that became the United States of America. Did their teaching about Christian marriage. penetrate into the Protestant culture in the new free churches that developed in Britain and in the United States?

Apparently not. The traditional formalism in British Christianity evidently won out. Even John Milton, who came under Puritan influence, was unable to apply their teaching about marriage in his own life. And in America, the later Puritans created such a bad impression because of the strictness of their moral standards that they made no lasting impact in the area of marriage and the family.

It seems, therefore, that the intermarital taboo was too strong, so that within the developing Protestant churches it was able, in time, to stifle the impact of the Puritan teaching on marriage. We have been unable to find any significant evidence that Puritans influenced the thought and teaching of Christian marriage in the main Protestant churches during the later centuries of the modern era. The Victorian era in England seemed, indeed, to reflect the very kind of moral rigidity that had been falsely attributed to the early Puritans in America.

THE PRESENT SITUATION

Where, then, are we today? What we seem to be seeing is the languishing of the power of the Christian churches to influence the principles and standards guiding the policies of the modern state. The result is that the Christian community, divided into separate, and often competing, denominations, is unable to act in unison and is steadily losing power and influence in the community at large. Today, secular standards tend to dominate political action generally, and these lower standards, particularly in the area of marriage and family life, are now invading the churches, which seem to be unable to resist, because the taboo lives on more powerfully in religious groups than in the general community. Only the fundamentalist sections of the Christian community seem to have the resolve to stand apart from pervasive secular influence, and their supposedly Bible-based teaching about marriage emphasizes the hierarchical concept, with the dominant husband and submissive wife—a message that carries no conviction either in the secular community, where women's liberation is developing rapidly, or in the more liberal Christian community, where the message of companionship marriage is now beginning to be widely heard.

Given this critical situation, what should Christians do? Perhaps we have no right to suggest a solution. But let us at least, in our closing words, share our own convictions.

What the Puritans tried to do was to make the local church a family. The Catholics, in their own way, had already done that. The priest was called *Father* and he focused all his activities in the church building, to which the members had to come in order to receive the sacramental blessings that alone kept them in favor with God.

For the Puritans, however, the idea was that the church was, in fact, a family of families. For them, the family unit was the core of human society, and they saw their task as that of making this unit a fully functioning *Christian* community. The pastor's major task, supported by his own family as a model, was to foster Christian family life both in the individual families in the congregation and in the congregation as a whole. And, of course, the foundation stone of Christian family life was a fully functioning Christian marriage.

What else, in reality, does the Christian church have to offer in today's world? Protestant churches have tended to place the focus on the *preacher*. That has been effective in the past. But today, how can the preacher compete with highly gifted television personalities using all the resources of the mass media? Besides, how far are sermons going to be the basis for Christian behavior, unless the church also provides the stimulus and the support necessary to put that behavior into practice? The Christian message is obviously of central importance, but only when it becomes the means of enabling those who hear it to change their behavior. In our opinion, this must be done mainly in group interaction, with continuing encouragement and support. It is a matter of historical interest that John Wesley did this by creating the concept of the Methodist class meeting!

An acid test of any Christian life is, and must be, how the person concerned manages his or her interpersonal relationships—in marriage first, then in the family group, and ultimately in wider circles. In a world in which the inability of people to live peaceably together now carries the threat of nuclear war, we can no longer escape the fact that our viable human future depends on our ability to relate constructively and creatively to one another. As we see it, the only effective answer to that challenge is the Christian message, applied in terms of action at all the levels at which people interact. This will be meaningless unless we can make it work first and foremost in Christian marriage, the closest of all human relationships.

BIBLIOGRAPHY

Over a period of three years, we have read and consulted a great many books. Where the authors are quoted, we normally recorded all publication data. In a very few cases, however, we regret that we omitted to do so, and were not able later to elicit the necessary information

Abelard, Peter. *A Story of Adversity*. Published in Latin in 1132. English version by J. T. Muckle, 1954.

Amstutz, H. Clair. *Marriage in Today's World*. Scottdale, Penn.: Herald Press, 1978.

Anonymous. *The Whole Duty of Man*. London: Society for Promoting Christian Knowledge (first published 1659).

Ariès, Philippe. *Centuries of Childhood: A Social History of Family Life* (translated from the French). New York: Random House, 1965.

Bailey, Derrick Sherwin. *The Mystery of Love and Marriage*. New York: Greenwood, 1977.

———. *Sexual Relation in Christian Thought*. New York: Harper and Brothers, 1959.

Bainton, Roland H. *Here I Stand: A Life of Martin Luther.* Nashville: Abingdon, 1978.

———. *Sex, Love, and Marriage: A Christian Survey.* New York: Collins-Fontana Books, 1957.

Barnhouse, Ruth T., and Holmes, Urban T. *Male and Female: Christian Approaches to Sexuality.* New York: Seabury Press, 1976.

Bassett, William W. and Huizing, Peter J., eds. *Celibacy in the Church.* New York: Crossroad, 1972.

Bassett, William W. and Huizing, Peter J., eds. *The Future of Christian Marriage.* New York: Crossroad, 1976.

Becker, Howard and Hill, Reuben. *Marriage and the Family.* Boston: D. C. Heath and Co., 1942.

Bell, Robert R. *Marriage and Family Interaction.* Homewood, Ill.: Dorsey Press, 1983.

Berry, W. Grinton, ed. *Foxe's Book of Martyrs.* New York: Abingdon Press, 1932.

Beveridge, Sir William. *Changes in Family Life.* London: Allen and Unwin, 1932.

Borer, Mary Cathcart. *People Like Us: A Social History of Britain.* London: Michael Joseph, 1960.

Botwin, Carol. *Is There Sex After Marriage?* Boston: Little, Brown, 1985.

Bowman, Henry A. *A Christian Interpretation of Marriage.* Philadelphia: Westminster Press, 1959.

Briffault, Robert. *The Mothers: A Study of the Origins of Sentiments and Institutions.* London: Allen and Unwin, 1927.

Brinton, Crane. *Anatomy of Revolution.* New York: Random, 1965.

Brown, Stanley C. *God's Plan for Marriage.* Philadelphia: Westminster Press, 1977.

Bureau, Paul. *Toward Moral Bankruptcy* (translated from French *L'Indiscipline des Moeurs*). New York: Richard R. Smith, 1930.

Caird, Mona. *The Morality of Marriage*. London: George Redway, 1897.

Calhoun, Arthur W. *A Social History of the American Family: From Colonial Times to the Present*. New York: Barnes and Noble, 1945.

Calverton, V. F. and Schmalhausen, S. D., eds. *Sex in Civilization*. New York: Macaulay, 1929.

Camden, Carroll. *The Elizabethan Woman*. New York: Appel, 1952.

Cervantes, Lucinus J. See Zimmerman, Carle C. and Cervantes, Lucinus J.

Chapman, Gary D. *Toward a Growing Marriage*. Chicago: Moody Press, 1979.

Chaucer, Geoffrey, *The Canterbury Tales of Chaucer*. English prose translation by R. M. Lumiansky. Washington Square Press, 1971.

Chavasse, Claude. *The Bride of Christ: The Nuptial Element in Early Christianity*. London: Religious Book Club, 1939.

Christenson, Larry. *The Christian Family*. Minneapolis: Bethany House, 1980.

Colacci, Mario. *Christian Marriage Today: A Comparison of Roman Catholic and Protestant Views*. Minneapolis: Augsburg Publishing House, 1958.

Cole, William Graham. *Sex in Christianity and Psychoanalysis*. New York: Oxford University Press, 1955.

Daly, Mary. *Gyn—Ecology: the Metaethics of Radical Feminism*. Boston: Beacon Press, 1979.

D'Arcy, M. C. *The Mind and Heart of Love*. London: Faber and Faber, 1945.

Davies, A. Powell. *The Meaning of the Dead Sea Scrolls*. New York: Mentor Books, 1956.

Denton, Wallace. *What's Happening to Our Families?* Philadelphia: Westminster Press, 1963.

De Coulanges, *The Ancient City*. Quoted in Zimmerman and Cervantes

Dolan, John P. *History of the Reformation*. New York: New American Library, 1967.

Dominian, Jack. *Christian Marriage: The Challenge of Change*. London: Darton, Longman, and Todd, 1967.

———. *Faith and Love: A Basic Guide to Christian Marriage*. New York: Crossroad, 1982.

Duvall, Sylvanus M. *Men, Women, and Morals*. New York: Greenwood, 1973.

Elmslie, W. A. L. See Robinson, Henry W.

Erikson, Erik H. *Young Man Luther*. New York: Norton, 1958.

Evans, Hugh Davey. *A Treatise on the Christian Doctrine of Marriage*. Cambridge: Riverside Press, 1870.

Fairchild, Roy and Wynn, J. C. *Families in the Church: A Protestant Survey*. New York: Association Press, 1961.

Fairchild, Roy W. *Christians in Families: An Inquiry into the Nature and Mission of the Christian Family*. Richmond, Va: CLC Press, 1964.

Farber, Seymour, et al. *The Family's Search for Survival*. New York: McGraw-Hill, 1965.

Feucht, Oscar E. *Helping Families through the Church*. St. Louis: Concordia, 1971.

Genne, William and Genne, Elizabeth. *Foundations for Christian Family Policy*. New York: National Council of Churches in the USA, 1961.

Gibbon, Edward. *Decline and Fall of the Roman Empire*. Ed. by Brian Tierney et al. New York: Random, 1977.

Goodsell, Willystine. *A History of the Family as a Social and Educational Institution*. New York: Macmillan, 1915.

Gordon, Michael, ed. *The American Family in Social-Historical Perspective*. New York: St. Martin's Press, 1983.

Graham, Billy. *Approaching Hoofbeats: The Four Horsemen of the Apocalypse.* Waco, Tex.: Word Books, 1983.

Grams, Armin. *The Christian Encounters Changes in Family Life.* St. Louis: Concordia, 1968.

Guerry, Edward B. *The Historic Principle of the Indissolubility of Marriage.* Sewanee, Tenn.: University Press, 1953.

Haw, Reginald. *The State of Matrimony.* London: SPCK, 1952.

Henson, H. Hensley. *Christian Marriage.* London: Cassel and Co., 1907.

Hertz, Joseph H. *A Book of Jewish Thoughts.* London: Oxford University Press, 1935.

Hiltner, Seward. *Sex and the Christian Life.* New York: 1957.

Hole, Christina. *English Home Life: 1500 to 1800.* London: Batsford, 1947.

Hosier, Helen. *The Other Side of Divorce: A Christian's Plea for Understanding and Compassion.* Nashville: Abingdon, 1975.

Howell, John C. *Equality and Submission in Marriage.* Nashville: Broadman, 1979.

Huizinga, Johan. *The Waning of the Middle Ages.* New York: Doubleday Anchor, 1954.

Hunt, Morton M. *The Natural History of Love.* New York: Alfred A. Knopf, 1959.

James, E. O. *Marriage and Society.* New York: John de Graff, 1955.

Janeway, Elizabeth. *Man's World, Woman's Place: A Study in Social Mythology.* New York: William Morrow and Co., 1921.

Johnson, James Turner. *A Society Ordained by God.* Nashville: Abingdon, 1970.

Joyce, G. H. *Christian Marriage: An Historical and Doctrinal Study.* London: Sheed and Ward, 1948.

Kay, F. George. *The Family in Transition: Its Past,*

Present, and Future Patterns. Newton Abbot, England: David & Charles, 1972.

Keck, Leander E. *Taking the Bible Seriously.* Nashville: Abingdon, 1979.

Kenkel, William F. *The Family in Perspective.* New York: Random, 1977.

Kerns, Joseph E. *The Theology of Marriage: The Historical Development of the Christian Attitude Toward Sex and Sanctity in Marriage.* New York: Sheed and Ward, 1964.

Kirk, Kenneth E. *Marriage and Divorce.* London: Hodder and Stoughton, 1948.

Lacey, T. A. *Marriage in Church and State.* London: Robert Scott, 1912.

Langdon-Davies, John. *A Short History of Women.* New York: Norwood Editions, 1928.

Lantz, Herman R. *Marital Incompatibility and Social Change in Early America.* Beverly Hills, Calif.: Sage Research Papers, 1976.

Laslett, Peter. *Family Life and Illicit Love in Earlier Generations.* Cambridge, England: Cambridge University Press, 1977.

Lea, Henry C. *History of Sacerdotal Celibacy in the Christian Church.* London: Watts and Co., 1932.

Lecky, William E. *History of European Morals from Augustus to Charlemagne.* Ayer Co., 1975.

Little, W. J. Knox. *Holy Matrimony.* London: Longmans, Green, 1900.

Lods, A. See Robinson, Henry W.

Lofthouse, W. F. *Ethics and the Family.* London: Hodder and Stoughton, (no date).

Lutheran Church—Missouri Synod. Family Life Committee. *Engagement and Marriage.* St. Louis: Concordia, 1959.

Mace, David R. *Hebrew Marriage: A Sociological Study.* London: Epworth Press, 1953.

Mackin, Theodore. *Marriage in the Catholic Church: Divorce and Remarriage.* New York: Paulist Press, 1984.

Macmillan, Arthur Tarleton. *What is Christian Marriage?: Present Teaching and Practice of the Church of England.* London: Macmillan, 1944.

Magoun, F. Alexander. *Love and Marriage.* New York: Harper, 1948.

Marshall, John. *The Future of Christian Marriage.* London: Geoffrey Chapman, 1970.

Martindale, C. C. *Wedlock.* London: Sheed and Ward, 1937.

Martinson, Floyd M. *Family in Society.* New York: Dodd, Mead, 1970.

Marty, Martin E. *A Short History of Christianity.* Philadelphia: Fortress Press, 1980.

Massachusetts Commission on Christian Unity. *Ecumenical and Pastoral Directives on Christian Marriage.* Mass.: Whitemore Associates, Inc., 1976.

Maston, T. B. *Biblical Ethics—A Survey: A Guide to the Ethical Messages of the Scriptures from Genesis Through Revelation.* Macon, Ga.: Mercer University Press, 1982.

May, Geoffrey. *Social Control of Sexual Expression.* London: Allen and Unwin, 1930.

McBirnie, William S. *The Search for the Early Church.* Wheaton, Ill.: Tyndale House, 1975.

McDonald, Cleveland. *Creating a Successful Christian Marriage.* Grand Rapids: Baker Book House, 1975.

McNeill, William H. *The Rise of the West: A History of the Human Community.* Chicago: University of Chicago Press, 1970.

Malinowski, Bronislaw and Briffault, Robert. *Marriage: Past and Present.* Boston: Porter Sargent (Extendng Horizons Series), 1956.

Messenger, E. C. *The Mystery of Sex and Marriage in Catholic Theology.* London: Sands and Co., 1948.

Meyendorff, John. *Marriage: An Orthodox Perspective.* St. Vladimir's Seminary Press, 1975.

Mollenkott, Virginia Ramey. *Women, Men, and the Bible.* Nashville: Abingdon, 1977.

Pagels, Elaine. *The Gnostic Gospels.* New York: Random, 1981.

Parker, T. H. L. *A Portrait of Calvin.* London: S.C.M. Press, 1940.

Pederson, J. T. E. see Robinson, Henry W.

Petty, Charles V. *A History of Marriage and the Family.* Fort Worth, Tex.: Southwestern Baptist Theological Seminary, 1967. Unpublished paper for the seminar "Christian Ethics '64."

Phipps, William E. *Was Jesus Married?* New York: Harper and Row, 1970.

Piper, Otto A. *The Biblical View of Sex and Marriage.* New York: Charles Scribner, 1960.

Power, Eileen. *Medieval People.* New York: Barnes and Noble, Inc., 1966.

———. *Medieval Women.* London: Cambridge University Press, 1975.

Queen, Stuart A. and Habenstein, Robert W. *The Family in Various Cultures.* New York: Harper & Row, 1974.

Rallings, E. M. and Pratto, David J. *Two-Clergy Marriages.* Lanham, Md.: University Press of America, 1984.

Richmond, Mary E. and Hall, Fred S. *Marriage and the State.* New York: Russell Sage Foundation, 1929.

Robinson, T. H. See Robinson, Henry W.

Robinson, Henry W., ed. *Record and Revelation.* New York: AMS Press, 1938.

Rosenberg, Charles E. *The Family in History.* Philadephia: University of Pennsylvania Press, 1975.

Ross, James B. and McLaughlin, Mary. *The Portable Medieval Reader.* New York: Penguin, 1950.

De Rougemont, Denis. *Love in the Western World.* Princeton: Princeton University Press, 1983.

Rumsey, Thomas R. *Men and Women of the Renaissance and Reformation: 1300-1600.* Wellesley Hills, Mass.: Independent School Press, 1981.

Sait, Una Bernard. *New Horizons for the Family.* New York: Macmillan, 1938.

Schücking, Levin L. *The Puritan Family: A Social Study from the Literary Sources* (translated from the German). New York: Schocken Books, 1970.

Schweitzer, Albert. *The Quest of the Historical Jesus.* New York: Macmillan, 1 68.

Scott, Donald M. and Wishy, Bernard. *America's Families: A Documentary History.* New York: Harper and Row, 1982.

Seiberg, Ilse. *Woman in Ancient Near East,* translated by Marianne Herzfeld. Leipzig: Edition Leipzig, 1974.

Shepherd, A. P. *Marriage Was Made for Man.* London: Methuen and Co., 1958.

Small, Dwight Hervey. *The Right to Remarry.* Old Tappan, N.J.: Fleming Revell, 1975.

Smith, C. Ryder. *The Bible Doctrine of Womanhood.* London: Epworth Press, 1923.

Stagg, Evelyn and Stagg, Frank. *Woman in the World of Jesus.* Philadelphia: Westminster Press, 1978.

Stenton, Doris Mary. *The English Woman in History.* New York: Macmillan, 1957.

Talmage, T. DeWitt. *The Wedding Ring: A Series of Discourses for Husbands and Wives and Those Contemplating Matrimony.* New York: Christian Herald— Bible House, 1896.

Taylor, Henry Osborn. *The Medieval Mind: A History of the Development of Thought and Emotion in the Middle Ages.* Cambridge, Mass.: Harvard University Press, 1962.

Thielicke, Helmut. *The Ethics of Sex,* trans. by J. W. Doberstein. New York: Attic Press, 1964.

Thomas, David M. *Christian Marriage: A Journey Together.* Wilmington, Del.: Glazier, 1983.

Troeltsch, Ernst. *The Social Teaching of the Christian Churches.* London: Allen and Unwin, 1931.

Tuchman, Barbara W. *A Distant Mirror: The Calamitous 14th Century.* New York: Ballantine Books, 1978.

Urwin, E. C. *Can the Family Survive?* London: S.C.M. Press, 1944.

Vicinus, Martha, ed. *Suffer and Be Still: Women in the Victorian Age.* Bloomington: Indiana University Press, 1972.

Waddell, Helen. *Peter Abelard: A Novel.* New York: Henry Holt, 1933.

———. *The Wandering Scholars.* London: B & N Imports, 1968.

Watkins, Oscar D. *Holy Matrimony: A Treatise on the Divine Laws of Marriage.* London: Rivington, Percival and Co., 1895.

Westermarck, Edward. *The History of Human Marriage.* London: Macmillan, 1925.

———. *A Short History of Marriage,* London: Macmillan, 1926.

———. *The Future of Marriage in Western Civilization.* London: Ayer Co., 1936.

———. *The Making of Man.* See Zimmerman, Carle C. and Cervantes, Lucinus J.

White, Ernest. *Marriage and the Bible.* Nashville: Broadman, 1965.

Wirt, Sherwood E. trans. *The Confessions of Augustine in Modern English.* Grand Rapids: Zondervan, 1971.

Wylie, William R. *Human Nature and Christian Marriage.* New York: Association Press, 1958.

Zimmerman, Carle C. *Family and Civilization.* New York: Harper, 1947.

Zimmerman, Carle C. and Cervantes, Lucinus J. *Marriage and the Family: A Text for Moderns.* Chicago: Henry Regnery Co., 1956.